Theories of Revolution:

An Introduction

Nelson's Political Science Library

Nelson's Political Science Library is under the general editorship of **Dr K. W. Watkins** of the Department of Political Theory and Institutions at Sheffield University.

Theories of Revolution:
An Introduction

A. S. Cohan

Department of Politics, University of Lancaster

A HALSTED PRESS BOOK

John Wiley & Sons
New York

Published in the USA
by Halsted Press, a Division of
John Wiley & Sons, Inc., New York

First published in Great Britain by Thomas Nelson & Sons Ltd, 1975

ISBN 0 470-16322-4
Library of Congress Catalog Card No. 75-62 59

Printed in Great Britain by
A. Wheaton & Company, Exeter

To

J. Ben Stalvey

for his kindness and encouragement
at the right times

Contents

Contents

Preface

Students are rarely far from the thoughts of academics. Indeed, students seem to have two not unrelated functions: to depress those whose job it is to teach them and to provide the real satisfaction that comes from a job providing security in lieu of financial reward. I have become acutely aware of these functions during the time that I have been teaching a course on revolution. Some students assumed—and I hasten to add incorrectly—that the course dealt with ways of overthrowing the government. The others, however, knew that we would explore those alleged reasons for revolutionary behaviour.

If the students in the former category caused me a great deal of anguish on occasion, those in the latter category have given me a great deal of pleasure. Over the past five years they have raised the types of questions with which we deal in this book. It is a truism that is not said often enough that the teacher learns as much from his students as his students learn from him. To several students I am particularly grateful. Anthony Mughan, Brian Heron, Keith McClelland, and James Hogan all suffered through the first few years of the course and contributed a great deal to the formation of my opinions on the subject. More recently, Richard Bober, who read this manuscript in rough form, and Betty White have added much to the joys of academic life.

Colleagues at Lancaster have also helped me in this enterprise. Peter Nailor and Richard Little have read and re-read drafts of this work, and their comments have been invaluable. R. H. Baker read and commented on several chapters, and R. D. McKinlay spent considerable time with me discussing the notions of social change and revolution. The views expressed in the final chapter reflect those discussions. Elsewhere, David Holloway of the University of Edinburgh has been a patient listener to new and not-so-new ideas, and K. W. Watkins, of the University of Sheffield and editor of this series, has been a constant source of help in this work. While we have disagreed frequently, the arguments were always entertaining. Finally, I would be remiss if I did not acknowledge the excellent work of Christine Bassett who has typed and retyped drafts of this book.

While I wish that I could blame the above for the flaws in this book, it is, alas, convention to excuse them from such responsibility and shoulder that burden myself.

A. S. Cohan

Chapter 1
Introduction and Overview

Studying and analysing revolutions is a fascinating and long-honoured tradition that philosophers, historians, social scientists and social commentators have relished for centuries. The sheer drama of the masses in motion has always been sufficient either to excite or horrify those whose business it has been to examine great social events and suggest why they occur. Curiously, however, since Aristotle first described to us 'the very springs and fountains of revolution',[1] the theorists who followed have raised considerably more questions concerning the nature of such occurrences than they have been able to answer. Most significantly, the theorists who have considered the phenomenon of revolution have differed about what revolutions are, and they have not yet reached any universally accepted conclusions why revolutions happen.

This lack of agreement should not suggest that they have been lax or have lacked conviction for the volume of work that has been produced would indicate great dedication to the study. Further, if we assume that at the heart of theorizing is the ability to answer the questions 'why?' and 'how?' when applied to particular events, or series of events, then it may be seen in virtually all of the works which the theorists of revolution have contributed that these are precisely the questions each believes he has answered; each author feels that he has discovered the basic reasons, or at least some of the reasons, for the growth and spread of a revolutionary situation.

But this assumption by the theorists about the fundamental correctness of their answers raises further questions principally because they disagree with one another about why revolutions occur. Marx, for example, argued that revolutions are the inevitable consequence of the structure of society. Revolutions are, therefore, 'normal' because they resolve the basic contradictions that are built into the social arrangements. Those who have

1

followed Marx, and have adhered to his view of society, have varied only with regard to where and when revolutions would be most likely to take place.

Countering this Marxian tradition are two schools of social and political thought which are related to one another. The first falls under the wide-ranging net of 'functionalism' and is generally concerned with what factors allow societies to persist over long periods of time. While the functionalist would admit that conflict is an endemic feature of society, he would reject the reasons given by the Marxist for the presence of conflict. Above all, he would reject entirely the Marxian idea of inbuilt contradictions in society. For the functionalist, the 'reality' of societal persistence would lead him to conclude such contradictions do not exist, and revolution, far from being inevitable, is altogether avoidable and generally undesirable.

Related to the functionalist view is the school of mass society theory whose exponents argue that the presence of certain structural characteristics in society provides the society with an inbuilt stability. If the traditional structural arrangements are suddenly swept away then the probability of mass revolution increases, with the possible consequence of the mass revolution being the institution of a totalitarian regime. Like the functionalist, the mass society theorist could not accept the view that inbuilt contradictions are contained in the social structure which lead to revolution. In fact, it is only the presence of the traditional social structure, widely adhered to and widely supported, that provides the societal continuity and stability necessary to prevent unattached masses from flocking to the new totalitarian movements. The totalitarian movements provide the masses with the sense of security previously supplied by the social structure.

Psychological explanations are also part of the theoretical tradition in the analysis of revolution and generally follow the non-Marxian line with regard to the inevitability of revolution. Two viewpoints emerge which attempt explanations about why the masses are likely to rise up against established or 'legitimate' rulers. The first holds that revolutions will occur when the population concludes that its situation is so unbearable that it can stand no more. In order to alleviate its situation it rises up to destroy the oppressors. The second suggests that the members of the population have some idea about what they ought to be receiving during the general course of their lives. When they find themselves confronted with a situation in which the gap between what they think they ought to be getting and what they actually are getting is growing wider and wider, they are likely to rise up. Subsumed by this 'general theory' is the more specific view that popular risings are most likely to occur when, after a long period of social and economic progress, either a downturn in that progress occurs or there are fears that the continued progress will be impeded.

A further series of psychological explanations is concerned not with the masses but with the leaders of revolutionary movements. These explanations raise the question why an individual is likely to become a revolutionary. Is there something about an individual's early childhood that predisposes him to a revolutionary career? Is there a basic 'flaw' in his personality? Or is he an individual who is so filled with a sense of injustice at the rottenness of the world that in a humane gesture of contempt for the repressive regime he acts to rid the world of such a cancer?

We are thus presented with a formidable range of literature from which the various theories have been derived, but as a cautionary note it is suggested that quantity is not to be equated with quality, and, although the literature is extensive, it is well to remember that it is flawed. Many of the weaknesses are not particularly significant and with some careful excisions they may be removed from the theories and still leave the theories generally intact. Other flaws, however, are fundamental and lead to serious questioning about the usefulness of the models and the validity of the theories. They involve many of the assumptions that are built into the theories, and the models from which the theories are derived; such weaknesses are our main consideration.

The purpose of this book is to provide a critical analysis of a number of theories and models of revolution. The works of some of the major theorists will be brought together in an effort to determine to what extent they have differed from one another and why these differences occur. Generally, we shall be concerned with developing an inventory of how far these theorists have brought us to an understanding of revolution. The study is by no means an exhaustive one. Many of the theorists of revolution and violence have not been included. But we shall be considering some of the most representative works of the theorists of the different schools that have been discussed.

The first problem to be confronted concerns what revolution is. This ostensibly simple question becomes exceedingly complex when the range of definitions is presented. While the descent into the definitional morass can be a tedious exercise, it is an essential starting point in the analysis of any of the theories and models because all begin with certain definitional assumptions. One of the more interesting revelations that is derived from the examination of definitions is that most of the theories deal not with revolution, even as defined by the particular theorists, but with violence. This problem will be examined in some detail in the next chapter.

Because considerable mystification surrounds the notions of 'theory' and 'model', what these terms mean will also be discussed in some detail. At the outset, however, it may be useful to think in terms of the theory helping to answer the question, 'why?' and the model aiding in explaining how the parts of the theory are related. This is a relatively simplistic approach yet much of the literature complicates the relative meaning of the two terms. Models and theories are closely related to one another for it is not possible to get to the 'why?' question unless we have some indication of how different factors are related to one another.

To approach the Marxian tradition in the study of revolutions it is best to begin with the original Marxist since all within the school begins with him. A two-pronged tradition of reverence and antipathy colours almost any picture that one may have of Marx and the view of society that he held. While no claims of objectivity or neutrality are being posited here, it is possible to look at Marx the social scientist in order to ascertain how useful his framework of analysis is for the study of revolution. This requires two steps: his model of revolutionary change must be understood so that the particular theory of revolution that is of greatest interest, the rise and eventual triumph of the proletariat, may be examined and tested.

While a host of revolutionaries followed Marx and carried his name on the banners that heralded their individual revolutionary movements, the Leninist and Maoist 'theories' have been of greatest influence because the movements that bore their names, in addition to Marx's, succeeded in gaining power. Thus, we shall concentrate upon the revisions that these leaders made to the Marxian theory when applying it to their own countries. It is, of course, imperative to place these theories in context and deal with some of the other Marxist approaches, and this will be done, albeit briefly. But both Lenin and Mao have had enormous influence on revolutionary theorists and activists throughout the world, and one can see in their writings the most obvious fusion of theory and practice. Perhaps as social conditions alter, further new Marxist thinkers will manage to leave their imprint upon the Marxian tradition, but for now, some understanding of Leninism and Maoism is vital for an appreciation of the evolution of Marxist thought with regard to revolution.

The functionalists present us with a far simpler task in selecting the work that should be analysed. Because their notion of revolution is derived from a tradition that includes a particular view toward societal persistence, relatively little work has been done within the functionalist school that enables us to examine why revolutions occur. Talcott Parsons, functionalism's major contemporary figure, would seem the appropriate thinker to consider in our analysis, but he has done relatively little work with regard to questions of revolution and why societies fall apart. In fact, Parsons has had serious doubts concerning the construction of a theory of social change (of which revolution would be considered one type). In relation to his theory of the social system, Parsons wrote:

> ' . . . while . . . we do not have a complete theory of the process of change in social systems, we do have a canon of approach to the problems of constructing such a theory. When such a theory is available the millennium for social science will have arrived. This will not come in our time and most probably never. But progress toward it is much more likely to be assured and rapid if we know what we want and need.'[2]

Parsons argued further that the way to develop an adequate theory of social change is through a proper understanding of the social system.

This is basically the argument that is taken up by Chalmers Johnson who has attempted to develop a model of revolutionary change within the functionalist framework. Beginning with the premise that an understanding of the properly functioning (i.e. stable) society is necessary before an understanding of the non-functioning society is possible, Johnson has constructed a model of revolutionary change that will serve as the basis of our analysis of the utility of this school in explaining why revolution occurs.

There is rather more choice among the mass society theorists for the focal point of our analysis, but they have all begun with basic premises concerning pluralist democracy. Through an analysis of what pluralist democracy is we shall apply the theory of mass society to the period of the rise of the Nazis in Germany and try to determine whether that theory is valid. This is one of the few cases in which the theory has been tested extensively by a variety of analysts, and the results of the tests are still not universally accepted as confirming or denying the theory. The theorists with whose work we shall be concerned particularly are Hannah Arendt and William Kornhauser.

While various analyses of revolutionary leaders are available, among the most interesting are the studies of Lenin and Hitler. We shall look at some of the assumptions that have been made about their personality development in order to determine whether they became revolutionaries, at least in part, because of their early childhood experiences. The backgrounds of these two leaders are particularly suitable for analysis because of the wealth of information that is available about them.

Dealing with the psychological theories that are concerned with the masses rather than revolutionary leaders, Pitirim Sorokin developed a theory of revolution that dealt with the 'cramped instincts' of the population. Sorokin believed that revolution resulted from the feeling on the part of members of the population that they were being repressed. Further, the conclusion of the revolution occurs when that same population understands its 'need' for a restoration of order.

Sorokin's approach is not widely accepted within the psychological school. The more enduring approach is the school of relative deprivation which has evolved out of the frustration-aggression hypothesis.[3] In order to understand the 'evolution' of the relative deprivation approach we shall begin with an analysis of de Tocqueville's study of the French Revolution and the later modification of de Tocqueville's theory by James Davies. The section will be concluded with a critique of the theory of relative deprivation as propounded by Gurr.

Finally, we shall consider how far the theories of revolution have taken us toward an understanding of why revolutions occur.

Notes and References

1 Aristotle, *Politics*, from *The Basic Works of Aristotle*, ed. by Richard McKeon, New York, 1941, Book I, 1301b. p. 5.

2 Talcott Parsons, *The Social System*, New York, 1964. First published 1951, pp. 534–5.

3 The seminal work in this area is John Dollard, Leonard W. Doob, Neal E. Miller, O. H. Mowrer and Robert S. Sears, *Frustration and Aggression*, New Haven, 1939.

Chapter 2
Dimensions of Revolutionary Change

Defining what constitutes revolution is the first and perhaps most critical problem to be confronted. The proliferation of literature dealing with the concept of revolution does not help matters. On the contrary, the usage of the term is varied enough to have provided very different meanings in each of the many works. Some studies have gone so far as to define revolution in different ways in different sections of the same book.[1] Amann suggests that there is no great cause for concern with the variations in the definitions. 'There is no "true" definition of an abstraction: such a term is a semantic device which may or may not be useful, not a reflection of some absolute Platonic prototype'.[2] Of course, Amann is correct in one sense; there is no 'true' definition. But this is no comfort to the student facing a wide range of options. And we shall see that some definitions are considerably more useful in the analysis of the concept than others.

The scope of the term, revolution, varies; it is not only used with reference to radical political change. In very broad terms the word has been applied to the transition from agricultural to industrial eras, especially in Western countries where the impact of industrialization, together with the resulting urbanization, upon the later development of the society was enormous. Hence, we had what is now known as the industrial revolution. More recently we have experienced a communications revolution of many dimensions. First, radio and television have revolutionized the transmission of information.[3] Second, the great advances in computer and telephone technology have allowed scientific enquiry to proceed at what can be described only as an exponential growth rate. Third, rapid population movement has been achieved through the development of mass transportation by train, car and aircraft.

In other aspects of life, advances in food technology have led to what has been termed a 'green revolution', especially in many

8

of the developing countries. While there are attendant problems, food yields have increased considerably in many places. We are currently embroiled in what appears to be a radical alteration of the values regarding sex roles in the industrial societies. This sexual revolution has produced groups such as Women's Liberation and Gay Liberation, and it has made family planning organizations respectable. Given the wide usage of the term it should come as no surprise that Crane Brinton began his own book with the thought that 'revolution is one of the looser words'.[4]

There is, of course, an intuitive appreciation that the term 'revolutionary change' conveys the notion of something radical happening, that old forms are disappearing, or are at least in the process of being displaced by new and usually untried approaches. Thus, when we speak about new techniques in medical science such as the use of an artificial kidney, or new literary forms such as James Joyce used, the word 'revolutionary' is certainly an apt description.

Even when speaking about new military techniques as being revolutionary, we are using an appropriate term. The German blitzkrieg of World War II effectively revolutionized warfare by coordinating for the first time attacks utilizing mechanized ground and air forces. The power and motion of the German attacks represented a complete reversal of the strategies utilized in the previous World War. In the earlier period attacks along a linear front by infantry and cavalry were the norm. In the 1939–45 war, the Germans concentrated troops in selected areas and used tanks as an offensive weapon. Other countries had to alter their military systems before they were able to confront the Germans successfully. Until they did, they were unable to compete with the German forces despite their generally superior strength in terms of numbers of divisions and weapons.

Thus it is in understanding the implications of these types of change that we may gain some appreciation of what revolution means. But among social theorists and social scientists no universally satisfactory conceptual definition has been agreed upon. For example, revolution defined as the change by violence of the ruling group in the state is not the same as revolution defined as a radical alteration of values in the community. But revolution is not the only term which raises problems. Heroic attempts have been made to inventory the many definitions that are current in political science.[5] These attempts have not, however, been effective, and conceptual confusion is still too common.

Power, for example, has been considered by many to be the central datum of political science since the very origins of the discipline.[6] Prior to the time of Plato philosophers were already concerned with the question of the distribution of power within a society. The normative consideration of who should and who should not have power in a particular community has been with us for over two thousand years. Given the fact of continuing—and increasing—popular clashes with authorities in virtually all societies, the answers seem no nearer today than when the Greek philosophers were worrying about the problem. In many ways the problem may be more complex today than in the past. The communications revolution has helped to create a more informed and knowledgeable populace. Leaders are more exposed to the views of those whom they govern. Since a sharp generational distance may exist between the rulers and the ruled, the answer to the question 'who should rule?' may differ considerably for the former than for the latter. In the more stable, less changing eras of the past a less informed population rarely called into question the right of a particular ruler or rulers to hold the main position of authority.

In more recent times the question 'who should rule?' or 'who should have power?' has been complemented by another question. Contemporary political scientists have concerned themselves with the empirical question of how power is distributed in the community. But these scholars have been unable to arrive at a definition of power with which the majority can agree. In fact, at the root of the dispute concerning the distribution of power in a community is this failure to come to terms with what is meant by the term 'power'. As a result of the differing definitions, findings in research have followed many patterns. The problem is that we are uncertain whether these findings reflect the different definitions from which they start or the particular conditions of the systems which they study. Some researchers have found hierarchical pyramidal arrangements while others have located rather diffuse power arrangements. Do these findings accurately portray the particular social arrangements of the communities analysed, or do they merely follow on from the particular definitions of power that have been utilized?[7]

Riker, in an article which is particularly concerned with an analysis of the many notions, or definitions, of power has noted that when dealing with the term, 'the classification has not proceeded as far as is needed so that we are still not at all sure of what we are talking about when we use the term'.[8] He goes on to examine five different formal definitions of power. By reducing each formula to mathematical terms he finds that 'these definitions have very little in common'.[9] Such ambiguity, he concludes, 'has no place in science or philosophy'.[10]

The reason why there is no place in a science of politics for conceptual cloudiness is that unless we are quite clear about what it is that we are studying the results of the study must always be considered suspect. Terms ought to be clear to those engaged in the same type of research for as Hempel states, explication of terms

'aims at reducing the limitations, ambiguities, and inconsistencies of their ordinary usage by propounding a reinterpretation intended to enhance the clarity and precision of their meanings as well as their ability to function in hypotheses and theories with explanatory and predictive force'.[11]

Hypotheses may be tested and results compared, and as these results are compared we may be in a position to develop fruitful generalizations that can lead to the formulation of theories. But comparison is rendered questionable, if not impossible, if the researchers are not defining their concepts in the same way. As Riker has stated, they are not really examining the same phenomenon if the definitions are different.

While many of the definitions of revolution have a number of factors in common there is a considerable variation among others, so wide in some cases that it may be concluded that the authors are not talking about the same phenomenon. Additionally, it should be noted that several aspects of revolutionary change which are particularly popular in the definitions that are utilized by most theorists—especially value alteration and violence—may, in fact, be the least useful in helping us to understand revolutions and why they occur. Value alteration and violence are such difficult concepts to measure and evaluate that from the perspective of trying to isolate causes and consequences of revolutions, other factors may be more amenable to systematic analysis.

Thus, two factors may be cited as adding to the difficulty of studying revolution. First, there is considerable variation among the many scholars of revolution regarding the definition. Second, those aspects of revolution with which most scholars tend to associate with the phenomenon are very difficult to measure. To deal with each of the theories and models that is discussed, the definition that serves as the starting point must be understood to explain not only what may be classified as a revolution for purposes of that theory or model, but also the consequences of that definition, i.e., what is not a revolution. This point becomes especially significant when dealing with those violent upheavals such as student demonstrations in Italy or Greece or Mexico which would not be considered revolutions in the sense that it will be discussed in this book. On the other hand, an election in Chile which brings to office a Marxist President who is committed to far-reaching social change may conceivably be one event in a revolution.

Defining Revolution

Generally speaking, definitions of revolution fall into two very rough categories with some of the definitions tending to straddle the fence between the two. The first category includes the types of change that may be usefully referred to as the Great Revolution. The theorists whose definitions would be located here include Crane Brinton, George Pettee, Sigmund Neumann, and those in the Marxian tradition such as Lenin, Mao and Castro. The revolutions include the French and American revolutions of the eighteenth century and the two major twentieth-century revolutions, the Russian and the Chinese. The Algerian, Cuban and Mexican revolutions could, arguably, also be included in this category. On the other hand, occurrences such as the Brazilian Army seizure of power in 1964 would not be included. This is not to suggest that all military coups are, by definition, eliminated from this group for the Egyptian army coup of 1952 could be considered part of a revolution for reasons that will be discussed later.

One example of such a definition of revolution is provided by Pettee who describes a great revolution as 'a reconstitution of the state'.[12] This type of revolution is perceived as having enormous consequences for a given society or societies. The results of the revolution are such that in a number of ways the end state no longer resembles the original state of the system. Such changes may occur in the 'myth' of the state, the structural arrangements, the leadership formations, or the political institutions.

The second category of definition is considerably broader and would, of course, include most of the major changes included in the first. It would also include all transfers of power that are extra-legal and/or violent. Theorists in this school would include Chalmers Johnson, Rudolf Rummel and Raymond Tanter, Peter Calvert, and James Davies. According to the view contained in this type of definition, the Greek army coup of 1967 in which the military seized power could be considered revolutionary while the Nazi takeover of Weimar Germany in 1933 would not: if the transfer of power was accomplished legally, it cannot be called a revolution. Nor would the Labour Party's electoral victory in 1945 and that ensuing programme of legislation which led to dramatic changes in aspects of British life be considered a revolution.[13] Such changes are considered to be part of the ordinary political processes of the two countries.

There is a tendency among virtually all writers in this field to look at revolutions in terms of upheavals or extra-legal change but not to see them as part of the 'normal' political process of that country. The end result of the 'normal' political process may be considerably different from the original state, but this is of no consequence. If the electoral procedure brought to power a new class of rulers which then proceeded to alter the political and social structures of that particular state, a revolution would not, according to the broader conception of revolution, be said to have occurred. This qualification is true of the 'great revolutions' school as well.

The essential difference between the two schools is that the theorists in the 'great revolutions' school tend to take what we may call an exclusivist view of what constitutes revolution. In their opinion only a few situations in which radical change occurs constitute revolution. The second school examines only two dimensions of social change. It asks 'how was the change accomplished?' Effectively, then, it is not so much concerned with what the change is about or how extensive the change is or, in fact, whether any other change occurs, as whether the change was effected 'legally' or 'illegally', 'violently' or 'nonviolently'. A revolution is, by definition, non-legal, violent change.

The 'great revolutions' school is only partly concerned with the legality of the process or with how the change occurs. The members of that school would generally accept the view that legal changes of power are not part of the revolutionary situation. But the 'great revolutions' theorists would go further and argue that there are numerous dimensions of revolutionary change. It is by taking account of some or all of these dimensions that one might be able to explain whether a revolution did occur in the past, is occurring at the present time, or will occur in the future.

The dimensions of revolution that have emerged include alteration in the value structure (or the myths of the particular system), alteration of the social structure, change in the political institutions, legality (or illegality) of the change, elite alteration (either in personnel or social composition), and violence. These dimensions have been derived from the numerous approaches to the subject. They indicate that there is some agreement among many of the scholars, but not each theorist in the 'great revolutions' school would agree with all of the dimensions of revolutionary change. A few definitions would include all of the dimensions, but most would include only a few. Several of the dimensions have much wider implications than others and they may, in fact, imply the presence or inclusion of the other dimensions.

Alteration of Values

Most theorists would consider the alteration of values to be a critical and perhaps most important feature of a revolution. This is particularly true of the non-Marxist theorists. Pettee, for example, has suggested that 'a great revolution is one in which the reconstitution of the state association is coincident with the substitution of one myth for another as the main integrating guide in the culture'.[14] Huntington, too, considers revolution to be 'a rapid, fundamental, and violent domestic change in the dominant values and myth of a society . . .'[15] Neumann looked at revolution in the broadest terms and, among other things, saw revolution as '. . . a sweeping, fundamental change in . . . the predominant myth of the social order'.[16] This is not to suggest that this is the only criterion of revolution that is used, for it is not. Personnel change and violence are also important, but within these conceptions the alteration of values is the primary measure of the degree of the change which happens as a result of the revolution.

Kuhn, in a work that has had considerable influence in political science as well as in the natural sciences, has suggested that political revolutions occur because the parties to revolution 'differ about the institutional matrix within which political change is to be achieved and evaluated . . .'.[17] Thus, the inability to resolve different ways of 'looking at the world' leads to the eventual overthrow of the prior way of evaluating the goals and problems of the community and to its replacement by a new view of the world. An example of such a change in the religious sphere might be the Lutheran revolution in early sixteenth century Germany or the shift away from the Church of Rome by the English monarchy in Tudor times. In scientific terms the Copernican revolution would represent such a change.

Even if the revolution does not alter the values of a society in totality—an event which would be considered an unlikely occurrence by most students of revolution given the resilience of cultural patterns—to the participant in the revolution there is a critical perception that the old order which is about to collapse will be swept away from the stage of history. Arendt has suggested that the 'modern concept of revolution' is 'inextricably bound up with the notion that the course of history suddenly begins anew, that an entirely new story never known or told before is about to unfold'.[18]

The view that revolution is in part a perception of a new beginning is tied to the particular changes that were occurring in the West in the period prior to the French and American revolutions. While not the only changing condition which might lead to a growing possibility of revolutionary change, a most significant change was the secularization of politics. In the previous era monarchs ruled by virtue of divine right, but during the sixteenth and seventeenth centuries the status of the role of kings was being called into question, and by the time that these early revolutions occurred the monarchy was already removed from its religiously covered cloak.[19] This secularization of politics culminated in the long process that is now known as the English Revolution as well as the American and French Revolutions.[20] During the English Revolution the roles of king and Parliament were altered permanently so that the monarch could no longer justify his power by reference to his God-given right to rule.

Thus, a critical dimension of any notion of revolution is to be found in the idea of a change in values. This may be demonstrated by a generally theoretical analysis of the philosophical underpinnings of the periods prior to and after the change in ruling groups. It may involve an attempt to ascertain the perceptions of those who participated in the revolution that the world is undergoing change. Or it may involve raising the question of whether the values which guide men's actions have changed. Were the value dimension to be the only one that is utilized then Chile during the Allende Presidency could have been experiencing revolution. On the other hand, Ireland, which experienced a period of considerable violence and eventual independence during the period 1916–23, may not have had a revolution at all. The values of parliamentary democracy fostered by the dominant British seemed to have been present prior to the war for independence, and this has not changed since. Irish parliamentary democracy has functioned uninterrupted since the founding of the state, and its success implies that the new system was planted in very fertile soil.

Interestingly, despite the primary importance of value change in the definitions of revolution it is a concept that has been hardly explored at all empirically. To speak of a fundamental alteration of values or the myth of a society is easy enough. When we speak about 'national character' we are actually implying that there are certain behavioural patterns that reflect the values that a people holds. If we speak about the changes in behaviour of Germans since World War II it is the value alteration that we are implying, but to demonstrate that these changes have occurred is quite another problem. It is difficult enough to determine what the values of a stable society are; dealing with values in transition is even more difficult. Fortunately, however, it is by exploring the other dimensions which follow that we are able to suggest—and the word suggest is used deliberately—that an alteration of the values of a community has occurred. Definitions that are clustered on the other dimensions are much more easily operationalized, i.e., examined in the 'real world', than the notion that revolution may be measured by the degree to which values in the society have changed.

Structural Alteration

The alteration of the existing social structure as a mark of revolutionary change is a second dimension which might be utilized in a definition of revolution for many of the theorists have considered structural change to be a major component of revolution. Neumann, for example, has suggested that alteration of the social structure and economic property control are the vital elements in the revolutionary formula.[21] But of all those who have looked at revolution as an alteration of the social structure none has been as influential as Marx.

The whole of the Marxian tradition of revolution is, as we shall discuss in detail later, wrapped up with the idea that revolution is the alteration of the social structure. Revolution is the passage, or transition, from one historical epoch to another. Each particular epoch is characterized by the mode of production. With the transition from one epoch to the next the relations between classes which reflect the particular mode of production are altered; as the mode of production develops, the situation of the exploited class deteriorates. Hence, 'the revolution, the transformation of an entire system, occurs when a class of men see no other way out of their misery than revolution'.[22] In Marxian terms the final revolution will end with the elimination of class conflict and the ultimate abolition of the state, the state being, after all, no more than a reflection of the dominant class interests in the given epoch.

The Marxian view has influenced a number of theorists. From the time that Marx began to write, a revolutionary movement grew up which has continued to involve his name in the many revolutionary situations in which such theorists have found themselves. Some theorists, such as Rosa Luxemburg, were particularly concerned with the activities of the working class.[23] Lenin had to confront the problem of dealing with both the working class and the peasantry.[24] Mao was forced to rely almost entirely upon the peasantry for the revolutionary support.[25] Yet each of these scholars/revolutionary theorists perceived of revolution almost exclusively in terms of the alteration of the previously existing social structure. It is not without significance, for example, that the first essay in the four volumes of Mao's collected works deals with an analysis of the classes in Chinese society; he attempted to determine which classes might be viewed as allies of the revolution and which classes were its enemies.[26] Despite the lack of an available proletariat after 1927 he still based his revolutionary analysis on the particular class antagonisms that were prevalent in China.

Although the Marxists are the most influential group to define revolution in terms of an alteration of the previously existing social structure they are not the only group of theorists which is so inclined. A significant non-Marxist contribution is provided by Dahrendorf who deals with what he terms the German Question.[27] The German Question is concerned with why the Nazis were able to come to power in the democratic Weimar era and why liberal democracy failed to take hold in Germany. Dahrendorf is interested in the particular factors that led the German people to vote for candidates of the National Socialist

Party and, by doing so, to give their support to Hitler. Significantly, he argues that in the early period of the Nazi rule a revolution did occur in Germany. In Weimar Germany, the social system was effectively built on authoritarian relationships so the attempt that Weimar made to build democracy was doomed to failure from the start:

> 'The social basis of German authoritarianism, thus of the resistance of German society to modernity and liberalism, consisted in a structural syndrome that held people to the social ties in which they had found themselves without their doing and that prevented them from full participation'.[28]

It was by replacing the 'organic social structures by mechanical formations',[29] that the Nazis were able to alter significantly traditional German society. The Nazis destroyed the states, the wellsprings of local loyalties. They rationalized the trade unions, and organized all facets of the life of the individual. This process will be discussed in more detail in Chapter 7.

Dahrendorf's study is not the only sociological-historical work which deals with revolution in terms of an alteration of the social structure. Various works which examine the new social structure in the Soviet Union following the revolution demonstrate that the problem of structural change is amenable to empirical analysis. Deutscher argued in a series of lectures that the original revolutionary working class in the Soviet Union was destroyed during the revolutionary-civil war period. The Soviet bureaucracy was forced to develop as it did in order to become the 'custodian' of the revolution for the new revolutionary proletariat which would grow to take the place of the class which had been destroyed. This bureaucracy 'has exercised power greater than that wielded by any possessing class in modern times . . .'.[30] But a critical distinction exists between this new ruling class and the old Tsarist order. The power of the Soviet bureaucracy is not rooted in the control or ownership of property; instead, the 'bureaucratic domination rests on nothing more stable than a state of political equilibrium' which is 'a far more fragile foundation for social dominance than is any established structure of property relations sanctified by law, religion and tradition'.[31] Thus, a new social structure has emerged in the Soviet Union, and its basis is vastly different than the previous system of social stratification.

Lane has come to roughly the same conclusion as Deutscher.

He argues that social stratification in the Soviet Union today is not unlike that of the Western industrial democracies. In fact, he hypothesizes that 'while the *origins* of the system of social stratification are to be found in the political order, after a revolutionary change many patterns of inequality come to approximate to the social stratification of other industrial societies'.[32] Lane's argument is different from Deutscher's for he is suggesting that the patterns of the social structure are likely to be similar in all industrial societies regardless of the dominant social myth. He does, however, argue like Deutscher that the system of social stratification that is found in Soviet society today does have political origins which stem from the revolution. Thus, he is able to state, 'it seems to me that the really significant difference in the system of social stratification compared with Western societies is the absence of a private propertied class possessing great concentrations of wealth'.[33] This, then, is a measure of the difference not only between other industrial societies and the Soviet Union, but between the Soviet Union and Tsarist Russia.

Institutional Change

Definitions of revolution may hinge on some notion of institutional change. Moore, for example, has constructed a continuum of social change on which revolution is placed at one end. He perceives of revolution as a type of change which is violent, 'engages a considerable portion of the population, and results in a change in the structure of government . . .'.[34] Institutional change is separated from the more general structural change because the former refers to some alteration in the political institutions while the latter may refer to an alteration of the general class relations of society. Thus, institutional change may include such diverse changes as an alteration of the monarchy or its abolition, or the establishment or abolition of a legislature, or a substantial alteration of the legislature's particular functions in society.

It is quite difficult to separate institutional change from either an alteration of values or the more general change in social structure, for it may be argued that the change of the political institutions may well reflect a change in the dominant values and the social structure. Edwards, arguing that in a revolution one system of legality replaced another, made this point when he stated :

'Any institution, no matter how foolish or pernicious, if only it is firmly fixed in the *mores*, will continue to exist in spite of the clearest demonstration of its harmfulness, until sheer necessity forces its abolition. Man is largely a creature of habit and tradition. Most of his institutions are the products of sentiment, not of reason. He will endure great suffering and loss rather than drop from his social order any institution to which he has been long accustomed. It means nothing that an alternative institution may be greatly superior to the old, but it is not the old, and so it will be admitted only grudgingly and under the pressure of urgent necessity'.[35]

Edwards believed that it takes at least three generations to bring people around to the idea that the only way out of an intolerable situation is to overthrow the existing government because of their deeply held values.[36]

Thus, according to this point of view, institutional change merely reflects the alteration in values and social structure, but particularly values, in the society. It implies that institutional change is a function of the alteration of values, and that value alteration must precede institutional change. Because value change in this view is a precursor of institutional change, it subsumes institutional change. Also implicit is the assumption that institutional change is an operational definition for the concept of value change. In other words, by examining the change in institutions we are actually measuring the degree to which values have been altered in the community.

An example of such a change is the Russian Revolution. One of the most remarkable features of the collapse of the Russian Monarchy is the apparent ease with which it was finally brought down in 1917. The Romanov Dynasty had dominated Russia for more than three hundred years, and in 1905 it had survived a major series of risings. Yet twelve years later it had been brought down by strikes in the capital, Petrograd. Surely this is validation of the thesis that value alteration between 1905 and 1917 preceded institutional change.

This, however, may represent an unduly restrictive view. We are using institutional change as a separate dimension of revolution because institutional change may, in fact, precede value change. Several generations may elapse before the dominant values in a society alter after the institutions have been changed. Among some segments of the population the values may never really change. The French monarchy may have been terminated for all time after 1848 but large portions of the population continued to hold the notion of monarchy or strong leadership in esteem for long periods afterwards.[37] This may have also been the case in Germany after the abdication of the Kaiser at the end of World War I. In spite of the establishment of an entirely new range of institutions, the values of German society remained what they had been prior to the fall of the Kaiser.[38] Another example of an alteration of the institutions preceding value change is to be found in Japan. When World War II ended, the Allied Forces insisted that the Japanese establish a parliamentary democracy in which the Emperor was demoted from a 'divine being' to a Western-style constitutional monarch.[39] Assuming that the values of constitutional monarchy and democratic-parliamentarism are now firmly established in Japan, this is a clear example of institutional alteration preceding value alteration.

For these reasons, institutional change is treated as a separate dimension. While it is closely related to value alteration it is not the same thing nor is it necessarily the result of a change of values; instead, the institutional change may effect an alteration of values.

Alteration of the Elite

One of the most useful dimensions of revolutionary change is what may be referred to as the 'elite dimension'. A definition utilizing this dimension examines the particular leadership formation in the society and to what degree the leadership has altered during the course of a revolution. This may seem a fairly obvious point; surely any revolution as we currently use the term is going to include a change in the ruling elite. But there are major variations among the different theories of revolutions with regard to what constitutes an alteration of the leadership.

If we construct a continuum of elite change, at one end there is what may be called personnel change. At the other end of the continuum is a radical alteration of the elite which would imply drawing the elite from different classes. The first view holds that

'A revolution may be said to exist where a group of insurgents illegally and/or forcefully challenges the governmental elite for the occupancy of roles in the structure of political authority. A successful revolution occurs where, as a result of a challenge to the governmental elite, insurgents are eventually able to occupy principal roles within the structure of political authority'.[40]

In this same vein, another theorist has suggested that 'revolutions are . . . violent civil disturbances that cause the displacement of one ruling group by another that has a broader popular basis for support'.[41]

Such a notion of revolution may not, however, be particularly fruitful. While it is true that if we include with elite change a condition that such change was accompanied by violence then we exclude from consideration the 'downfall' of governments in the parliamentary democracies such as the United Kingdom and the Netherlands, we do not exclude many cases in which nothing else occurred. If we were to examine Thailand since 1950, we would find that three military coups have taken place. Utilizing this definition we would conclude that three revolutions have occurred despite the fact that each coup involved very little beside the personnel change. Certainly little change has occurred in the day-to-day life situation of the people. Further, the new leadership groups have tended to come from precisely the same class as the previous groups. A similar argument could be made with reference to countries such as Syria and South Viet Nam.

Ultimately, to reduce the dimension of elite alteration to simple personnel change is to weaken the concept of revolution. When we think about revolutionary change we have an image of radical change, of a major alteration, not a mere change of actors performing unchanging roles. It is, of course, possible that personnel change might be part of a revolutionary situation, but it would seem to be insufficient as a single or comprehensive indicator of a revolution.

At the other end of the continuum Lasswell has provided a definition of revolution that takes us considerably further than the idea that revolution hinges on a simple change of personnel. He defines revolution as 'a shift in the class composition of elites'.[42] The simplicity of this definition ought not hide its ramifications. The elite dimension in any social formula, be it one for social stability or for social change, is a vital one. Changes in the elite may well reflect enormous changes in the value orientations or social structure of a particular society. Such changes may also be a harbinger of a coming change in the values of that society. Lasswell is suggesting that examining class background to determine the degree of change within the ruling personnel is not the primary issue. What is of greatest concern is what that change represents in social terms.

If Lasswell's definition is used, then the Nazi seizure of power in 1933 and what followed may be considered a revolution given the pronounced differences in general and class background between the Nazi leadership and the previous German elite groups.[43] Lerner has argued that the Nazi elite was certainly a 'marginal' group when analysed with reference to the previous German leadership, a point that we shall discuss in Chapter 7. The group that came to power in Ireland following the break with Great Britain was considerably different in its collective background and social class from the earlier leaders of the old Irish parliamentary party.[44] The Egyptian coup could also be considered part of a revolution if Lasswell's definition is used, since the army colonels that deposed King Farouk in 1952 did not come from the same class as those that had ruled Egypt prior to the coup.[45]

The definitions that accepted personnel change as an indicator of revolution would not have categorized the German case as a revolution for no force was used in the takeover. The Irish and Egyptian cases would probably have been included as would each of the recent Syrian coups and the Greek military coup of 1967. These latter coups would not be included in the revolution category if Lasswell's definition were to be used, since the new rulers were drawn from the same classes as the rulers that they displaced.

Legality and Legitimacy

A fifth dimension follows from those notions of revolution that are reflected in the Syrian-type coup. It is concerned with the contrast between legal and illegal transfers of power. Peripherally related to this is the very broad and elusive question of legitimacy. When we speak of legal change as opposed to non-legal, or illegal change, we are referring to changes made according to the constitutional and/or traditional rules of a society. Legitimacy is a somewhat different concept which tends to subsume legality. It refers to the support given by the people of that society to the political system and that system's political roles. The support that is demonstrated gives the rulers the 'moral' right to rule.

Legitimacy is a particularly vexing problem for all but the

Marxian theorists who see authority resting largely upon force. Rose states 'the type of authority that a regime exercises can be distinguished by the degree to which its population acts in accord with regulations concerning the maintenance of the regime and for diffuse cultural orientations approving the regime'.[46] Hence, if a regime is widely supported by the populace, or by the 'politically significant' members of the populace, only minimal force is required by the government to keep order in the society. If, however, there exists widescale opposition to that regime, then force will be needed in a rather large measure. One of the sociological schools, the functionalists, utilize as their central theme with regard to revolution this question of legitimacy.

On the point that 'all revolutions are definitionally failures of political control by an existing ruling elite',[47] most theorists of revolution could agree. The real problem that they must face is how one goes about measuring and analysing this failure of political control. But on a second point they could not necessarily agree. Dunn has stated, 'there can be no revolutions, however abortive, except where the previous regime, whether by its weakness or by its viciousness, has lost the right to rule'.[48] This particular argument would be the reverse of that which sees certain revolutions occurring largely as the result of action by groups without broad-based support. Depending upon the particular point of view one holds, the Viet Cong revolution in South Viet Nam could be interpreted in at least two ways. The fighting could be considered an indigenous popular uprising or it could be seen as part of an international communist conspiracy with its direction being plotted by forces outside of South Viet Nam and which lacks the support of the terrorized population.

Nor could the view that a revolution represents regime failure or viciousness on the part of the regime be held without question by those who look at revolutionary change as non-legal or illegal transfer of power. First, a real problem is raised when we accept illegal transfer as revolution because of the vast number of cases that are likely to be included. As with the notion of revolution-as-personnel change, each coup in Dahomey or Sierra Leone would constitute a revolution. So, too, would each military take-over in Latin America. Second, such a transfer of power is illegal only in the eyes of the previous ruling groups (and, perhaps, foreign governments that recognized the original group), not by the new group that gains control or, indeed, even by the masses. Constitutions that have little moral basis are easily replaced, and the replacements may be replaced as well. If we may reiterate a point that was made by Edwards: in a revolution one system of legality is substituted for another. Once the old regime is gone, the new regime is in a position to institute its own legal base. Whether moral support follows is another question.

Violence and Violent Events

Not all theorists of revolution accept the idea that revolutions are, by definition, violent acts. Edwards, for example, has argued that revolutionary change is 'brought about not necessarily by force and violence'.[49] By taking this view, Edwards is in a lonely position. It is understandable that Edwards should stand alone because the image of the masses rushing from the countryside and cleansing the towns and cities of the villains is a popular one, dramatized by revolutions such as the Mexican and Chinese. The picture of the Russian Revolution that has been depicted by contemporary Soviet art is one of the masses rising to throw the tyrants out physically.

Scholars who write about revolution generally accept this view, for violence has become an integral part of the revolutionary situation. Dunn has argued that 'revolutions are a form of massive, violent and rapid social change'.[50] Violence is a major component of Huntington's definition as well.[51] Calvert goes further than either of these theorists by utilizing only the dimension of violence to define revolution. He states that revolution is 'simply a form of governmental change through violence'.[52] This view is not far from the argument that revolution is a form of illegal change.

Violence is an integral part of the Marxian notion of revolution as well, but the conceptions of what constitutes violence are considerably different than among non-Marxian scholars. The theorist in the non-Marxian tradition is as likely to place the blame for violence on the revolutionary as he is to blame the government. If the state responds with force to combat revolutionary behaviour it is merely acting in response to the violent provocation of the rebels. On the other hand, the Marxian theorist looks at the state as the instrument, or tool, of the dominant class. Thus anti-revolutionary behaviour on the part of the leadership is violence. When the proletariat, or dominated class, finally revolts, it is only as a reaction to the calculated violence done to it by the bourgeoisie.

As early as 1927 Mao was writing that 'a revolution is not a dinner party, or writing an essay, or painting a picture, or doing embroidery, it cannot be so refined, so leisurely and gentle, so temperate, kind, courteous, restrained and magnanimous. A revolution is an insurrection, an act of violence by which one class overthrows another'.[53] In more recent terms Debray saw revolution not only as containing elements of violence or military action but as a process in which the military leaders within the revolution, the instruments of violence, become the nucleus and givers of revolutionary theory rather than the party theorists as in the more 'traditional' Leninist-Maoist conception. Debray believes that the Maoist idea of revolution is outdated. Today, 'under certain conditions, the political and the military are not separate, but form one organic whole, consisting of the people's army whose nucleus is the guerrilla army. The vanguard party can exist in the form of the guerrilla *foco* itself. The guerrilla force is the party in embryo'.[54] Thus, instead of the party preceding the development of the fighting forces, the reverse is now the case. The military, i.e., the instrument of violence, becomes the basis of the party theory.

Among those who see violence as an integral part of revolutionary social change, not one would argue that all violent acts are revolutionary acts for it is obvious that this is not the case. As Dahl has said, 'when I read that looting TV sets from neighbourhood stores is an act of revolutionary violence, I wonder whether politics and the theatre are not converging—to the detriment of both'.[55] Most violent acts are not revolutionary, or in support of a revolution, although it may well be the case that the factors that are responsible for an adolescent's violent acts may also be at the base of the revolutionary's behavioural tendency. According to some notions of revolution such a tendency may reflect a general syndrome of anti-social behaviour.

Yet there is difficulty in basing a definition of revolution largely on the presence of violence in the transfer of power. As in the case of the term, revolution, a clear, concise, and widely accepted definition of violence does not appear to have been derived. In an article dealing with revolutions as the politics of violence, for example, Calvert never really tells us what he means by violence. He argues, however, 'that violence is politically inefficient'.[56] Not being certain what he means by violence it is difficult to determine whether he is correct. One may argue, for example, that while the violent act may have grave consequences, it may also be the fastest and least costly, i.e., most efficient, way to achieve the desired end, either the destruction of the existing regime by the revolutionaries, or the destruction of the revolutionaries by the existing regime.

The difficulties that may be encountered by an imprecise or broad definition of violence may be seen in the work of Chalmers Johnson. Johnson sees any attempt to separate the notion of revolution from the commission of an act or many acts of violence as absurd. His view of revolution is based on the argument that one way of approaching 'the concept of revolution is to examine it as a form of violence'.[57] At another point in his work he suggests that revolution is a form of social change. In other words, revolution is at the end of a continuum of social change, and it is also possible to place it on a continuum of violent behaviour. But violence and social change may be mutually exclusive phenomena. The degree of social change does not necessarily increase in proportion to the degree of violence that is present. Either may occur in the absence of the other.

When Johnson does define violence, he has more difficulty. He does not define violence as the simple use of force by the government or by the revolutionary party or army; instead, he sees it 'as action that deliberately or unintentionally disorients the behaviour of others'.[58] This definition has profound consequences. In recent years writers in the Soviet Union have been jailed, sent to work camps, mental institutions, or exiled. These writers have offended the community by pursuing their art. According to Johnson's definition it would be argued that the writers have committed violent acts, for they are, by definition, anti-social. The young black entering a previously all-white school in the United States is engaged in violent behaviour. If the governor of a Southern state stands in the doorway to prevent the entry of the black child and a crowd gathers, and a person in the crowd strikes that child, then according to Johnson's definition of violence, the child has committed a violent act. By pursuing a course which defies social convention the child has disorientated the behaviour of the population. The physical act of striking the child is not a violent act because it is not disorientating the behaviour of other whites in the crowd and done in response to the violent act committed by the 'revolutionary' child.

Johnson's concept of revolution as a violent act—as well as those of most other theorists—has further implications. During

the twentieth century we have become increasingly familiar with
the notion of the non-violent revolution. The mass movement
that Gandhi led which helped to gain independence for India
was based on a philosophy of non-violence taught by its leader.
It is true that violent acts occurred, but these violent acts may
have been reactions to the passive resistance campaigns. Such
was the case with the civil rights movement that was led by
Martin Luther King in the United States in a crucial period.
King lived by the credo of non-violence that Gandhi preached;
a violent act ended both their lives. Perhaps it is the counter-
revolution rather than the revolution that raises the spectre of
inevitable violence.

Because of the requirement for violence by most theorists of
revolution the idea of the non-violent revolution must become,
for them, a contradiction in terms. Given this view the independence movement in India and the civil rights movement in the
United States would be excised from the category of revolutionary change. Or, using Johnson's definition of violence, such
movements could be seen as revolutionary with both Gandhi
and King losing the title of non-violent men and joining the
ranks of the violent revolutionaries such as Mao and Castro.

So despite the fact that most theorists of revolution would
include violence as a requisite part of the revolutionary formula,
its inclusion does not present us with a trouble-free concept. Nor
does it easily delineate the revolutionary process. As has been
suggested, the definition of violence is imprecise, and this imprecision brings difficulty. It would imply, amongst other things,
that radical alterations of existing societies might not be included
in the category of revolutionary change because of the absence
of violence while violent acts entailing considerably less change
than non-violent situations could be called revolutionary simply
because the elite has been altered through violent means.

The difficulty encountered here is made entirely clear by
Arendt. She argues that

'Violence is no more adequate to describe the phenomenon
of revolution than change; only where change occurs in the
sense of a new beginning, where violence is used to constitute
an altogether different form of government, to bring about the
formation of a new body politic, where the liberation from
oppression aims at least at the constitution of freedom can we
speak of revolution'.[59]

Thus, some violent behaviour might be revolutionary, but not all violent behaviour can be classified in this way. As suggested, those who study revolutions are, by virtue of definitions which hinge on violence, forced to reject the idea of a revolution occurring if no violence has happened even if there has been radical change. Further, their attention will be riveted to the violent act even though it may be nothing more than a violent event with no lasting significance. But this fascination with violent events leads to a second point.

If a revolution is defined as the violent overthrow of the government then it is not seen as a process of radical change; instead, the revolution is, by definition, the point in time when the old regime collapses and the new ruling group takes over. As long as this one change is accompanied by violence then a revolution is said to have occurred. In this usage of the term 'revolution' we can see some of the terminological confusion that is present in the literature. An example of this confusion may be found in the categorization of coups. Some would argue that no coup is a revolution because it involves almost no violence in the transfer of power. Others would hold that all coups are revolutions because they inevitably involve an illegal transfer of power. Another example of confusion involves the attempt to date revolutions. In the Russian case, we speak of the February revolution and October revolution to differentiate the collapse of the Autocracy from the Bolshevik seizure of power. It is, of course, not always so easy to 'date' a revolution. The Chinese revolution seems to defy such a simple process since the 'seizure of power' by the Communists occurred after more than twenty years of warfare. To suggest that the revolution occurred on October 1, 1949, when the Chinese People's Republic was formally declared is to ignore years of revolutionary struggle.[60]

The major problem that occurs with the elevation of violence and the violent event as the primary dimension of revolution is that it rejects the idea that the extent of a revolution may be measured by the amount of change that occurs over a particular time span, a feature that is either explicit or implicit in most of the other definitions of revolution that we have examined. If the change is minimal, then a revolution cannot be said to have occurred. If, on the other hand, the change is 'radical', then, it may be said that a revolution has occurred. The mechanism by which the transfer of power occurred is not in itself of great significance. Thus some coups may be part of a revolution but a coup, in itself, is not a revolution simply because it represents illegal change. Further, if we think of revolutions as processes rather than events then the Russian revolution(s) occurred not on a specific occasion(s) but over a period between 1905 to about 1939, 1905 being the year of the first workers' revolt and 1939 being the year that the Stalinist purges ended. But even this dating is imprecise.

We have seen that one of the hallmarks of revolution when compared with other forms of social change is the degree to which the end state of the systems differs from the original state of the system. Thus, by examining Russia over a thirty year period, the full magnitude of the change may be seen.

Curiously, when the idea of violence is mixed into the formula, or the discussion of the events leading to the revolution (as the event which marks the overthrow of the regime) is also brought in, this notion of the degree of change tends to be forgotten. This is unfortunate : if a revolution is an event then it is difficult to connect it to a change in values, structures, elites or institutions over time. If, on the other hand, a revolution is a radical alteration of a particular society, or group of societies, then an understanding of how the change was accomplished is only one aspect of the revolution that must be considered.

More important is the extent to which the society has been undergoing change over the given time span; this includes the period prior to the transfer of power and perhaps more significantly, the period after the new group is in power. Arendt has dealt with this point :

'If one keeps in mind that the end of rebellion is liberation, while the end of revolution is the foundation of freedom, the political scientist at least will know how to avoid the pitfall of the historian who tends to place his emphasis upon the first and violent stage of rebellion and liberation on the uprising against tyranny, to the detriment of the quieter second stage of revolution and constitution, because all the dramatic aspects of his story seem to be contained in the first stage, and, perhaps, also because the turmoil of liberation has so frequently defeated the revolution'.[61]

Most of the theorists and model builders with whom we deal in this study are not really concerned with revolutionary change as defined by Marx and Arendt. Instead, they have developed schemes of regime collapse which are associated with degrees of violence in the society. Sadly, most of these scholars do not even follow their own definitions. While the definitions do seem to be concerned with the degree of change in the final state, the models and theories only serve to illustrate how and why a prior regime comes apart rather than focus on the period in which the new regime is establishing itself.

Conclusion

Definitionally, the dimensions along which revolutionary change tends to be placed are as follows:

1 The alteration of values or the myths of the society
2 The alteration of the social structure
3 The alteration of institutions
4 Changes in the leadership formation, either in the personnel of the elite or its class composition
5 Non-legal or illegal transfer of power
6 The presence or dominance of violent behaviour made evident in the events leading to the regime collapse.

Most of the definitions will include more than one of these dimensions of change. Several of the dimensions, notably the alteration of values and social structure may imply or be implied by the other dimensions. It should also be noted that two of the dimensions, value change and violent events, easily the most popular dimensions among the model-builders and theoreticians may be the least useful and helpful in explanation since they are so difficult to deal with on an empirical basis.

If these two dimensions are not included in the definition, or not used when moving from the conceptual to operational definition, then revolution may be examined more readily: revolution could be defined as that process by which a radical alteration of a particular society occurs over a given time span. Such alteration would include (a) a change in the class composition of the elites, (b) the elimination of previous political institutions and their replacement by others (or by none), or an alteration of the functions of these institutions, and (c) changes in the social structure which would be reflected in the class arrangements and/or the redistribution of resources and income. The magnitude of the revolution may be measured by the extent to which changes have occurred in any of the above dimensions or in some combination of them.

Each of the three dimensions suggested is amenable to

empirical analysis, i.e., they may be studied with minimal difficulty in the real world. Through empirical analysis theories of revolution may be developed. If, on the other hand, certain aspects of revolution cannot lend themselves to study on the part of researchers, or, if they bear no resemblance to the terms of the model, then they remain only concepts with no further contribution possible to our understanding of revolutionary change generally.

It is, however, not easy to excise value change and violence. Revolution is a very evocative term, and the twin notions of violence and values contain much of the 'romance' that is normally associated with dramatic social change. All that is being suggested is that the other aspects of revolution may tell us more about the degree and significance of changes than the more elusive components. Further, it may move us to include in the revolutions category societal alterations of great magnitude that heretofore have been excluded because of the absence of violence and our lack of understanding of changes in values.

Notes and References

1 See Chalmers Johnson, *Revolution and the Social System*, Stanford, 1964, esp. Part 2. This problem will be examined in detail in Chapter 6.

2 Peter Amann, 'Revolution: a redefinition', *Political Science Quarterly*, 77, 1962, p. 36.

3 See, for example, H. L. Nieburg, *Political Violence*, New York, 1969.

4 Crane Brinton, *The Anatomy of Revolution*, New York, 1960, p. 4. First published 1938.

5 See Harold Lasswell and Abraham Kaplan, *Power and Society*, New Haven, 1950.

6 *Ibid.*, p. 76.

7 See, for example, some of the 'classic' studies of community power. Floyd Hunter, *Community Power Structure*, Chapel Hill, 1953; Robert Dahl, *Who Governs?*, New Haven, 1961, and Nelson Polsby, *Community Power and Political Theory*, New Haven, 1963. The first two works are representative of the two 'main' schools, the 'elitist' and the 'pluralist'. The latter work falls into the 'pluralist' category, but provides a useful introduction to the subject.

8 William Riker, 'Some ambiguities in the notion of power', *American Political Science Review*, 59, 1965, p. 341.

9 *Ibid.*, p. 343.

10 *Ibid.*, p. 343.

11 Carl Hempel, *Fundamentals of Concept Formation in Empirical Science*, Chicago, 1952, p. 12.

12 George Sawyer Pettee, *The Process of Revolution*, New York, 1971, p. 3. First published 1938.

13 See Brinton, *The Anatomy of Revolution*, p. 4.

14 Pettee, *The Process of Revolution*, p. 22.

15 Samuel P. Huntington, *Political Order in Changing Societies*, New Haven, 1968, p. 264.

16 Sigmund Neumann, 'The international civil war', *World Politics*, 1, 1948–9, pp. 333–4.

17 Thomas S. Kuhn, *The Structure of Scientific Revolutions*, Chicago, 1962, p. 93.

18 Hannah Arendt, *On Revolution*, New York, 1965, p. 21. First published 1963.

19 *Ibid.*, pp. 18–9.

20 See Lawrence Stone, *The Causes of the English Revolution 1529–1642*, London, 1972.

21 Neumann, 'The international civil war', pp. 333–4.

22 Franz Schurmann, 'On revolutionary conflict', *Journal of International Affairs*, 23, 1969, p. 41.

23 There are a number of works that one can choose to examine the social and political thought of Rosa Luxemburg. A very useful work is edited and introduced by Robert Looker, *Rosa Luxemburg: Selected Political Writings*, London, 1972.

24 See V. I. Lenin, 'The two tactics of social-democracy in the democratic revolution', from *Selected Works*, Vol. III, London, 1936, pp. 39–133. This work is the major statement that Lenin made with regard to cooperation with the peasantry. It is discussed in detail in Chapter 5.

25 Perhaps the best introduction to the Maoist view toward the peasantry is found in his very famous 'Report on an investigation of the peasant movement in Hunan' from *Selected Works of Mao Tse-Tung*, Vol. I, Peking, 1967, pp. 23–59.

26 See Mao Tse-Tung, 'Analysis of the classes in Chinese society', from *Selected Works of Mao Tse-Tung*, Vol. I, pp. 13–21.

27 See Ralf Dahrendorf, *Society and Democracy in Germany*, Garden City, New York, 1969. First published 1967, pp. 3–60.

28 *Ibid.*, p. 381.

29 *Ibid.*, p. 385.

30 Isaac Deutscher, *The Unfinished Revolution: Russia 1917–67*, London, 1967, p. 57.

31 *Ibid.*, pp. 56–7.

32 David Lane, *The End of Inequality?*, Harmondsworth, Middlesex, 1971, p. 132.

33 *Ibid.*, p. 69.

34 Wilbert E. Moore, *Social Change*, Englewood Cliffs, New Jersey, 1963, p. 81.

35 Lyford P. Edwards, *The Natural History of Revolution*, New York, 1965, first published 1927, p. 21.

36 *Ibid.*, p. 16.

37 See, for example, William Shirer, *The Collapse of the Third Republic*, London, 1970; Harvey Waterman, *Political Change in Contemporary France*, Columbus, Ohio, 1969; and Henry Ehrmann, *Politics in France*, Boston, 1968.

38 See, for example, Dahrendorf, *Society and Democracy in Germany*, Elizabeth Wiskemann, *Europe of the Dictators*, London, 1966; A. J. Nicholls, *Weimar and the Rise of Hitler*, London, 1968; William Shirer, *The Rise and Fall of the Third Reich*, New York, 1960.

39 See, for example, Ardath W. Burks, *The Government of Japan*, New York, 1961; Nobutaka Ike, *Japanese Politics: An Introductory Survey*, London, 1958; and Chitoshi Yanaga, *Japanese People and Politics*, New York, 1964, pp. 129–43.

40 Raymond Tanter and Manus Midlarsky, 'A theory of revolution', *Journal of Conflict Resolution*, *11*, p. 267.

41 James C. Davies, 'Toward a theory of revolution', *American Sociological Review*, 27, 1962, p. 6.

42 Harold Lasswell, *Politics: Who Gets What, When, How*, New York, 1958. First published 1936, p. 113.

43 Daniel Lerner, 'The Nazi elite', from *World Revolutionary Elites*, ed. by Harold Lasswell and Daniel Lerner, Cambridge, Mass, 1966, pp. 194–318.

44 See A. S. Cohan, *The Irish Political Elite*, Dublin, 1972.

45 See P. J. Vatikiotis, *The Egyptian Army in Politics; Pattern for the New Nations?*, Bloomington, 1961. The viewpoint expressed by Vatikiotis is not universally accepted. Hrair R. Dekmejian has suggested that the Free Officers did not come from the 'humble background' that is normally attributed to them. See *Egypt under Nasir*, Albany, 1971.

46 Richard Rose, 'Dynamic tendencies in the authority of regimes', *World Politics*, 21, 1969, p. 604.

47 John Dunn, *Modern Revolutions*, London, 1972, p. 13.

48 *Ibid.*, p. 246.

49 Edwards, *The Natural History of Revolution*, p. 2.

50 Dunn, *Modern Revolutions*, p. 12.

51 See Huntington, *Political Order in Changing Societies*, p. 264.

52 Peter Calvert, 'Revolution : the politics of violence', *Political Studies*, 15, 1967, p. 2.

53 Mao Tse-Tung, 'Report on an investigation of the peasant movement in Hunan', p. 28.

54 Régis Debray, *Revolution in the Revolution?*, Harmondsworth, Middlesex, 1967, p. 105.

55 Robert Dahl, *After the Revolution?*, New Haven, 1970, p. 4.

56 Calvert, 'Revolution : the politics of violence', p. 9.

57 Chalmers Johnson, *Revolutionary Change*, Boston, 1966, p. 7.

58 *Ibid.*, p. 8.

59 Arendt, *On Revolution*, p. 28.

60 For a discussion of the Chinese 'model' of revolution, see Huntington, *Political Order in Changing Societies*, pp. 270–4.

61 Arendt, *On Revolution*, p. 140.

Chapter 3
Theories and Models in the Analysis of Revolutions

Because two terms, theories and models, are used extensively, a logical next step is to determine with somewhat greater precision what these two terms mean. We should, however, approach the task with caution for there is considerable disagreement about what the terms imply or whether 'theories', in fact, differ at all from 'models'. Additionally, many of the scholars who deal with theory and/or model construction needlessly complicate matters by failing to utilize the types of examples in their works which might make their ideas clear to the student who is unfamiliar with such terms. In this section, then, the basic idea of what is meant by theories and models in this book will be described and applied by looking carefully at the extensive research of one political scientist, some of which dealt with the origins of revolution.

To simplify our task, it should be made clear that certain types of theory are of no concern to us. When speaking about theory, 'what might be more appropriately labelled the history of social thought, or the study of sociological classics'[1] will not be included. Hence, the traditional theories that have been developed in political science in particular and the social sciences generally will be excluded. Van Dyke has stated, 'a political theorist might concern himself with the council-manager system of municipal government not with a view to assessing its efficiency or its chances of survival but rather with a view to determining how it relates to the general proposition that democracy is good'.[2] As suggested earlier, the interest of political theory was the question of what was the right and proper form of the state or what were the proper qualifications of the just or good rulers. This exercise was the chief concern of social thinkers for centuries and, it might be added, universally agreed answers were not given to the basic question of the proper form of the

36

state. Today, however, political scientists are less concerned with this question.

Instead, contemporary analysis is geared to the explanation of social phenomena. In other words, contemporary social science is very largely—but not entirely—concerned with explaining how and why certain events happen. It is interested primarily in discovering 'laws' of political or social behaviour which might explain the social patterns that occur and recur. So in this book, the Marx that says 'Let the ruling classes tremble at the Communistic revolution. The proletarians have nothing to lose but their chains. They have a world to win'[3] does not really interest us. We are interested instead in the Marx who hypothesized, 'In proportion as the bourgeoisie, i.e., capital, is developed, in the same proportion is the proletariat, the modern working class, developed'.[4] The first Marx is the political philosopher-propagandist. The second Marx is the social and political scientist who created, and left to the generations that followed him, a model and theory of revolution.

In taking this particular approach we are not suggesting that the social sciences are value-free. As Gross has asked, with specific reference to sociology,

'Is it possible to have inquiry without the motivation of curiosity, or practical interest? Can the sociologist safely proceed with an inquiry without being prepared to defend it against those who hold opposing attitudes, and in doing so must he not use rational or persuasive methods which require evaluate (normative) judgments?'[5]

The answers to these questions are reasonably obvious and are dealt with in sufficient detail elsewhere not to concern us here.[6] In fact, we would accept the notion 'that in principle there is no difficulty in applying the scientific method to the social sciences, but in practice we run up against severe difficulties'.[7] The difficulties will reveal themselves in later chapters when we consider the biases of some of the approaches. And, as we shall see, the natural sciences are not free from biases either. But for now, an appreciation of the meaning of the terms, theories and models, is most important.

Theories and Models

As suggested, the terms, theories and models, are used differently by different social scientists. Because of this non-agreement, the distinction that is being made here is not universally accepted nor, indeed, the final word on this subject. Yet it is necessary to distinguish between the two terms so that in our analysis of the approaches taken in a quest for an understanding of revolutions we shall have criteria by which we may judge the validity of the theories and the usefulness of the models. 'Validity' and 'usefulness' are the twin yardsticks by which we may assess the theoretical enterprise.

In a sense, there are two basic 'types' of theory. 'A Theory is a set of ideas *about ideas*; and theory is a set of ideas about *concrete data* observed in the real world'.[8] The former 'Theory' seems to fit into the category of world view and might be a reasonable description of the Marxian or Functionalist Theories. The scope of these Theories is such that they are largely untestable and, therefore, to their proponents, unassailable. In terms of their validity, anything and everything may be used as evidence of this correctness or lack of correctness depending upon whether one accepts or rejects the particular viewpoints that give rise to such Theories.

A 'theory', on the other hand, does not allow its proponents to make such grandiose claims. Instead, the theorist purports to examine some aspect of human behaviour (in the case of the social scientist) rather than to develop a Theory of All Human Behaviour. While the theorist might accept the argument that it is possible to develop some form of 'general Theory', he would probably insist that such Theory could be built only through the cataloguing of a very wide range of 'theories', all of which, when taken together, would lead to the establishment of a grand Theory of All Human Behaviour. This type of 'theory' is frequently referred to as 'low' or 'middle' level theory, but the distinction between 'low' and 'middle' level remains somewhat obtuse.

Essentially, the theory is testable in the real world. If, for example, we wish to consider some aspect of social class and its relation to attitude or behaviour, we might consider why it is that a given group of people to whom we ascribe certain social 'class' attributes vote in a particular way. Here a critical problem is raised. The term 'class' has no particular real world meaning. It is a concept which, in order to analyse, we must define operationally before we are able to test our theory. Thus, in the case of 'social class', we must utilize certain 'real world' characteristics such as occupation, income level, or level of education as our indicators of the 'social class' of a particular individual or group of individuals. Thus, we confirm or deny the validity of our conceptual theory through the use of our operational terms. How successful we are depends largely upon the amount of confidence we are able to place in our operational definitions. It should be borne in mind, however, that we choose our operational terms with great caution; there must be reasonable justification for their use. Nevertheless, theories that may appear to be confirmed are frequently very questionable when we consider the operational indicators that the theoretician uses. This, for example, will be seen when we consider the theory of relative deprivation.[9]

Generally, the mechanism through which we structure our different operational terms, or variables, is referred to as a model. The model may be seen as an analogue, or an *'interpretation* of reality, not the reality itself'.[10] Thus, if we take our basic theoretical formulation that social class is related to attitude or behaviour, the model is the structure of that relationship that suggests that class adherence leads to certain types of attitudes or behavioural patterns. From this we may deduce that a member of a particular social class is likely to vote in a certain specified way, and this becomes our theory of voting. Hence, 'in general, we learn something about the subject-matter *from* the theory, but not by investigating properties of the theory. The theory *states* that the subject-matter has a certain structure, but the theory does not necessarily *exhibit* that structure in itself.[11] In other words, it is the model that provides the structure through which the theory—with its content—is derived or examined.

While it can be very difficult at times to tell the difference between a theory and a model, for analytical purposes it is probably desirable to do so. Thus a model is conceived as 'a rather general image of the main outline of some major phenomenon, including certain leading ideas about the nature of the units involved and the patterns of the units involved and the patterns of the relations'.[12] A theory, on the other hand, is 'a heuristic device for organizing what we know, or think we know, at any particular time about some more or less explicitly posed question or issue'.[13] With this particular distinction in mind, the element of content becomes an integral part of the formula, and a basic way of judging a theory and a model becomes clearer. With its content, a theory may be judged right or wrong, at least through its operational terms. A model may be judged useful or not useful when aiding us to determine whether a theory is valid or invalid.

David Willer has very usefully distinguished between the two terms. A theory, for Willer, 'is an integrated set of relationships with a certain level of validity'.[14] This suggests that in the social sciences a theory may not be demonstrated to be 'true' in all cases; instead, in a larger number of instances it is found to be correct. Because of the imperfect testing environment the researcher cannot hope for the 'perfect' theory. The crucial point, however, is that the theory is validated. Thus, 'before validation it is improper to refer to this set of statements as 'theory' regardless of their purity of form'.[15] Consequently, prior to validation we would refer to this set of relational statements as 'a set of hypotheses',[16] not as a theory. It is only when the hypotheses are validated, i.e., tested in the 'real world' and found to be 'correct', that we can begin to refer to such hypotheses as theories.

A model, on the other hand, 'is a conceptualization of a group of phenomena, constructed by means of a rationale, when the ultimate purpose is to furnish the terms and relations, the propositions of a formal system which, if validated, becomes theory'.[17] In effect, the model is structural and without content, but the content is supplied when the model is being utilized to test particular hypotheses which, when they have been validated, may be considered theories. If these hypotheses are not validated then they are either eliminated from further consideration or modified to take into account factors that might explain why they were not validated the first time. The introduction of such factors modifies the model whose terms may not have included those variables which are now thought to be influential in the determination of certain outcomes.

A model is 'comprised' of two critical parts, the rationale and the mechanism. The rationale has been defined as 'an explanation of the nature of the included phenomena and leads to the nominal definitions of the concepts of the model'.[18] Thus, for our purposes, the way in which a society changes radically might be considered the rationale for a model of revolution. The mechanism, on the other hand, is the structure of the concepts and how they are related to one another. In a model of revolution the mechanism would consist of the different variables that lead to revolutionary changes. Factors to be considered might include hunger, poverty, new values, alienation or a host of other variables.

Ultimately, the theoretical enterprise consists of answering the questions of 'how?' and 'why?'. The model is the mechanism through which we see how the various components of the theory relate to each other and in what particular sequence. The theory, on the other hand, represents an attempt to understand causes 'of a phenomenon or of the interrelation between classes of phenomena'.[19] As such it purports to explain why certain phenomena have occurred. Realistically, the 'how' and 'why' considerations cannot be separated, and if we are able to explain why certain events or processes have taken place we have, at least implicitly, explained how. Thus, if we have a theory of revolution which explains why the Russian or French Revolution happened we also understand how the different factors which were responsible are related to each other.

Causation

A further question that we must consider is what we mean when we speak of 'causes of revolution' since this question is closely related to the general problem of the analysis of revolutions through the use of models. If models are to be useful in the development of theories, a number of cases must be examined to determine if an underlying series of factors or 'causes' are present in each case. If the researcher finds in all of the cases that are examined that certain factors are present, then he may begin to believe that he has discovered a theory of revolution that is able to explain why revolutions occur generally. He may claim that he has discovered the cause, or causes, of revolutions.

But to speak of causal relationships and causes of particular occurrences is a very chancy exercise. Strictly speaking, it is impossible to establish causal relationships in the social sciences just as it is not possible to do so in the natural sciences, for the conditions that are set to establish causation are so stringent that it is unlikely that such conditions will ever be met. They require the researcher to demonstrate that if A is the cause of B then it is invariably true that whenever A happens B will happen as well, a requirement that may never be fulfilled. Yet despite this stringency, we do speak in causal terms fairly freely. In daily conversation we might speak about rising commodity prices throughout the world as the cause of higher prices at home, or the high unemployment figures as the cause of a particular government being turned out of office in an election, or a bad harvest with resulting food shortages having caused a revolution to occur in a certain country. But the scientific criteria for establishing a causal relationship are such that one must approach a problem containing causal terms with extreme caution. The distance between the 'causal' conversation and scientific analysis is very great indeed.

Nagel has suggested that there are four conditions that must be met in order to establish causality between two objects or events. First, the relation must be invariable and uniform. This means that such a relationship must always be the same way. Second, the events must be spatially contiguous; A must be next to B. Third, the relations must have a temporal character; A must come before B. A cannot be a cause of B if B occurs first. Fourth, the relations must be asymmetrical; if A is cause of B, B cannot be a cause of A.[20]

In the formula that Nagel establishes, it must be demonstrated that the prior event (or events) is both the *necessary* and *sufficient* condition for what follows. This means that a certain set of factors must occur prior to the event that is being 'caused' and that no other factors are needed or, indeed, occur before that event happens. Thus, if B has occurred then A has come immediately before.

But this demonstration of necessity and sufficiency is very difficult. In a passage that refers to historians but which is of relevance to both political scientists and sociologists. Nagel has remarked that social researchers

> 'are rarely if ever in a position to state the *sufficient* conditions for the occurrence of the events they investigate. Most if not all historical explanations, like explanations of human conduct in general—and indeed, like many explanations of concrete events in the natural sciences—mention only some of the *indispensable* (or, as is commonly also said, *necessary*) conditions for these occurrences'.[21]

Why, then, even attempt to establish causality given the severe limitations that are always present?

Kemeny has suggested that it is really a convention, and that scientists like to put their laws into causal form.[22] In agreeing with this point of view, Blalock, who has done extensive work on the question of causation, cautions that causal thinking belongs on a theoretical level and that causal laws can never be demonstrated empirically. He does, however, suggest that it is 'helpful to think causally and to develop causal models that have implications that are directly testable'.[23]

Timasheff, writing in a book which deals with the growth of revolutionary situations, has stated that

'a logical causal model . . . is designed for relatively closed systems, where the perception of the observer is focused upon :
(a) an original or initial state of the system, including all its relevant traits,
(b) a final state of this same system, and
(c) an operator eventually interchangeable with at least some of the traits in the initial state of the system'.[24]

But working with a closed system in the social sciences—at the point of development that has been reached—is a luxury that is almost too good to be imagined and certainly something that cannot be envisaged in the study of revolutions. When setting up a causal model or chain 'there is no way of knowing for sure whether or not one has located all of the relevant variables'.[25] In the 'real world' of political science and sociology this is especially true; the social researcher is not working in laboratory conditions.

So we must return to the point that was made by Nagel and reiterated by Meehan. If it is not possible to state the conditions that are sufficient to generate a particular event, it is still probably within the grasp of the social scientist to discover the necessary conditions. As Meehan says, 'most of the attempts at causal explanations in political science, in relation to war, for example, are more an exercise in ingenuity than attempts at formal explanation'.[26] Because accurate prediction requires knowledge of both the necessary and sufficient conditions, we may make probabilistic or tendency statements about what might or might not occur. But these predictions, based as they are on the necessary conditions, still are of considerable value and, as evidenced by voting research, can be reasonably accurate.

Yet the question that must be uppermost in the student's mind is whether a sound case is made by any of the theory and/or model builders with regard to the very basic explanation of how and why revolutions occur, and, much more difficult, whether any of the models or theories are useful in aiding the prediction of revolutionary events. Ultimately this is the real test of the theories and the models.

The Relationship Between Theories and Models

It has been suggested that included in each theory is the model, at least implicitly, since the theory is comprised the 'fleshy' relationships derived from the skeletal model. To be useful, a model must aid in prediction and 'the *predictive* performance of a model involves the three properties of rigor, combinatorial richness, and extended relevance or organizing power'.[27] The model must be able to account for the numerous patterns that a researcher is likely to find in the real world. If the model is unable to account for certain patterns then it must be modified in light of new information that cannot be processed in the original model.

The medical researcher, at the beginning of his work, may adopt a model that suggests that external factors are responsible for changes in the system. Such a model may be diagrammed in the following way:

$$\text{External Factors} \longrightarrow \text{Changes in the System}$$

Testing a variety of factors, the researcher finds that people who have had heart attacks tend to have a high level of cholesterol in the blood. While at this early stage of research he is unable to confirm the possibility that a high cholesterol intake is a 'cause' of heart attacks, he is able to state that he has found a positive relationship between the level of cholesterol in the blood stream and the incidence of heart attacks.

On further examination, however, the medical researcher finds that in some areas of the world cholesterol intake is very high but the incidence of heart attacks is quite low. The primary difference appears to be that when high cholesterol intake is unaccompanied by a relatively fast-paced and highly pressured life-style, the incidence of heart attacks is low. Thus, the budding theory becomes somewhat more refined. According to what the researcher has found, a high incidence of heart attacks tends to be found among people with a high intake of cholesterol and a life-style with considerable tension brought about by pressures in work or in the home. The model is still adequate at this point because both factors which have been identified are external to the system and when placed in relation to that system seem to be responsible for heart attacks.

Upon further research, the scientist finds that among some groups of people who have both high cholesterol intake and experience great tension, there is a very low incidence of heart attacks. The model which suggests that external factors are responsible for changes in the system state is inadequate, for no other external factors can be located which might explain the differences in the incidence of heart attacks. So the researcher might add a section to the mechanism of the model which suggests that internal factors might be partially responsible for changes in the system state. The modified model could enable the researcher to broaden his frame of reference.

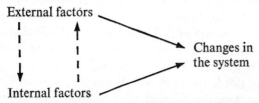

Using this revised model the researcher may find that those individuals who have a high incidence of heart attacks tend to be descended from people who also had heart attacks, thus suggesting that heredity is an explanatory factor in such occurrences. Since what is passed on by past generations is included in the genes of the individual this would be considered an internal factor to that person. But the model in its previous form was unable to take account of such factors since its mechanism contained only external factors. It is only through the empirical process that the model may be found to be adequate or inadequate, useful or non-useful. Once this model is altered to take into account different patterns or combinations of variables, then the theory-deriving exercise becomes viable once again. The result is that the researcher is able to tell us that the individual who has a high intake of cholesterol, a relatively high degree of tension in his every day life situation, and is descended from a family with a history of heart attacks is more likely to have a heart attack than others who do not meet any or all of the above criteria. According to this view, heart attacks are not random occurrences.

Many questions remain unanswered by this exercise. We have not commented on whether the external factors are more important than the internal factors.[28] Do the external factors 'trigger' the internal factors? Does the presence of the internal factor create a tendency to prefer foods with high cholesterol? Thus, considerably more research is necessary before theories may be derived. But the development of theories is not possible before the construction of adequate models.

An Early Model of Revolution

The writings of Aristotle provide a suitable way to apply the notions of model and theory that have been suggested to the study of revolutions. It is, of course, appropriate to begin with Aristotle because he was the first political scientist. It was Aristotle who first brought empirical analysis into the field of politics, and it has been suggested that he 'is the true founder of the study of revolution'.[29] The reason for this is that he created an intricate formula for measuring revolutionary change with a clear and elegant model of revolution.[30] Additionally, he derived several theories from the model. When they were in hypothetical form, these aspiring theories were validated by reference to a careful empirical analysis of the numerous states that Aristotle studied during the course of his 'research career'.

Aristotle looked at revolutions principally by dealing with two of the types of states that he had classified, oligarchy and democracy. He was particularly interested in these states because, as far as he could tell, since they were imperfect, they already had the seeds of instability in them.[31] He was not suggesting that these states were particularly bad, or totally without justice, justice being the critical element of what constituted the good state for Aristotle. He would, however, have argued that if these states were placed against an absolute standard of justice, they would have been found to be deficient, for each type of state contained numerous weaknesses.

Revolution for Aristotle consisted of political change of two types. The first type concerned the possibility of a change in the constitution of the state which would occur 'when men seek to change from an existing form into some other, for example, from democracy into oligarchy, and from oligarchy into democracy, or from either of them into constitutional government or aristocracy, and conversely'.[32] A second type of change did not involve an alteration of the constitution; instead, it would be considered what we have earlier referred to as a change of personnel in government. Aristotle described it as the situation in which the revolutionary group tries 'to get the administration into their own hands'.[33] While this type of revolution might have certain social consequences, for Aristotle it essentially constituted a change in the political situation rather than the arrangement of the state.

He also suggested that revolution might simply refer to the degree of change that occurred. In other words, a democracy may become less of a democracy or an oligarchy less of an oligarchy, but the essential nature of the system of government remained in the particular category in which it originally could be classified. It is also possible in this formula that the revolution 'may be directed against a portion of the Constitution only'.[34] Thus, an attempt could be made to overthrow a monarchy or establish a new council, but no effort is made to alter the basic political arrangements of the existing constitution, other than that one particular part.

For Aristotle there was one basic cause of revolution. If one were to scrutinize all of the cases that Aristotle examined, this ultimate cause becomes clear. 'Everywhere inequality is a cause of revolution, but an inequality in which there is no proportion —for instance, a perpetual monarchy among equals; and always it is the desire of equality which rises in rebellion'.[35] This notion of equality may present itself in two ways. First, men may think that they are equal to those who have more power or goods than they themselves have. Second, men who think that they are superior to others may find that, in fact, they have only the same power or goods or, in some instances, even less than those they consider inferior to themselves. A variety of factors arise that may be considered the immediate causes of revolution. Aristotle identified 'insolence, fear, excessive predominance, contempt, disproportionate increase in some part of the state; causes of another sort are election intrigues, carelessness, neglect about trifles, dissimilarity of elements'.[36] Each of these, however, may be considered operational definitions of the basic concept of inequality.

To examine revolutions in the context of the individual types of political systems, Aristotle found it necessary to say what it was that characterized the particular systems. Democracy is a system in which there is government by the many while an oligarchy is one in which there is government by the few. Aristotle recognized that the distinction was likely to be one based on the issue of wealth. He stated that

'the real difference between democracy and oligarchy is poverty and wealth. Wherever men rule by reason of their wealth, whether they be few or many, that is an oligarchy, and where the poor rule, that is a democracy. But as a fact the rich are few and the poor many; for few are well-to-do, whereas freedom is enjoyed by all, and wealth and freedom are the grounds on which the oligarchical and democratical parties respectively claim power in the state'.[37]

Because the basic constitutions or arrangements of the two types of states are different, the immediate factors which lead to revolution are likely to be different too. 'The democrats think that as they are equal they ought to be equal in all things; while the oligarchs, under the idea that they are unequal, claim too much, which is one form of inequality'.[38] As can be seen, however, both are based on notions of inequality.

In a system which is oligarchical, a democratic party, aware of the presence of inequality, in the distribution of wealth and/or political power, is not going to be satisfied with this situation for an extended period of time. Consequently, when the opportunity presents itself, this group is likely to move to overthrow the existing order and to establish a new constitution, i.e., a democracy. Just the opposite may be what occurs in a democracy. A group of men, motivated by a belief that they are superior to others in spite of the constitutional formula which establishes equality, band together. When they feel that they are in a proper position to achieve a victory they strike, and when they are successful they alter the constitution so that they become legally superior.

If we utilize Willer's definition of a model, the rationale of the Aristotelian model of revolution is a study of the way certain factors in a society lead to a revolution. The mechanism, or structure, consists of the following 'nominally defined concepts':[39]

1 Revolution is defined as a change of the Constitution of a state;
2 Equality is defined as the situation in which each citizen in the state has the same voice in the decision process; and
3 Inequality is defined as the situation in which the citizens have different voices in the decision process.

The model that Aristotle develops may be described diagrammatically in the following way:

Perception of
Inequality $\Big\}$ ⟶ Revolution

While this model has a rationale and a structure which defines the arrangement of the variables and pattern of their relationships, it lacks 'content' in so far as it does not refer to particular cases. It is only when the inclusion of content occurs that we are able to derive theories of revolution. From what has been described thus far it is possible to develop at least two theories of revolution from Aristotle's work. These theories might or might not be generally acceptable today although it may be said that they have contemporary connotations. They were, however, derived from tested hypotheses at the time Aristotle lived, for he had a number of examples to test empirically his two basic hypotheses which, once validated, would gain the status of theories.

The first theory may be stated in the following manner: if a political system is a democracy then revolution will be brought about by men who consider themselves to be superior to the multitude (who rule). Since theories are derived from models by applying a set of propositions to that model the theory that has just been propounded would include these propositions:

1 A democracy is a political system in which citizens are politically equal.
2 A democracy is a political system in which the poor (who are numerous) rule.
3 A democracy is a political system in which the majority of citizens are poor.
4 A democracy is a political system in which a minority of citizens are wealthy.
5 Those who are rich in a democracy will perceive themselves to be superior to the majority who are poor (and who rule).

If this series of propositions is linked together by using the model of revolution then the theory that was suggested will be derived. For Aristotle it was a valid or proved theory because in all cases in which the above situation existed, revolutions occurred, and these factors seem to have been responsible for the revolutions.

A second theory that Aristotle derived from his model of revolution deals with what might occur in the oligarchical state.

If a political system is an oligarchy then a revolution will be brought about by men who consider themselves to be the equals of those who rule (the minority). The series of linked propositions that would lead to this theory are the following:

1 An oligarchy is a political system in which men are politically unequal.
2 An oligarchy is a political system in which men are unequal according to wealth.
3 An oligarchy is a political system in which the minority of men who are wealthy govern.
4 An oligarchy is a political system in which the multitude are poor.
5 Those who are poor in an oligarchy will perceive of themselves as being equal to those who are wealthy (and who rule).

Once again, Aristotle would have claimed that by using these propositions with his model a particular theory of revolution had been derived. He tested and validated hypotheses that were based on the model and these propositions.

These derived formulae could be considered theories according to the criteria that were set earlier because they answer the question 'why?'. A revolution occurs in a democracy because a party of men believe that they are superior to the multitude. A revolution occurs in an oligarchy because a party of men believe themselves to be equal to the minority who rule. Obviously we have not answered all of the possible 'why?' questions. We still do not know why these men consider themselves superior or equal. The theory would be that much stronger and more convincing if we could answer this type of 'why?' question. But at a particular point in time we find ourselves back to an original 'why?', or fundamental 'why?', and, at that point, we can only offer the exasperating explanation 'because', or 'I don't know'.

The model, on the other hand, helps us to structure our thought and categorize the various phenomena included. Being without content, its main function is to help to explain 'how it is put together and how it works'.[40] So it was with Aristotle's model of revolution. It placed certain variables in a structural arrangement that the researcher activated when he put into this structure the content that produced theories. The later writers with whom we will be concerned are not always so rigorous, or obliging, as Aristotle.

Conclusion

While the notions of theory and model that have been discussed are not universally accepted or agreed upon, they would seem to be an adequate starting point in our analysis of the revolutionary formula. The fundamental question is whether the works that we shall analyse meet the basic criteria as proper theories and models. Do they isolate the reasons why revolutions occur? Do the models from which the different theories of revolution are derived adequately account for all possible explanations of revolutionary situations? Or are there other possible explanations that cannot be deduced from particular models? These are the questions that must be considered when examining the efforts of the theorists of revolution.

Notes and References

1 Hubert Blalock, *Theory Construction*, Englewood Cliffs, New Jersey, 1969, p. 2.

2 Vernon Van Dyke, *Political Science: A Philosophical Analysis*, Stanford, 1960, p. 58.

3 Karl Marx and Frederick Engels, *Manifesto of the Communist Party*, from *Selected Works*: in one volume, London, 1968, p. 63.

4 *Ibid.*, p. 41.

5 Llewellyn Gross, 'Sociological theory: questions and problems', from *Sociological Theory: Inquiries and Paradigms*, ed. by Llewellyn Gross, New York, 1967, p. 44.

6 See, for example, Peter Winch, *The Idea of a Social Science and its Relation to Philosophy*, London, 1958; and Alan Ryan, *The Philosophy of the Social Sciences*, New York, 1970.

7 John Kemeny, *A Philosopher Looks at Science*, Princeton, New Jersey, 1959, p. 247. For a further discussion see pp. 247–58.

8 Robert T. Golembiewski, William A. Welsh, and William J. Crotty, *A Methodological Primer for Political Scientists*, Chicago, 1969, p. 430.

9 See Chapter 8.

10 Carlo L. Lastrucci, *The Scientific Approach: Basic Principles of the Scientific Method*, Cambridge, Massachusetts, 1963, p. 61.

11 Abraham Kaplan, *The Conduct of Inquiry*, San Francisco, 1964, p. 264.

12 Alex Inkeles, *What is Sociology?*, Englewood Cliffs, New Jersey, 1964, p. 28.

13 *Ibid.*

14 David Willer, *Scientific Sociology: Theory and Method*, Englewood Cliffs, New Jersey, 1967, p. 9.

15 *Ibid.*, p. 9.

16 *Ibid.*

17 *Ibid.*, p. 15.

18 *Ibid.*, p. 17.

19 Lastrucci, *The Scientific Approach: Basic Principles of the Scientific Method*, p. 115.

20 Ernest Nagel, *The Structure of Science*, London, 1961, p. 74.

21 *Ibid.*, p. 559.

22 Kemeny, *A Philosopher Looks at Science*, p. 51.

23 Hubert Blalock, *Causal Inferences in Nonexperimental Research*, Chapel Hill, North Carolina, 1961, p. 6.

24 Nicholas Timasheff, *War and Revolution*, New York, 1965, p. 36.

25 Blalock, *Causal Inferences in Nonexperimental Research*, p. 14.

26 Eugene Meehan, *The Theory and Method of Political Analysis*, Homewood, Illinois, 1965, pp. 118–9.

27 Karl Deutsch, *The Nerves of Government: Models of Political Communication and Control*, New York, 1966, p. 17.

28 A very interesting 'layman's' presentation of the problems inherent in the use of different models may be found in the debate between P. Burch and R. Doll with regard to cigarette smoking as a cause of lung cancer. See *New Scientist*, *61*, No. 886, 1974.

29 Peter Calvert, *Revolution*, London, 1970, p. 39.

30 Aristotle, *Politics*, from *The Basic Works of Aristotle*, ed. by Richard McKeon, New York, 1941, esp. Book V, 1301a–1316b.

31 *Ibid.*, 1301a.

32 *Ibid.*, 1301b.

33 *Ibid.*

34 *Ibid.*

35 *Ibid.*

36 *Ibid.*, 1302b.

37 *Ibid.*, 1270b–80a.

38 *Ibid.*, 1301a.

39 Willer, *Scientific Sociology*, p. 18. For a discussion of nominal definition, see Carl Hempel, *Fundamentals of Concept Formation*, pp. 2–6.

40 Inkeles, *What is Sociology?*, p. 28.

Chapter 4
Marx's Model and Theory of Revolution

The Marxian revolutionary tradition is perhaps the most significant of any of the schools of revolutionary thought. Its importance stems at least in part from the understanding that its 'founder', 'Karl Marx, was *the* social and political thinker of the nineteenth century. Within the classic tradition of sociology, he provides us with the most basic single framework for political and cultural reflection'.[1] Because of the mountainous body of literature by Marx and which interprets what Marx said or is supposed to have said we have the uncomfortable feeling of dealing not with one man but with a committee of scholars. The members of this committee generally agree with the theme that they have suggested, but there is some divergence on critical issues. It becomes difficult at times to determine which is the Marx that is being studied.[2]

Although Tucker has argued that 'as a form of socialist doctrine . . . Marxism was inseparable from the idea of revolution',[3] it is only through careful analysis of numerous works that the theory of revolution presents itself. Marx did, however, outline his theory of revolution in a number of places. The most famous of these was *The Manifesto of the Communist Party* which is required reading for any student of revolution. It is not only an ideological tract, but a sociological treatise as well. Later, in his 'Preface' to *A Contribution to a Critique of Political Economy*, he outlined in very brief form the process of how society changes. This suggests the first problem in studying Marx's theory of revolution. We must dig through various works that Marx wrote casting aside Marx the propagandist and Marx the ideologue in order to determine why and how Marx thought revolution occurred.

Further complicating matters is the wide array of Marxist groups or scholars in the Marxian tradition. Aron has remarked that 'it is really no more difficult to present Marx's leading ideas

54

than those of Montesquieu or Comte; if only there were not so many millions of Marxists, there would be no question at all about what Marx's leading ideas are or what is central to his thought'.[4] Aron may be exaggerating the simplicity of Marx's thought; nevertheless, it is a point well taken. There are Leninists, Stalinists, Maoists, Trotskyites, and followers of Marxist humanism exemplified by Rosa Luxemburg. In addition there are assorted socialists and anarchists who would want to be considered part of the Marxian tradition. Fortunately, none of the individual Marxist groups disagree on the fundamental aspects of what may be termed the Marxian model of revolution; the component parts and the particular mechanism are generally accepted with little disagreement. The concepts of alienation and class consciousness fit into all of the Marxian schemes of revolution; it is when we confront the operational definitions of these concepts that we find differences.

There are at least three ways in which disagreement arises in the Marxian revolutionary tradition. First, if the Marxian idea of revolution is considered a theory of revolution, then disagreement can be found concerning some of the propositions and definitions that are components of the theory. Are the definitions that Marx utilized of 'alienation' and 'class' adequate for contemporary analysis? Second, if the Marxian model of revolution is taken as a causal model, then the relevant question focuses on the place of *necessary* and *sufficient* conditions. Is the Marxian model a full causal model? Does it contain all of the factors that lead inevitably to revolution, or does Marx provide only the necessary conditions, i.e. the basic structure of society before a revolution may take place? If this is the case then it is left to revolutionary theorists such as Lenin and Mao to provide the sufficient conditions which will complete the causal chain.

A third approach also examines the Marxian model of revolution rather than the theory. The model has a structure, but effectively, no content. The content is provided when using the model in an examination of various cases of revolutionary change. Through this process theories are derived from the model. Among the 'validated' hypotheses that may be considered theories would be the Leninist and Maoist approaches. Other partially tested theories might include the Luxemburg approach or the more recent approach developed by Castro in Cuba and propagated by Guevara and Debray in Latin America. The Marxian model becomes particularly flexible here because of the variety of propositions that may be used in the analysis of revolution. It is through the use of this third approach that we shall explore the development of the Marxian revolutionary tradition.[5]

The Marxian model of revolution is a relatively simple one as it is a uni-causal rather than a multi-causal model. By this we mean that instead of a variety of factors that are responsible for revolution Marx specified only one, albeit a broad one; it is the particular structural arrangements of society. The economic structure 'causes' certain social relations to develop and from these 'causes' the particular class arrangements are derived. In each society there will be two basic classes: one class rules and exploits, and the other class is ruled and is exploited. Members of the exploited class become 'alienated' from the dominant values and/or ways of doing things and eventually form a large group which is drawn together by common class consciousness, i.e., awareness of its common situation. Once the exploited class is strong enough it overturns the ruling class and becomes the ruling group in place of the former group. The model of society and of revolutionary change may be diagrammed in the following way:

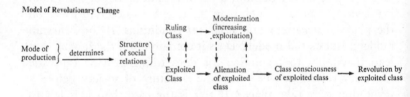

Model of Revolutionary Change

In order to understand the implications of the Marxian model of revolution we shall look first at the development of the theory of revolution and the propositions that Marx included in his theory.

The Marxian Theory of Revolution

What distinguishes Marxian social science from contemporary 'bourgeois' social science was Marx's emphasis on social change. His entire social science was concerned with the idea that society was basically unstable and changing and could not be understood as a cohesive structure or combination of structures. As Mills has said

'The social scientists study the details of small-scale milieus; Marx studied such details too, but always within the structure of a total society. The social scientists, knowing little history, study at most short-run trends; Marx, using historical materials with superb mastery, takes as his unit of study entire epochs. The values of the social scientists generally lead them to accept this society pretty much as it is; the values of Marx lead him to condemn his society—root, stock and branch. The social scientists see society's problems as matters only of 'disorganization'; Marx sees problems as inherent contradictions in the existing structure. The social scientists see their society as continuing in an evolutionary way without qualitative breaks in its structure; Marx sees in the future of this society a qualitative break : a new form of society—in fact a new epoch —is going to come about by means of revolution'.[6]

Essentially, the Marxian theory of revolution is derived from his conflict model of society. A conflict model is based upon the assumption that society is characterized by continual conflict among groups. Basically, this model is one in which 'conflict is explained in terms of concrete and specific social relationships'.[7] Through the analysis of the particular types of social relationships an understanding of why revolutionary situations occur emerges. It is through the addition of the particular Marxian propositions to the model that Marx's theory is derived.

Marx argued that society is based upon the particular economic structure, or mode of production. For this reason Marx is frequently referred to as an economic determinist, a view that, as we shall see, probably represents an oversimplification of his position. He stated that

'In the social production of their life, men enter into definite relations that are indispensable and independent of their will, relations of production which correspond to a definite stage of development of their material productive forces. The sum total of these relations of production constitutes the economic structure of society, the real foundation, on which rises a legal and political superstructure and to which correspond definite forms of social consciousness'.[8]

So each aspect of society must be examined in terms of how it reflects the economic structure. This refers to the individual in society as well. As Avineri said, 'the individual cannot be conceptually isolated from his social context : by definition any meaningful sentence about an individual must simultaneously refer to his environment'.[9] Marx recognized that there were factors in society other than the economic structure that might be seen as shaping the consciousness of the individual in society. The state, for example, could be conceived as that which shapes the psyche of the members of a social organization. But Marx rejected the idea of the state as being a separate and independent structure. Even the state was no more than a reflection of the economic structure.

What is critical in Marxian analysis is the separation of society into classes. Avineri has stated that 'class differentiation becomes for Marx the decisive factor in the formation of the body politic'.[10] In Marxian analysis classes reflect property ownership. Those that own property in society become the dominant or ruling class, and those who hold no property are the dominated, or exploited class. So state and property are inter-locked with each other. The state reflects, according to Marx, the property relations and, therefore, the class differences. The state is the instrument of the ruling class for exploitation and dominance : it is, in effect, an instrument of violence and control open only to the ruling class.

For Marx, the entire movement of history has been one of revolutionary change. As suggested, the fundamental basis of any society has been the mode of production and the arrangement of classes. In ancient times the mode of production was slave labour. In that period the slave was a commodity that could have been passed from one owner to another.[11] In feudal times, the serf was tied to the land, but not owned by the landowner. 'He does not receive a wage from the owners of the land; rather the owner of the land receives a tribute from him'.[12] In exchange for this tribute the serf was permitted to retain some of the food that he raised. In modern bourgeois society, the worker 'belongs neither to an owner nor to the land, but eight, ten, twelve, fifteen hours of his daily life belong to him who buys them'.[13] In effect, the worker sells a part of himself as a commodity to the capitalist who owns the means of production.

Each particular epoch is defined, then, in terms of the mode of production of that epoch. The three epochs identified by Marx were :

1 The ancient epoch in which the mode of production was slave labour,

2 The feudal society in which the mode of production was serf labour, and

3 The modern, bourgeois society, in which the mode of production is wage labour.

So, for Marx, 'a social revolution is a change in the mode of production with consequent change in all subordinate elements of the social complex'.[14] Revolution refers to the movement, or transition, from one particular epoch to the next epoch. Although Marx used the term 'revolution' to refer to any rising, the real meaning of the term is to be found in the idea of the alteration of the mode of production that characterizes each epoch.

Marx seemed to be fairly explicit about when the revolution would occur. He stated, 'No social order ever perishes before all the productive forces for which there is room in it have developed; and new, higher relations of production never appear before the material conditions of their existence have matured in the womb of the old society itself'.[15] This passage has proved to be particularly troublesome to revolutionists in the Marxian tradition and is a point to which we will return later. Suffice it to say that the 'real' Marx seemed to be saying that revolution could not occur until all of the particular conditions that he had specified were present. Only the presence of those conditions that Marx outlined could trigger the revolution because it is the presence of those factors which brings the people to a realization of their situation and an understanding that only common action will alter that situation. As he said elsewhere, 'Society . . . has in truth first to create for itself the revolutionary point of departure, the situation, the relations, the conditions under which alone modern revolution becomes serious'.[16] Despite this apparent clarity by Marx, the identification of the point when a society is 'ready' for revolution is a question that has occupied Marxists since Marx himself was writing. It is a very difficult problem when we consider which countries have undergone Communist-led revolutions for they have not been the technologically and economically advanced societies.

The conditions for revolution occupied a considerable portion of Marx's work, but his strongest interest was focused on the particular epoch which was emerging at the time that he was writing. That epoch was the capitalist one which was dominated by the growing bourgeoisie. In keeping with Marx's view of society, the presence of the emerging bourgeoisie did not eliminate class antagonism, it simply developed 'new conditions of oppression'.[17] But, Marx argued, the capitalist period had resulted in one major change from previous epochs:

'Our epoch, the epoch of the bourgeoisie, possesses, however, this distinctive feature : it has simplified the class antagonisms. Society as a whole is more and more splitting up into two great hostile camps, into two great classes directly facing each other : Bourgeoisie and Proletariat'.[18]

The bourgeoisie itself was perceived as a revolutionary class which was constantly altering the situation in society. It was this class also that was responsible for rooting out the old forms or residues of the past and those aspects that were destroyed would include any remnants of the feudal society that had come before. In addition, the bourgeoisie was constantly revolutionizing the instruments of production, i.e., the particular technology of industry of the period. This is a factor of the epoch that has enormous ramifications; the result of this continual revolutionizing of society was the planting of the seeds of the coming revolution.

Critical to the bourgeois epoch is the development of capital which is seen as 'a social relation of production. It is a bourgeois production relation'.[19] Effectively then, 'the only relation which bound men together was money payment'[20] in the bourgeois epoch. But this capital, or money payment, is possible only in a society in which labour power is available for 'Capital presupposes wage labour; wage labour presupposes capital. They reciprocally condition the existence of each other'.[21] This is a most significant point for it is here that we are able to identify the other class that develops in society. Marx hypothesized, 'In proportion as the bourgeoisie, i.e., capital, is developed, in the same proportion is the proletariat, the modern working class, developed—a class of labourers, who live only so long as they find work, and who find work only so long as their labour increases capital'.[22] Elsewhere he wrote :

'The development of the industrial proletariat is, in general, conditioned by the development of the industrial bourgeoisie. Only under its rule does the proletariat gain that extensive national existence which can raise its revolution to a national one, and does in itself create the modern means of its revolutionary emancipation. Only its rule tears up the material roots of feudal society and levels the ground on which alone a proletarian revolution is possible'.[23]

Marx referred to the organic composition of capital which is seen as the 'relation of constant to variable capital'.[24] Constant capital includes investment in plant and materials as well as depreciation on fixed capital. It is called constant capital because it is a relatively stable part of the eventual cost of the product being manufactured. Variable capital, on the other hand, refers to that part of capital which is spent on wages, or that which buys the 'commodity' that the worker is selling. It is referred to as variable capital because it continually changes as a part of the cost of the product. What the capitalist receives from the sale of the product which is above the combined cost of constant and variable capital is the profit.

But profit actually grows or diminishes in relation to the wage that the worker is receiving because constant capital is a fixed figure. The worker sells his commodity, labour power, at a particular wage, but he produces a value which is in excess of what he actually receives. The difference between what his 'commodity' costs and what the value is of that which he produces is called surplus-value. Thus the profit is the equivalent of the surplus-value. It is in the interest of the capitalist to increase his profit while it is in the interest of the worker to increase his wages so that his living standards increase. But since the cost of items is rising (by virtue of the capitalist's desire to maximize profits) at a faster rate than wages, in relative terms the worker's deprivation increases.[25]

With the development of the working class, or proletariat, and the weakening of the worker's position, we may identify the beginnings of the coming revolution. Marx saw the proletariat as the mechanism for the elimination of the conflictual society that man had always known. This latest 'exploited class' would grow 'alienated' as the epoch of the bourgeoisie progressed from stage to stage. Alienation, then, is a major step on the way to revolution.

Alienation

Alienation is a theme that runs through much of Marx's works, but it is a subject that has recently enjoyed a greater interest by scholars than in the past.[26] Whether it is referred to specifically as alienation or by other terms such as the division of labour, Marx was concerned with the effects of the particular mode of production, i.e., the capitalist mode on the worker. While a rather wide literature exists which deals with alienation,[27] it will be treated here in simple terms as it relates to the theory of revolution.

Israel has identified three social conditions which are responsible for creating the process of alienation.[28] The first is where 'man and his working power is transformed into a commodity'.[29] The worker 'sells' his labour to the capitalist who is in the business of garnering more capital. But as we suggested, the variable capital, or the worker's wage must be kept relatively low. Marx said the 'profit can only increase rapidly if the price of labour, *if* relative wages, decrease just as rapidly'.[30] Thus, even if real wages grow, they are constantly dropping in relative terms. Thus a contradiction is found here. 'If capital is growing rapidly, wages may rise; the profit of capital rises incomparably more rapidly. The material position of the worker has improved, but at the cost of his social position. The social gulf that divides him from the capitalist has widened'.[31]

The second factor in the process of alienation is the division of labour. As a society becomes more complex and the technology in the society develops, the function of the individual worker becomes more narrowly constrained. Thus, from the worker who used to assemble an entire automobile with a group of workers in a garage, we have the individual who stands on the assembly line waiting for the incomplete automobile to pass by so that he may turn a screw or spot weld a particular joint in the car. As Marx said,

'Owing to the extensive use of machinery and to division of labour, the work of the proletarians has lost all individual charm for the workman. He becomes an appendage of the machine, and it is only the most simple, most monotonous, and most easily acquired knack, that is required of him. Hence, the cost of production of a workman is restricted, almost entirely, to the means of subsistence that he requires for his maintenance, and for the propagation of his race . . . In proportion therefore, as the repulsiveness of the work increases, the wage decreases. Nay more, in proportion as the use of machinery and division of labour increases, in the same proportion the burden of toil also increases, whether by prolongation of the working hours, by increase of the work exacted in a given time or by increased speed of the machinery, etc.'.[32]

This problem is obvious to anyone who has been faced with the particular tedium of a repetitive job. Interestingly, modern capitalists have become increasingly aware of this problem and have attempted to rectify the problem by giving the workers more of a creative role in production. Automobile manufacturers in Sweden faced with labour shortages and absenteeism have been particularly active in trying to overcome the difficulties by making work more interesting. By putting workers into groups which build the entire product rather than a small part of the product the management hopes that increased interest in the work will develop. This same technique has been utilized in many electronics firms.

The third reason that Israel gives for the growing alienation of the worker is that of private property. The worker develops and builds objects, but these objects are not owned by him. Thus the fruit of the labour of the worker is only a commodity just as the labour itself is. So, 'when Marx says that existing conditions of production dehumanize the worker he implies that, once the products of the workers' creative self-realizing activity have been taken away from him, he retains only his biological animal-like functions'.[33]

Thus in the Marxian theory alienation is that process by which the members of the working class find themselves to be nothing more than commodities in the general scheme of things. A relative impoverishment continues as the capitalist society becomes more and more advanced technologically.[34] It is with this growing sense of a loss of humanity and function that the worker begins to look around and finds that other workers are in the same situation while other groups, the bourgeoisie, are in the position of getting relatively richer while the worker is getting relatively poorer. It is at this point that the second feature of the Marxian theory, class consciousness, emerges.

Class Consciousness

As seen earlier, classes are defined in terms of property ownership. Those that have property are the exploiters, and those that do not are the exploited. But the exploited class has no particular political role in the society until its members are aware of the exploitation they endure. This is important because in the Marxian model, 'Classes do not constitute themselves as such until they participate in political conflicts as organized groups'.[35] Organized groups will not develop until the individuals themselves are aware of their common situation. This does not necessarily mean that when they have first joined together they are completely aware of their common goal which would, in the Marxian theory, be the destruction of the existing state and, therefore, of the bourgeoisie. But once the members of the working class are knowledgeable about their common situation, they will start developing such common goals.

According to the Marxian theory at the beginning of the epoch of bourgeois dominance, the working people, or labourers, in society 'still form an incoherent mass scattered over the whole country, and broken up by their mutual competition'.[36] The workers, when they do battle for better living conditions, are not accruing gains for themselves. Instead, they are helping to accentuate the power of the bourgeoisie which is still destroying some of the remnants of the past epoch. Once the industrial growth becomes more pronounced, however, the workers become concentrated in the great industrial centres. With economic cycles affecting the lives of the workers, conditions deteriorate for the workers more rapidly. Thus, they form unions and trade associations and begin to do battle with the bourgeoisie. Generally they are defeated, but occasionally they taste the fruits of victory for a brief time which only whets their appetites for more gains.

Sooner or later the bourgeoisie is forced to make certain concessions to the more militant working class such as shorter working days or recognition of workers' parties. But realistically, the bourgeoisie may only give so much and no more before their own position becomes untenable. With each concession it is merely weakening its own hold on the social situation. Thus, increased repression occurs when the ruling group feels that it is becoming unacceptably weaker. As far as the working class is concerned, 'after every revolution marking a progressive phase in the class struggle the purely repressive character of the state power stands out in bolder and bolder relief'.[37]

Once the critical stage is reached Marx focuses on the number of former members of the ruling class that begin to go over to the soon-to-be-victorious working class. But even with these new recruits to the struggle, 'of all the classes that stand face to face with the bourgeoisie today, the proletariat alone is a really revolutionary class'.[38] More to this point, it is not possible to achieve the revolutionary success with only a small group of people opposed to the ruling authorities. 'The time of surprise attacks, of revolutions carried through by small conscious minorities at the head of unconscious masses is past. When it is a question of a complete transformation, the masses themselves must also be in it, must themselves already have grasped what is at stake, what they are going in for (with body and soul).'[39]

Earlier we mentioned that while Marx is frequently referred to as an economic determinist this probably represents an over-simplification of Marx's actual view of the development of revolutionary consciousness and the growth of the revolutionary movement. Nevertheless, how revolutionary consciousness de-velops is a question that is never fully confronted despite Marx's view that there is nothing mechanistic about the movement of history.[40] By the time that Marx was describing the events in France in the period between 1848 and 1851 he was comment-ing on the unreadiness of the proletariat both because of a lack of proper objective conditions in the underdevelopment of the bourgeoisie and the lack of understanding by the proletariat of its historical mission. He wrote :

'As soon as it has risen up, a class in which the revolutionary interests of society are concentrated finds the content and the material for its revolutionary activity directly in its own situation : foes to be laid low, measures dictated by the needs of the struggle to be taken; the consequences of its own needs drive it on. It makes no theoretical inquiries into its own task. The French working class had not attained this level; it was still incapable of accomplishing its own revolution'.[41]

After the failure of the Paris Commune in 1871, he commented that the working class 'know that in order to work out their own emancipation, and along with it that higher form to which present society is irresistibly tending by its own economical agencies, they will have to pass through long struggles, through a series of historic processes, transforming circumstances and men'.[42] Thus, while there is a belief that even if objective circum-stances are correct, i.e., the epoch of the bourgeoisie has reached a high stage of development, the subjective condition must be met before the revolution can occur, and the subjective condition is defined in terms of the development of class consciousness which is not only widespread, but leads to organization as well. But its development is dependent upon the progressive tendencies of the bourgeoisie itself. As the original 'revolutionizing' class, it is the growth of the bourgeoisie that allows for the growth of the working class, the class which will eventually destroy the class upon whose very existence it depends for its own growth and development.

The End of Revolution

The particular values that Marx, the humanist, held became very pronounced when he dealt with the period following the overthrow of the bourgeoisie and the eventual formation of the new society. Freed from the antagonisms and hatreds that stemmed from class-based society, men would be permitted to live in harmony with one another. As was indicated earlier, Marx's definition hinged not only on the destruction of the previous mode of production which was responsible for the particular structure of social relations, but also upon the establishment of the new epoch which would be free of class antagonisms. But the period of transition from capitalist to Communist society is a critical one which is, unfortunately, dealt with only very briefly by Marx. Yet its significance should not be underestimated. It forms a vital component of the Leninist interpretation of Marx when applied to the Russian case as well as an important part of the Maoist theory when dealing with the 'proletarianization' of Chinese society.

This period of transition was to be based upon the dictatorship of the proletariat. It was first identified in a letter in which Marx described what he believed he had accomplished in his work. He wrote:

> 'What I did new was to prove: (1) that the *existence of classes* is only bound up with *particular historical phases in the development of production*, (2) that the class struggle necessarily leads to *the dictatorship of the proletariat*, (3) that this dictatorship itself only constitutes the transition to the *abolition of all classes* and to a *classless society*'.[43]

Later, he wrote that 'Between capitalist and Communist society lies the period of the revolutionary transformation of the one into the other. Corresponding to this is also a political transition period in which the state can be nothing but *the revolutionary dictatorship of the proletariat*'.[44]

One of the outcomes of the revolution and movement to the Communist society is the eventual abolition of the state. The state, after all, is no more than the instrument of the ruling class used in order to keep the exploited class in its place. Once no classes exist, there is no reason for the state to continue to exist since it is merely a reflection of the class structure.

But in the period immediately following the seizure of power by the proletariat remnants of the old order will still exist for the 'instantaneous conversion' of the members of the bourgeoisie is not likely to occur. Thus, the proletariat will rule, but it will have to be on guard against all of the enemies of the working class, and those enemies are the remaining bourgeoisie. It is only when the bourgeois elements disappear from the society that the state, the instrument of oppression, disappears as well. The antagonisms of all of the previous epochs will be gone because the modes of production that characterized each of the previous epochs will be gone. 'In place of the old bourgeois society, with its classes and class antagonisms, we shall have an association, in which the free development of each is the condition for the free development of all'.[45]

Summary and Critique of the Marxian Theory

The Marxian theory of revolution is thus derived from a model which rests on the idea of contradictions in society. 'For Marx, society is not primarily a smoothly functioning order of the form of a social organism, a social system, or a static social fabric. Its dominant characteristic is, rather, the continuous change of not only its elements, but its very structural form'.[46] In this model, the contradictions lead to class struggles. The exploited or ruled class becomes alienated and develops class consciousness which eventually leads it to take action to overturn the dominant, or ruling class.

The theory posits the growth of the bourgeoisie, a class that is revolutionary itself as evidenced by its modernization of society. With the growth of this class and its successful destruction of feudal society, a new impetus is felt in society. It is an impetus that grows out of the dynamic tendencies of the bourgeoisie. As the bourgeoisie advances by improving the technology of the means of production and by continuing investment, the working class or proletariat grows as well. With the growth of the industrial side of the society the proletariat is increasingly exploited and grows more dissatisfied. The increase in dissatisfaction leads to an awareness that at the root of these problems is the mode of production which determines the structure of social relations. This awareness leads members of the proletariat to form groups which oppose the rulers. Eventually when the means of production have reached their most advanced stage and the proletariat realizes its revolutionary potential, the bourgeoisie is overthrown and the proletariat is ascendant. Once the proletariat has succeeded in overturning the bourgeoisie, it must deal with the class antagonisms that remains, which it does in the period of the dictatorship of the proletariat. The revolution has succeeded when these antagonisms are destroyed, and the classless society emerges.

The Marxian theory may be described as simple, elegant, and to the point. It has been the most influential theory of revolution in the past hundred years. Yet, strangely, as a way of predicting outcomes it has not been validated with reference to industrial societies. Revolutions generally have not occurred in the societies of the West that were most advanced industrially and technologically in spite of the early expectations of Marx and Engels. They have not happened in Great Britain, Germany and the United States. Where Marxist inspired risings occurred in France, they failed. Instead, the great Marxist-orientated revolutions have occurred in the technologically less advanced societies where the bourgeoisie was barely developed, and the working class, where it was to be found, was small as well.

Why has this happened? The best clue is provided by Lichtheim who argues that there is a need to examine Marx in his particular social context and 'to relate Marxism to contemporary thought in general—in other words, to criticize it'.[47] Marx developed his propositions in the context in which he was writing, and much of the criticism of the Marxian theory of revolution is not really directed toward the model; instead, it is concerned with the propositions that Marx utilized. The notions of class that he held, especially with regard to the working class, and his expectations concerning how the working class would develop class consciousness have particularly been vulnerable to criticism. The criticism is easily mapped out if we describe several of the propositions that Marx utilized in the theory of revolution that he developed from his model.

Zeitlin identified some thirty theoretical propositions from Marx's work in the *Communist Manifesto*.[48] Marx modified these propositions as his work developed; nevertheless, some of them are particularly useful in describing the theory of revolution that he utilized. While Zeitlin feels that Marx's analytical framework is still a useful way of examining social change, he argues that 'Marx's theoretical approach enabled him to explain the past but failed him in his predictions. His method was encumbered with difficulties which are inherent in any attempt to comprehend a whole society in the process of rapid change'.[49]

Some of the critical propositions that Zeitlin identified follow, and to these propositions several have been added from other works. They are derived largely from the *Communist Manifesto*, *Wage, Labour and Capital* and the Preface to *A Contribution to a Critique of Political Economy*. These do not represent all of the propositions that are relevant to the theory of revolution. But they are critical to an analysis of why the theory has never been validated. The propositions deal largely with Marx's notion of class and the development of class consciousness.

1 Modern society, i.e., capitalist society, 'has simplified class antagonisms. Society as a whole is more and more splitting up into two great hostile camps, into two great classes directly facing each other: bourgeoisie and proletariat'.[50]
2 The bourgeoisie is a revolutionary and revolutionizing class. It is revolutionary because it has destroyed the vestiges of the old epoch. It is revolutionizing because it is constantly modernizing the technology of the era in order to improve its own position.
3 The bourgeoisie is defined as the class that owns the means of production, which, in turn, may be defined as property.
4 The growing industrialization brings with it the growth of a new class, the proletariat. The members of this class must sell their labour, which is a commodity, to the capitalist. The working class does not own property.
5 Because of the lack of control over his own life, the tedium of work due to the division of labour, and his continually more impoverished position, the worker becomes alienated from the particular social process.
6 The worker finds other workers who share his situation and his point of view. From this contact with workers an awareness of his possibilities with other workers for reforming or changing society becomes obvious. This is class consciousness.
7 The proletariat eventually overturns the bourgeoisie. It must be the proletariat that does this because 'Of all the classes that stand face to face with the bourgeoisie today the proletariat alone is a really revolutionary class'.[51]

Two criticisms may be levelled at Marx with regard to his definition and conception of class. The first criticism concerns the Marxian concept of class based on property ownership or non-ownership. Dahrendorf argued that 'A theory of class based on the division of society into owners and non-owners of means of production loses its analytical value as soon as legal ownership and factual control are separated'.[52] Dahrendorf's position follows on from a view that was expressed by Burnham although, generally, Dahrendorf is very critical of Burnham's formulation.[53] Still, the managers in contemporary society are not necessarily the owners of the means of production. Thus, authority flows from factors other than property ownership.

More evidence of this was provided earlier when we dealt with Lane's analysis of the Soviet Union.[54] That private property no longer exists in the Soviet Union has not prevented the emergence of class stratification based on other factors such as party membership. 'Whoever tries, therefore, to define authority by property defines the general by the particular—an obvious logical fallacy. Wherever there is property there is authority, but not every form of authority implies property. Authority is the more general social relation'.[55]

The second aspect that appears to be in error is the particular idea of class consciousness that Marx developed. According to the propositions that are derived from Marx's work, the proletariat in the advanced industrial societies ought to have risen up much before other groups in less developed societies. But it has not happened that way at all. Workers in the United States, Great Britain and France still operate within the particular social systems and, in fact, tend to be strongly supportive of those systems. Whatever radicalism existed among workers in the United States appears to have disappeared during the Depression. The impetus for the rising in France in 1968 came largely from students, a decidedly bourgeois group, although workers did join in. That Marx was mistaken about the readiness of the worker to revolt should be no mystery.

Mills said :

'In his notion of class, Marx tends to confuse the object fact of it, a statistical aggregation of people, with the psychological developments that may occur within its membership. He seems to believe that class consciousness is a necessary psychological consequence of objective economic development which includes the polarization of owners and workers. To Marx there is no ambiguity about this, because the psychological and political results are, in some way not fully explained, the product of economic changes. But the connection between economic facts and psychological changes are not well considered as empirical questions'.[56]

This is a crucial point. The Marxian theory of revolution is based on the conception of the working class that Marx held and the necessary development of class consciousness. Without such an occurrence the revolution could not happen. But class consciousness was supposed to follow the growing alienation of the worker which would occur in response to the growing technological advancement of society and increasing impoverishment of the worker in the capitalist era. The failure of the empirical cases to confirm the Marxian hypothesis destroys the validity of Marx's theory assuming, of course, that enough time has elapsed to consider the hypothesis 'tested'.

Both Marx and Engels were aware of the questions that were raised by the failure of the working class to rise up and turn out the bourgeoisie. Following their more hopeful period of the late 1840s when revolution seemed imminent throughout the industrializing and industrialized world, they began to reassess their previous position. Gregor remarks, 'When faced with the necessity of explaining contemporary behaviour, both Marx and Engels seem to have modified the simplistic 'echo' or 'reflex' theory of consciousness which is found in the early statements. Consciousness in the more mature documents is derived, complex; interests are multivaried and multidimensional'.[57]

Engels wrote that 'we make our history ourselves, but, in the first place, under very definite assumptions and conditions. Among these the economic ones are ultimately decisive. But the political ones, etc., and indeed even the traditions which haunt human minds also play a part although not the decisive one'.[58] He condemned those who suggested that he and Marx were economic determinists although he conceded that the economic 'cause' may have been overstated in many of their works. Nevertheless, there was no suggestion that there was an automatic movement from point to point in history. A variety of factors interacted to bring about social change. Yet the link between the particular social conditions and the awareness of the worker that he is in a particular situation does not seem to have been established. If there is no automatic movement from alienation because of material conditions to a condition of class consciousness, then we do not actually know how the transition comes about or why it eventually happens, and until we are able to understand why the working class in the industrial society has not revolted, then the theory may not be considered valid.[59]

One more point with regard to the theory and its weaknesses may be mentioned. It is related to the question of when class consciousness has developed to the point that revolution may occur. Marx was not at all clear about when the revolutionary change might happen. He did say, as we suggested earlier, that the revolution could not occur in society before 'all the productive forces for which there is room in it have developed'.[60] This stage of development implies that the revolution could occur only when the subjective readiness of the proletariat meets the objective conditions. When attempts at revolution fail, then, the reason is always that the objective condition did not exist or the subjective conditions were not adequate. This smacks of tautology. What Marx was saying was that the revolution may succeed because the stage of development is right. If it fails it failed because the stage of development was not right. But this is, by definition, true. It is not based on infallible powers of analysis.

Ultimately, the major weakness of the theory that Marx propounded is that he was, first and foremost, a nineteenth century man. His appreciation of what the classes were and therefore what they might become was based on his perspectives of his particular time. This would certainly limit any social scientist. But that these predictions do not seem to have worked out as he had expected does not detract from the *model* of social change that he bequeathed. Only the propositions that were utilized in order to derive the *theory* from the model are seemingly inadequate.

The model of revolution has also been criticized, but it is a considerably different type of criticism than that which is directed to the theory. The criticism of the theory is concerned with the content, i.e., the particular definitions and propositions that Marx utilized. The criticism of the Marxian model is based on the components of the model. It may be argued that the structure of class antagonisms, however defined, is only one possible factor in conflict.[61] This, however, is an open question. Earlier, it was suggested that models are not right and wrong, only useful or not useful. We may only determine if a model of revolution, whether it is a unicausal or multicausal model, is useful in the analysis of how revolutions occur. How useful the Marxian model is may be examined by analysing the Leninist and Maoist 'theories' of revolution which are derived from the model that Marx produced.

Notes and References

1 C. Wright Mills, *The Marxists*, Harmondsworth, Middlesex, 1962, p. 37.

2 Avineri raises this point at the beginning of his major work on Marx. He argues that it is difficult to place Marx in perspective because of the different 'roles' in which he has been cast. 'This confusion arises mainly from two causes. First, the recent renaissance of interest in Marx concentrates almost exclusively on his earlier writings; his later works have hardly been reconsidered and scrutinized in the light of the new discoveries. A gap between the "young" and "older" Marx is almost taken for granted. Secondly, much of what is traditionally considered orthodox Marxism is based on the more popular of Engels' later writings. If they seem to differ widely from those of the young Marx, the conclusion usually drawn from this disparity is a statement about a difference between the early and later Marx'. See Shlomo Avineri, *The Social and Political Thought of Karl Marx*, London, 1968, p. 2.

3 Robert C. Tucker, *The Marxian Revolutionary Idea*, London, 1970, p. 3.

4 Raymond Aron, *Main Currents in Sociological Thought*: I, Harmondsworth, Middlesex, 1965, p. 111.

5 Admittedly, this is an approach that would be criticized by Marxist analysts for eliminating the values that are an inherent part of Marx's work. In the effort to separate out the 'ought' component, we are doing something that Marx certainly never intended. Israel has argued that in Marx's work 'there is a mixture of sociological-economical analysis and of normative-ethical discourse'. Further:

'Thus Marx has two intentions : (1) the description and analysis of society and its conditions, and (2) the specific goal of creating critical knowledge as a means of freedom and emancipation. In its eagerness to be considered as science and to create a self-image of strictly scientific orientation, sociology in its modern version has abandoned the second task. It is the price paid for being "scientific". The question is whether the results are worth the costs'.

Joachim Israel, *Alienation: From Marx to Modern Sociology*, Boston, 1971, p. 80.

But it may be argued that in this work we are focusing on the 'sociological-economical' analysis. While there is an awareness that it is an 'artificial' separation, Marx's work does represent a view of what society is about and why it is as it is.

6 Mills, *The Marxists*, pp. 12–3.

7 Irving M. Zeitlin, *Marxism: A Re-examination*, Princeton, New Jersey, 1967, p. 8.

8 Karl Marx, 'Preface' to *A Contribution to the Critique of Political Economy*, from Karl Marx and Frederick Engels, *Selected Works in One Volume*, London, 1968, p. 182.

9 Avineri, *The Social and Political Thought of Karl Marx*, p. 17.

10 *Ibid.*, p. 25.

11 Karl Marx, *Wage, Labour and Capital*, from Karl Marx and Frederick Engels, *Selected Works*, Vol. 1, Moscow, 1962, p. 83.

12 *Ibid.*

13 *Ibid.*

14 Tucker, *The Marxian Revolutionary Idea*, p. 15.

15 Karl Marx, 'Preface' to *A Contribution to the Critique of Political Economy*, p. 183.

16 Karl Marx, *The Eighteenth Brumaire of Louis Bonaparte*, from *Selected Works in One Volume*, p. 100.

17 Karl Marx and Frederick Engels, *Manifesto of the Communist Party*, from *Selected Works in One Volume*, p. 36.

18 *Ibid.*

19 Karl Marx, *Wage, Labour and Capital*, p. 90.

20 A. James Gregor, *A Survey of Marxism*, New York, 1965, p. 141.

21 Karl Marx, *Wage, Labour and Capital*, p. 92.

22 Marx and Engels, *Manifesto of the Communist Party*, p. 41.

23 Karl Marx, *The Class Struggles in France 1848 to 1850*, Moscow, 1968, p. 37.

24 Zeitlin, *Marxism: A Re-examination*, p. 44; see also John Eaton, *Political Economy*, New York, 1963.

25 This concept of 'immiseration' of the proletariat is not original with Marx. See Gregor, *A Survey of Marxism*, pp. 146–9.

26 Avineri, *The Social and Political Thought of Karl Marx*, p. 2.

27 See, for example, Avineri, *The Social and Political Thought of Karl Marx* (cited above); David McLellan, *Marx's Grundrisse*, London, 1971; and Istvan Mészáros, *Marx's Theory of Alienation*, London, 1970.

28 Joachim Israel, *Alienation: From Marx to Modern Sociology.*

29 *Ibid.*, p. 53.

30 Karl Marx, *Wage, Labour and Capital*, p. 97.

31 *Ibid.*, p. 98.

32 Marx and Engels, *Manifesto of the Communist Party*, p. 41.

33 Avineri, *The Social and Political Thought of Karl Marx*, p. 106.

34 Israel points out that it is not a type of alienation that develops from conflict with society. Instead, 'for Marx society is the sum total of all human relations . . . a conflict between the individual and society is usually implicit in theories of alienation, but . . . Marx rejects such a view and places the conflict *within* society—between social classes whose interests clash with each other'. Israel, *Alienation: From Marx to Modern Sociology*, p. 72.

35 Ralf Dahrendorf, *Class and Class Conflict in Industrial Society*, Stanford, 1959.

36 Marx and Engels, *Manifesto of the Communist Party*, p. 42.

37 Karl Marx, *The Civil War in France*, from Karl Marx and Frederick Engels, *Selected Works in One Volume*, p. 289.

38 Marx and Engels, *Manifesto of the Communist Party*, p. 44.

39 Frederick Engels, 'Introduction' from Karl Marx, *The Class Struggles in France: 1848–50*, New York, 1964, p. 25.

40 Gregor, *A Survey of Marxism*, see particularly pp. 158–69.

41 Marx, *The Class Struggles in France*, p. 37.

42 Marx, *The Civil War in France*, pp. 294–5.

43 Karl Marx, 'Letter to J. Wedemeyer in New York', from Karl Marx and Frederick Engels, *Selected Works in One Volume*, p. 679.

44 Karl Marx, 'Critique of the Gotha Programme', from Marx and Engels, *Selected Works in One Volume*, p. 679.

45 Marx and Engels, *Manifesto of the Communist Party*, p. 53.

46 Dahrendorf, *Class and Class Conflict in Industrial Society*, p. 27.

47 George Lichtheim, *Marxism: An Historical and Critical Study*, New York, 1961, p. xvii.

48 Zeitlin, *Marxism: A Re-examination*, pp. 69–72.

49 *Ibid.*, p. 142.

50 Marx and Engels, *Manifesto of the Communist Party*, p. 36.

51 *Ibid.*, p. 44.

52 Dahrendorf, *Class and Class Conflict in Industrial Society*, p. 136.

53 James Burnham, *The Managerial Revolution*, New York, 1941; see also *Ibid.*, pp. 87–91.

54 See Chapter 2.

55 Dahrendorf, *Class and Class Conflict in Industrial Society*, p. 137.

56 Mills, *The Marxists*, p. 112.

57 Gregor, *A Survey of Marxism*, p. 184.

58 Frederick Engels, 'Engels to J. Block in Königsberg', from Marx and Engels, *Selected Works in One Volume*, p. 629.

59 One possible answer to the question is found in the concept of false consciousness. See Israel, *Alienation: From Marx to Modern Society*, pp. 80–96.

60 Marx, 'Preface' to *A Contribution to the Critique of Political Economy*, p. 183.

61 Dahrendorf, *Class and Class Conflict in Industrial Society*, pp. 126–30.

Chapter 5
Marxist Theories of Revolution

Although both Lenin and Mao would not fall into the category of social scientists, it is appropriate to treat their theories of revolution in our analysis of approaches to revolutionary change for two reasons. First, both theorists would have argued that Marx's work represented scientific analysis of the progression of history. Marx had, after all, developed what we have called a model of social change and had built into the model all of the factors relevant to an explanation of why revolutionary change would occur and what the particular sequence of that change would be. Second, both Lenin and Mao examined their own societies from the perspective of the Marxian sociological framework and constructed very detailed pictures of what their own societies were like and why, within the context of the Marxian model, revolutions of a particular type were bound to occur.

It is with such considerations that we approach the Leninist and Maoist contributions as proper 'theories' of revolution which have been derived from the Marxian model of revolution. We shall examine each of the theories in turn with particular reference to those features which distinguish the theories from Marx's theory of revolution as well as some of the more recent Marxist theories. We shall conclude with a brief evaluation of how the Marxian model is still suggestive of numerous possibilities for revolutionary change.

The Leninist Theory of Revolution

Marx was ambivalent when it came to identifying the country in which the first socialist-led revolution was to occur. It has been said that 'twice at least Marx seems to have been inclined to suggest that the revolution will break out first in countries with less developed industrial structures, and not in the most highly industrialized areas'.[1] The two countries in which Marx appeared to be interested were Germany and Russia. Germany,

77

which was not industrialized at the time, had been identified
when the *Manifesto of the Communist Party* was written in
1847–8. Then in 1882 Marx wrote in the 'Preface' to the
Russian Edition of the *Manifesto* that the work 'had as its object
the proclamation of the inevitably impending dissolution of
modern bourgeois property'.[2] But Russia did not appear to be
ripe for such a dissolution. While capitalism was developing
rapidly it was in its early stages. Existing side by side with this
nascent capitalism was a huge peasantry which owned more
than half of the arable land in common. Thus, Marx believed
that two possibilities were presented. On the one hand the type
of common ownership could lead to the 'higher form of Communist common ownership'[3] without first going through the
stages leading to the development of Communism. On the other
hand, the Russian Revolution might have to pass through all of
the stages on the road to Communism.

Marx seemed uncertain which would be the direction taken.
He concluded his Preface by arguing that

> 'If the Russian Revolution becomes the signal for a proletarian
> revolution in the West, so that both complement each other,
> the present Russian common ownership of land may serve as
> the starting point for a Communist development'.[4]

Marx here may have been suggesting that the boundaries of a
country are not the crucial element in defining the revolutionary situation. If the Russian rising was tied to events in the West
then it may be seen in a wider context, as a world, or at least
a European, revolution. He may also have been trying to remain
aloof from the disputes that punctuated the various Russian
socialist movements and which continued to characterize Russian
socialism until the Bolshevik seizure of power in October, 1917.[5]

The reasons for the confusion among the Russian socialists
are legion. No country was more ready for a revolution than
Russia, but it would be stretching Marxian analysis to assume
that Russia was ready for a socialist revolution. In the late
nineteenth century it was a large, semi-feudal state which was
beginning to enter the capitalist era. Investment in Russian
industry was only starting to turn St Petersburg and Moscow
into industrial centres. With the growth of industry came a new
class, the urban proletariat, which could have eventually become
the group that made the revolution. But in the late nineteenth

century this was considered a possibility only in the distant future.

A strong revolutionary tradition did exist in Russia, for few societies have seen challenges such as those against the Tsarist regime in the nineteenth century. And since the Decembrist Rising in 1825, the political situation was very unstable. In 1861 Tsar Alexander freed the serfs and 'thereby secured for the dynasty the peasantry's unwavering allegiance for decades ahead'.[6] But among the growing middle classes a restlessness developed that frequently led to the forming of radical organizations that struck occasionally through bombs or by means of political assassination as in the killing of Tsar Alexander II in 1881. Lenin's older brother was executed for his alleged part in an abortive plot to assassinate Alexander III, and efforts have been made to suggest that it was this execution that converted Lenin into a revolutionary, although this is probably unlikely.[7]

If these different groups had one thing in common, it was a lack of any real popular following. They could explode bombs if they wished and assassinate the odd Tsar but ultimately if success rested on the possibility of rallying a disgruntled population, then they were operating in apparently sterile ground. This, however, changed in the late nineteenth and early part of the twentieth century. The loss of the war with Japan unleashed a wave of discontent which was aggravated by the Bloody Sunday massacre in 1905. Risings occurred throughout the country which resulted in a series of Tsarist concessions, including the setting up of a constituent assembly, the Duma. While it turned out that this was not quite the concession that those who pressed for it had wished, it opened the door to more demands for change which ultimately brought down the Tsar. The very nature of the autocracy made it unlikely that the last Tsar could adjust to what had become a new situation.

Few were to weep over the departure of the Tsar. His regime was a repressive one, both rigid and ossified. It made extensive use of the secret police to infiltrate political organizations whether revolutionary or not; even moderate political groups had difficulty operating openly in this type of repressive environment. Revolutionary groups needed to be extremely cautious if they were to operate in Russia at all for the penalty for failure to keep the activity secret was exile in Siberia or abroad, or worse. It is within this context, a repressive and increasingly restless society, in which Leninism or the Leninist theory of revolution, was born.

Leninism may be approached from two standpoints. First, it may be seen as flowing logically from Marxism. Certainly this is the viewpoint that Lenin held. He did not think of himself as a revisionist or a deviationist. The second view does suggest that he was a revisionist: he converted Marxism in order to make it apply to the Russian situation, and the end result of this process may have been a betrayal of the views that Marx held. Whichever view is taken, few Marxist thinkers approach Lenin dispassionately, and the particular line that he took has led to one of the dominant themes in contemporary Marxism, but one which is not universally accepted.

The Leninist theory of revolution hinges on the addition of several propositions to the Marxian theory, and the careful avoidance of several other propositions. Basically what Lenin said is that in the society in which capitalism is not fully developed, but in which there is a growing working class, a revolution led by the proletariat is possible provided several conditions are met. The proletariat must seek allies for the revolution. In the case of Russia (as is possible with other societies) the peasantry may be the likely ally. But the peasantry is not necessarily capable of seeing the benefits of a socialist revolution. Interestingly, neither is the working class likely to develop to a mood of revolutionary consciousness on its own. Instead the proletariat is prone to develop trade unionist tendencies which lead to demands for reforms and economic benefits rather than revolution. Thus, in order to coordinate the revolution, a vanguard party is needed to bring revolutionary consciousness to the potentially revolutionary mass and to coordinate the revolution even after the old regime is overthrown. It is in this way that the development of socialism will occur.

The Leninist theory of revolution raises two critical problems for Marxian analysis, and these must be examined in order to understand Lenin's particular place in the Marxian revolutionary tradition. First, there is the very serious question about when the revolution must occur. How far must capitalism develop before the objective situation is such that a revolution in which the proletariat plays the leading role may break out? This first question leads to a second: how is the revolution to occur? Lenin raised the possibility of a vanguard party organizing the revolution and leading the mass to a successful conclusion of their crusade. At the opposite end of the scale it was assumed that the revolutionary spontaneity of the new proletariat would insure eventual revolutionary success, a view that Lenin rejected entirely.

Stages of Revolution

Revolutionary Marxism is based on the notion that revolution progresses in stages. As we have seen, the Marxian notion of revolution is defined as the change from one epoch to another which is characterized by the dominance of a new class. Lenin agreed, arguing that 'the transfer of state power from one class to another class is the first, the principal, the basic sign of a *revolution*, both in the strictly scientific and in the practical political meaning of the term'.[8] There is no disagreement among the Marxists on this definition. Where the disagreement occurs is in the question of how these stages occur and which is the dominant group in each stage.

One view of progression by stages has been labelled 'vulgar' Marxism by those in the tradition of Lenin and Trotsky. This view was based on a literal interpretation of what Marx had to say. As we have seen, the Marxian view seemed to be quite clear that the transition from one epoch to another would happen when the productive forces of the particular epoch had grown, or developed to the highest stage possible and when there was no room for further development of those productive forces. Thus, revolution would occur when feudalism had gone as far as it could and when, in the capitalist period, the development of capitalism had reached its full fruition. This growth would be accompanied by the growth of the proletariat to the degree that the new complexity of society, i.e., the technical aspects, would lead to a greater division of labour which, in turn, would lead to alienation, the growth of class consciousness and the inevitable revolution.

Each stage was to be in orderly progression. The feudal stage would give way to the capitalist stage, and this would eventually give way to the socialist stage. If one was a patient Marxist at the end of the nineteenth century this implied that those who represented or were part of the proletariat at this stage of development would have to subordinate their basic aims to those who would lead the liberal-bourgeois democratic revolution that had to occur before any notion of a socialist revolution was possible. Only when the bourgeois democratic era had developed to its full modernity could the proletariat rise to lead the next revolution.

There is an implicit assumption built into this view that the proletariat would not be ready or willing to make (or lead) the next revolution in any event. Class consciousness which would follow on from growing alienation could not really be expected to happen until the productive forces had grown to their fullest extent. After all, the Marxian prescription was quite clear that class consciousness, i.e., the understanding by the workers that they were being exploited, was a function of the growing modernization of the society's economic sector. Thus, the revolution would occur only when the time was right, or when the highest stage of capitalist development had been reached.

Lenin, however, was not a patient Marxist. Had Lenin accepted the idea that a revolution could not occur until the productive forces reached their highest level of development, then the seizure of power that he led would never have happened. Lukacs argued in 1924

> 'The actuality of the revolution: this is the core of Lenin's thought and his decisive link with Marx. For historical materialism as the conceptual expression of the proletariat's struggle for liberation could only be conceived and formulated theoretically when revolution was already on the historical agenda as a practical reality; when, in the misery of the proletariat, in Marx's words, was to be seen not only the misery itself but also the revolutionary element "which will bring down the old order" '.[9]

What Lukacs was saying was quite simple. Lenin recognized that the revolutionary movement of which he was a part had to take advantage of the situations as they developed. At the turn of the century in Russia, the revolutionary possibility was growing. How it would be confronted was the vital question that was facing the revolutionary groups of the socialist persuasion.

In one of his more important works,[10] Lenin approached the problem of the different stages of the revolutionary process. He agreed that the revolution must come in stages and accepted the view that a democratic revolution had to occur before it was possible for a socialist revolution to happen. Nor did he reject the idea of the necessity of the bourgeois-democratic revolution. As a traditional Marxist he accepted the idea that the bourgeois revolution was advantageous to the proletariat. What Lenin did argue for, however, was an activist proletarian role in carving out its rightful place in the coming revolution. The proletariat could not live simply by the reforms that the bourgeoisie might make if the bourgeoisie led the revolution. So while other Marxists were arguing that the proletariat should stand aside while the revolution progressed as Marx predicted that it would through the efforts of the bourgeoisie, Lenin pushed the argument further :

> 'Marxism teaches the proletarian not to keep aloof from the bourgeois revolution, not to refuse to take part in it, not to allow the leadership of the revolution to be assumed by the bourgeoisie, but, on the contrary, to take a most energetic part in it, to fight resolutely for consistent proletarian democracy, to fight to carry the revolution to its completion'.[11]

Lenin described the bourgeoisie as inadequate for the task of overthrowing the Tsar and instituting a programme that incorporated the types of reforms that the proletariat demanded. In this semi-feudal country, how could the bourgeoisie which was tied to the feudal element, hope to overthrow the Tsar? The answer was simple for Lenin : it could not.

Lenin believed that 'only the *people*'[12] were powerful enough to combat the Tsarist forces successfully. While it was obvious that the proletariat would be too small to accomplish this aim, it could succeed if tied to the rest of the exploited population. If such an alliance could be forged, the overthrow of the Tsar would follow. As Lenin said, 'A decisive victory of the revolution over tsarism is the *revolutionary-democratic dictatorship of the proletariat and peasantry*'.[13] Lenin recognized that this would not be a socialist revolution, but that it would facilitate the eventual socialist revolution more easily than any bourgeois democratic revolution in which the proletariat did not participate : 'Only the proletariat can be a consistent fighter for democracy. It may become a victorious fighter for democracy only if the peasant masses join it in its revolutionary struggle'.[14]

Thus, Lenin was not denying the need to progress through the various stages or epochs. Where Lenin did differ from many Marxists is in the notion that the proletariat ought to be playing an activist role right from the start of the revolutionary struggles. This was possible—in fact, imperative—largely because the bourgeoisie was inadequate for the task of democratizing society. Lenin was not the only Marxian thinker to advocate the activism of the worker at this time. Trotsky, too, had preached such a course. But Trotsky had gone further than even Lenin. In his theory of the permanent revolution, Trotsky argued that 'the proletariat grows and becomes stronger with the growth of capitalism'.[15] This did not mean that the worker had to wait until capitalism had reached its final stages before he could take over the society. To the contrary, Trotsky believed that the worker in an economically backward society could conceivably come to power sooner than in the advanced society. He rejected out of hand the idea that the workers must wait their turn:

> 'To imagine that the dictatorship of the proletariat is in some way automatically dependent on the technical development and resources of a country is a prejudice of 'economic' materialism simplified to absurdity. This point of view has nothing in common with Marxism'.[16]

He held that the particular situation in Russia was such that power could be held by the workers '*before* the politicians of bourgeois liberalism get the chance to display to the full their talent of governing'.[17]

Where Trotsky and Lenin disagreed was in the role that the peasant was to play. Lenin was advocating the dictatorship of the proletariat and peasantry while Trotsky left it to the workers to 'revolutionize' the society; it was from this ongoing 'revolutionizing' process that the title 'permanent revolution' was derived. The peasants would be included only if they were true to the workers' direction. Lenin was to come around to Trotsky's way of thinking on the eve of the Russian Revolution and justified this modification of his original view by recourse to his usual appeal for practicality and tactical flexibility. By 1917 he perceived that much of the peasantry was not collaborating with the worker, but with the bourgeoisie.[18] Since the peasantry had 'gone over' to the bourgeoisie, Lenin could no longer advocate the joint dictatorship of the proletariat and peasantry, 'words which have become meaningless'.[19]

The events of early 1917 also forced other alterations in the Leninist theory. As we have seen, Lenin argued for a democratic revolution in which the workers participated, not one in which they stood in the background and waited. But when Lenin returned to Russia from his long exile, he found that a revolution had indeed occurred which left the bourgeoisie and the liberal remnants of the feudal aristocracy in power, albeit not very securely. Many socialists argued that the workers should co-operate for the time being with the new regime and accept the prospect of reforms which would better the lives of the workers and lay the foundations of the type of society which the proletariat would eventually inherit. Capitalism would follow its normal course, and the proletariat would mature to the point at which they could lead the next revolution.

Lenin rejected this idea in the *April Theses*, which were presented just after he arrived back in Petrograd from his exile in Switzerland. Lenin argued that the workers should seize power immediately. He justified this argument by relying on a traditional Marxian viewpoint; the revolution was to proceed by stages. Lenin argued that

> 'The specific feature of the present situation in Russia is that the country is *passing* from the first stage of the revolution —which, owing to the insufficient class-consciousness and organization of the proletariat, placed power in the hands of the bourgeoisie—to its *second* stage, which must place power in the hands of the proletariat and poorest section of the peasants'.[20]

Lenin had originally argued for the proletarian participation and eventual leadership of the democratic revolution. But when the February Revolution happened, Lenin had to reassess his position. He could only justify the continued agitation by the workers if they had reason to revolt. This could only happen if the revolution were to be carried to a further stage. So, in effect, Lenin reduced the length of time it was thought had to elapse between the stages of revolution and brought the revolutions closer together than anyone thought possible. He argued that Russia had gone through the bourgeois-democratic revolution and there was no reason to wait any longer before instituting the worker-led revolution.

Thus, Lenin contributed two novel ideas to the notion of stages of revolution. First, he argued that the workers should participate in all stages of the revolution, not merely the final stage, for the bourgeoisie could not be trusted to effect the democratic revolution. Basically, this meant that the political revolution need not wait for the economic revolution. Second, given the existence of a large, socially and politically conscious proletariat, the stages of revolution need not be so spaced apart as other socialists had thought. Instead, once the workers were in a political position to seize power—whether the highest stages of capitalism had been reached or not—they should do so.

The Vanguard Party

Marx was not very clear about how class and revolutionary consciousness was to be developed. He saw a twofold role for the Communist Party in the working class. In the first place the Communist Party spells out the interest of all workers in the world, and, second, the party represents the interests of the working class.

> 'The Communists, therefore, are on the one hand, practically the most advanced and resolute section of the working-class parties of every country, that section which pushes forward all others; on the other hand, theoretically, they have over the great mass of the proletariat the advantage of clearly understanding the line of march, the conditions, and the ultimate general results of the proletarian movement.'[21]

But while this brief description really serves as a grab-bag for a number of different viewpoints, there does seem to be an indication that the Communist Parties must play the dominant role in the revolutionary process. There is, however, no indication about how this role is to be interpreted. Does the party play a dictatorial role or one of guidance? Here is where the disagreement is most profound.

One school of thought might be called the 'spontaneity school'. Those who are in this school would hold to the most mechanistic of interpretations. They would argue that class consciousness comes to the worker as the society becomes more advanced in the capitalist era. The revolution would occur when that development has reached its highest stage and not before. It is referred to as a spontaneity school because the party really plays no role in the rising. Rather, the workers, through their own development, would eventually rise up and destroy the existing regime.

Experience appeared to have demonstrated that this school had been inaccurate in its expectations about how the workers would develop. In the most advanced countries technologically, trade unionism and participatory politics have prevailed and revolutions have not occurred. Marcuse, for example, has rejected the traditional Marxian proposition which specifies the proletariat as a revolutionary class.[22] Contemporary trends have, for him, ruled out any possibility of the workers rising against the capitalist masters. The members of the working class have been in collusion with the business groups rather than in opposition to them.[23] Interestingly, and as we shall see, the events in France in the 1968 revolt may have given new life to the spontaneity school.

A second school is that which Lenin himself founded. As we have seen, it was difficult for a revolutionary or even anti-government party to operate in the very repressive Russian state. Additionally, Lenin's lack of faith in the possibility of the bourgeoisie turning out the Tsarist regime was complicated by his early belief in the Marxian notion that revolution must come in the particular stages that Marx identified. But, as we have seen, the manner in which these stages might be accomplished was not so clearly spelled out that differences in opinion could not arise over the methods. Finally, Lenin faced the very real problem of how the small proletariat was to develop class consciousness at a period in which capitalism was only in its formative stages, much less its final stages by which time it might have been expected that class consciousness would have developed. By dealing with this question, Lenin produced what might be considered his most important work, in terms of its later influence, *What is to be done?*. First appearing in 1902, it contained the kernel of Lenin's thesis of how the revolution could come about, a thesis that remained substantially unchanged. Essentially it had but one basic aim : to explain how the revolution was to be brought about in the Russian-type society.

The theme that Lenin developed is that the class consciousness that will lead to revolution cannot happen if the workers are left to their own devices. Instead, 'the history of all countries shows that the working class, solely by its own forces, is able to work out merely trade-union consciousness, i.e., the conviction of the need for combining in unions, for fighting against the employers, and for trying to prevail upon the government to pass laws necessary for the workers . . .'.[24] Lenin was not suggesting that there is no such thing as spontaneity, for the workers will feel aggrieved and unhappy. But this spontaneity will lead to the desire for short term rewards, not revolutionary activity. This is particularly true in those countries in which the working class is not very strong, i.e., in those systems where capitalism is developing fairly quickly from its early stages.

Lenin argued that a mass movement was developing in Russia on its own, but that this new mass movement did not have the proper guidance. Therefore, either the social democratic movement of which Lenin was a part would subordinate itself to the workers and the labour movement, or the mass movement would inspire these conscious revolutionaries to get busy with the 'new theoretical, political and organizational tasks'[25] which now awaited. For Lenin there was no choice at all : 'The greater the spontaneous upsurge of the masses, the wider the movement becomes, so much the more rapidly does the demand increase for a mass of consciousness in the theoretical, political and organizational work of Social-Democracy'.[26] The revolutionaries not only had to keep abreast of the workers' movements, they had to stay ahead of the movement in order to anticipate each step in the revolution.

Lenin urged political education for the workers which was to go further than merely pointing out the kinds of problems and contradictions that existed in the society. Such education had to consist of agitation and preparation for the struggle with the authorities. It would have to bring to the workers the understanding that they were engaged not only in an economic struggle, but, Lenin stressed, if the revolution succeeded then the reforms were guaranteed in any event. Thus, the Leninist emphasis 'subordinates the struggle for reforms to the revolutionary struggle for freedom and for Socialism, as a part to the whole'.[27]

But the real question that Lenin's analysis raised is this : if spontaneity among the working class leads only to trade unionism and the demand for better economic conditions, how, then, is the worker going to be drawn into a revolutionary struggle? Here, perhaps, is the most controversial part of the Leninist scheme. Lenin argued that 'class political consciousness can be brought to the worker *only from without*, that is, from outside the economic struggle, outside the sphere of the relations between the workers and the employers'.[28] Lenin argued further that the social democratic agitators would have to work among all classes for the workers to gain the knowledge that they would need to carry out the revolution. But basically, Lenin advocated an organization that was small and cohesive, of professional revolutionaries, who would direct the activities of the workers.

He therefore distinguished between the workers' group, or unions, and the revolutionary organization. The union was a trade organization that is broad and as open as it could possibly be. The revolutionary group, on the other hand, must consist of 'people whose profession consists of revolutionary activity'.[29] It could not be wide and open for the most obvious reason; in autocratic Russia open activity would be suicidal. While it is true that open organizations allow the workers to have greater access to the organization, they also permit greater access to the police of the society. Above all, if the revolutionary organization is satisfactorily established 'then we shall be able to guarantee the stability of the movement as a whole and to realize both the Social-Democratic and properly trade-unionist aims'.[30] Once again Lenin subordinated the part to the whole. The people who belong to the revolutionary party may be drawn from all classes. The main concern is not their class background but their revolutionary devotion to the eventual triumph of socialism.

Lenin then suggested five propositions that went into his theory of revolution. After accepting the Marxian analysis of what society is like and what the general causes of revolutions are, he argued

'(1) that no revolutionary movement can be durable without a stable organization of leaders which preserves continuity; (2) that the broader the mass which is spontaneously drawn into the struggle, which forms the basis of the movement and participates in it, the more urgent is the necessity for such an organization, and the more durable this organization must be (because the broader the mass, the easier it is for any demagogue to attract the backward sections of the mass); (3) that such an organization must consist mainly of people who are professionally engaged in revolutionary activities; (4) that, in an autocratic country, the more we *narrow* the membership of such an organization, restricting those who are professionally engaged in revolutionary activities and have received a professional training in the art of struggle against the political police, the more difficult it will be to "catch" such an organization; and (5) the wider will be the category of people, both from the working class and from other classes of society, who will have an opportunity of participating in the movement and actively working in it'.[31]

Lenin could argue that he was keeping solely within the Marxian tradition. As we have seen, Marx and Engels were not certain how class consciousness would develop, but with his theory of the revolutionary party he seems to have gone considerably further. Nothing in Marx indicates the need for, or indeed the desirability of, an elitist party to the degree that Lenin proposed. Nevertheless, Lenin was dealing with a concrete situation, and this was his particular solution to the Russian problem.

His idea of the vanguard party was widely criticized, the most trenchant criticism coming from Rosa Luxemburg. Luxemburg is frequently considered one of the theorists who believed in spontaneity, but this surely represents a misinterpretation of her views toward the party. She believed in the party and the role that the party needed to play, especially in the society that had not undergone the capitalist transformation; the party would perform both an educational and leadership role. Inherent in her work was a greater faith in the masses than Lenin expressed. In fact, her work anticipated the attitude that Mao has held with regard to the mass line. Luxemburg believed that Lenin's particular thesis of centralism and the revolutionary party had two clear principles. The first was what she referred to as the 'blind subordination'[32] of all parts of the party to this small nucleus. Second, Lenin's plan involved the separation of the nucleus, or party, from the movement itself. The Leninist notion of the party did not merely provide for the leadership of the proletariat, a role that she would have ascribed to the revolutionary party. It also drew a barrier between the leadership and the followers, fatal to any socialist movement. She hit this point very hard : 'The fact is that the Social Democracy is not *joined* to the organization of the proletariat. It is itself the proletariat'.[33] The leadership drew its inspiration and momentum from the masses; it could not function properly as a socialist group without this enthusiasm.

It is important to understand that Luxemburg and Lenin had much in common. Both represented the radical wing of Marxism at a time when the revisionists were enjoying considerable success. Both Lenin and Luxemburg adhered to the principle of democratic centralism which permitted debate within the party ranks but insisted on subordination to the decision once it was taken. However, according to Frolich, Luxemburg cast her net further than did Lenin with regard to those involved in the debates; she wanted more interaction between the party and the workers. But she did believe that once decisions were taken by the party, all, including the parliamentary party, were bound by the decision. Still, a fundamental distinction may be drawn between Luxemburg and Lenin :

'She believed, rather too optimistically, that the pressure of the revolutionary masses would correct any political errors of the party leadership . . . with certain reservations it may be taken that Rosa was more strongly influenced by the historical process as a whole, and arrived at all her political conclusions exclusively from this source, whereas Lenin's eye was more concentrated on the aim before him, for whose achievement he then sought the necessary political means. For her the decisive political factor was the mass : for him it was the party, and he aimed at forging into the spearhead of the movement as a whole. He resembles the Chief of Staff of a highly organized army, she rather the standard bearer in the front rank of a broad class host'.[34]

Her faith in the masses, and her continued belief in the need for contact with and responsiveness to them probably cost her her life. In the 1919 Spartacist Rising in Germany she did not encourage the revolutionary action of the workers because she perceived that the rising was premature and, therefore, doomed to failure. Luxemburg quite rightly understood that the workers needed the support of the soldiers to succeed, a lesson made obvious by the Russian Revolution, but she also believed that such support would not be forthcoming. The bulk of the German army was drawn from peasant and rural backgrounds, people not necessarily sympathetic to the goals of workers. But she went along with the rising because she believed that there was a moral obligation to do so given her political philosophy concerning the relationship that must exist between the party and the mass.

She saw in the Leninist theory of the elitist party its possible outcome, the authoritarian society. The party that Lenin founded would inevitably lead to a basic conservatism at its highest levels and would demonstrate a sterility of thought that reflected a lack of concern for the ideas and hopes of the people. She charged that 'Lenin's concern is not so much to make the activity of the party more fruitful as to control the party—to narrow the movement rather than to develop it, to bind rather than to unify it'.[35] In this action of binding the mass to the party were the seeds that would eventually doom the revolution to failure.

Luxemburg, then, represented a third Marxist school with

regard to the type and role of the Communist Party. It is the school which may be closest to what Marx himself was suggesting. It supports the idea that the Communist Party is at the forefront of revolutionary ideas, but its dependence upon the workers is never forgotten. In fairness to Lenin, however, no revolutionary movement could ever develop in a vacuum. His party could not have thrived in a non-revolutionary environment, a point that he always made. If the objective conditions for revolution did not exist then the subjective conditions were of no consequence whatsoever. Additionally, Russia was not Germany and the workers in Germany may not have required the guidance that the Russian workers did given the relative levels of maturity of the capitalist forces in each society. While the socialists did have problems growing to maturity in Germany —and the workers drifted mainly to trade unionism rather than to revolution—the shackles provided by the Russian authorities made free association considerably more difficult.[36]

The question whether type of party that Lenin proposed would lead to an authoritarian regime which eventually betrayed the proletariat is largely unanswerable. Lenin and his colleagues clearly expected revolution in the West to follow the Russian Revolution. This never happened, and they were left with one backward country led by a revolutionary party. Perhaps the Stalinist regime that followed was inevitable, but when Lenin was planning the revolution he was concentrating on the destruction of the previous regime rather than the trends and tendencies of the following regime once the revolutionaries had succeeded. What is significant is that of all the 'theories' that flowed from the Marxian model, Lenin's was the first to overturn the prior regime. Until the Chinese revolution, and the communist take-overs in Europe following World War II, no other approach could compete with the Leninist which, after all, had been the first successful Marxist-orientated revolution.

Summary of Leninism

Perhaps more so with Lenin than with any Marxian thinker— including Marx—it is unjust to reduce his life's work on revolution to several pages of a general text on revolution. Yet there is a remarkable consistency in Lenin's work that allows one to do precisely this. Despite his enormous output, it is not difficult to distil the basic themes that run through most of what he wrote. He accepted the correctness of Marxian analysis, i.e., the

Marxian model of society and revolutionary change. But he saw as perhaps no other Marxist thinker before him did that different situations required different approaches to revolutionary change. Thus, it can be said that Lenin was the first to understand the 'actuality of revolution'. To deal with the Russian problem, however, Lenin was forced to reject certain Marxian propositions that had been considered articles of faith by the majority of Marxists. These propositions were concerned largely with the stages of revolution, the degree of proletarian participation at the early stages, and the role of the vanguard party.

Gregor describes the significance of these changes very succinctly:

> 'The proletariat was not to mature to responsibility; it was to be marshalled to it. It was not to take up its tasks; its tasks were to be imposed upon it. It was not to come to know; it was to be told its purpose. It might come to appreciate its *immediate* interest, but only the revolutionary cadre could understand its ultimate interest'.[37]

Lenin thus removed Marxian revolution as a possibility only in advanced capitalist societies and placed it within the realm of possibility for virtually any country provided a revolutionary situation existed and a revolutionary party was present that could guide the society on the road to socialism. By particularizing Marxian analysis to Russia, Lenin taught that the Marxian model was useful in any society. It was a lesson that other revolutionaries, including the Chinese, were to learn well.

The Maoist Theory of Revolution

If a Marxian thinker in the early part of the twentieth century was to have chosen the most unlikely country for a Marxist orientated social revolution, it is likely that China would have been one of his first selections. When the Manchu Dynasty finally collapsed in 1911 China was a country with virtually no working class, save some small concentrations of workers in a few cities, and a centuries old tradition of land ownership which created the world's largest peasantry. To further depress the Marxian theorist no evidence of any Marxian influence existed in the centres of learning, nor had the working class been inspired to participate in any militant revolutionary activity. Yet some forty years later the most populous country in the world had come under the domination of a revolutionary movement which took its influence from Marx and based its ideology on Marxian class analysis. This movement took less than thirty years to develop and grow to full strength. In 1920 it did not exist; by 1950 it had mastered all of China with the exception of the offshore islands. Few revolutionary movements anywhere in the world have succeeded so rapidly, and none has achieved the magnitude of the Chinese Communist revolutionary mass movement.

China had been in a state of almost continual turmoil since 1851, the year of the beginning of the Taiping Revolution which nearly overthrew the Manchu Dynasty. The revolt eventually failed, but the Dynasty never actually recovered. When the Dynasty finally did collapse, no group emerged that could unify the diverse elements in Chinese society. By the time the Chinese Communist Party (CCP) was founded in 1921, the confusion within the country was very great indeed. The nationalist forces, the Kuomintang (KMT) of Sun Yat Sen and later Chiang Kai Shek did represent a potential ruling group, but they never mastered the whole country. They had to contend with the divisions in their own party as well as invasion by the Japanese. On the other hand, after 1935, the CCP came to present to the populace a stable and well-led movement in sharp contrast to the KMT. Above all, the CCP was concerned, and was seen to be concerned, with the well-being of the population under its control, which no other previous movement had demonstrated.

The concern for the people involved in the movement, and for the poor population generally, was a reflection of the views of the leader of the movement, Mao Tse-Tung. The CCP might have succeeded had Mao not been the leader, but this is a doubtful proposition for Mao brought to the leadership a determination rarely encountered as well as a sensitivity to the particular problems China faced, and in doing so, added a new dimension to the tradition of Marxism-Leninism. He contributed little to Marxist-Leninist philosophy; his works in the philosophical area are not impressive. But in the area of revolutionary strategy and theory he added an entirely new concept of mass revolution. Much of what Mao wrote now sounds trite, but it should be remembered that he was the first to write about what so many have written about since and which is now fairly conventional wisdom. Its surface triteness masks the incisiveness of his analysis and tends to cloud the influence that Mao has had on many other revolutionaries that have followed him. As Schram has stated :

> 'He has given the CCP its own strategy and tactics, rooted in Chinese conditions, and he has made Communism infinitely more familiar and acceptable to his countrymen by writing about it in a style heavily coloured by allusions to classical writings and precedents from Chinese history'.[38]

Mao's great lesson to the underdeveloped countries of the world was the need to bend Marxism to the particular situation rather than the particular situation to Marxism.

Much more than in the Russian Revolution, the environment in China closely resembled what was to be found in other developing systems. A large peasantry combined with a colonial or despotic rule in the cities was to be found in countries other than China. Huntington, for example, has analysed types of revolution and calls one of his two types the eastern revolution. This is no more than the Chinese Revolution generalized so that it may be applied to other systems.[39] Tactically, what occurred in China has also occurred to some degree in Algeria, Cuba, Indo-China, Malaya, the Philippines, and the Portuguese Colonies in Africa. Some are still occurring, and Maoism as a doctrine of revolution is still influential despite the attempts of younger Marxists like Debray to modernize or alter it. The theory that Mao developed may well be the most widely applicable of any of the Marxist theories, and its implications have not been lost on those who have actively opposed Marxist-inspired revolutionary movements.[40]

The Maoist theory of revolution holds that in a country where the working class is unavailable or unable to participate in the revolutionary movement, other classes which may be in a similar relationship with the dominant class as the proletariat is with the bourgeoisie may have class consciousness and, therefore, revolutionary potential. When such a class (or combination of classes) is present, a revolution can occur. In a system where the peasantry has been dominated, and exploited, and has a growing class consciousness, then the peasantry is the revolutionary class. But the presence of a large peasantry and absence of a working class is an indication that the society has failed to develop to the degree that it eventually will (i.e., entered into an industrial era). Because the society has not reached the stage of development it must eventually attain, the revolution should be guided by the representatives of the working class (that is yet to develop), the party. Thus, revolution can occur in the pre-capitalist society if guided by the party, which then leads that society through the various stages of development.

The Maoist theory differs from the Leninist theory principally because of the absence of the working class in Mao's theory and, as we shall see, a greater humanism. Lenin's theory is founded on the existence and availability of the working class. The working class may be aligned with a disgruntled and politically aware peasantry, but no doubt exists about which group is the centre of the revolution. Without the presence and availability of this working class the revolution is not possible. In the Maoist vision, it is the peasantry that plays the vital role. Indeed, given the particular level of development in the society it is only the peasantry that can play such a role. Mao is convinced about the inevitability of revolution and the role that the working class will eventually play as befits a theorist in the Marxian tradition.[41] But for the time being the proletarian contribution is minimal and the revolution will come about with guidance.

'It is like a ship far out at sea whose mast-head can already be seen from the shore; it is like the morning sun in the east whose shimmering rays are visible from a high mountain top; it is like a child about to be born moving restlessly in its mother's womb.'[42]

The Maoist theory of revolution evolved over a fairly long part of Mao's career. At least fifteeen years were to elapse from the time of the founding of the CCP before the theory of revolution that was to be known as Maoism was to reach fruition. Before it did the CCP was to spend many years in the wilderness as a result of mistakes in tactics in the early years. It is from these mistakes that the CCP learned how revolution in China would be possible.

Mao added three basic ideas to the Marxian model. First, he expanded the class analysis to include in the revolution classes that may previously have been thought hostile to the revolutionary movement. Second, he developed ideas of strategy for China's revolutionary war and ways of developing strategy that would be applicable to other revolutionary situations. Third, he adopted a humanist attitude with regard to the masses by insisting that the ideas that fuelled the revolution must stem from the masses who were participating in the revolution.

Origins of Maoist Thought

Although the CCP was officially founded in July 1921, Marxism began to take hold among certain groups in China slightly before that time. Nationalism influenced large numbers of people fairly early as a direct result of the imperialist powers' activities in China since the 1840s. Thus, a willing population was available. Students in Peking and Shanghai were in an especially volatile mood following the Japanese demands which would have reduced China to colonial status in 1915. The October Revolution in Russia could not fail but arouse interest in a country which had been in the midst of turbulence for many years. Additionally, a small but well-located working class was beginning to develop in the major cities. It has been suggested that by 1919 there were nearly 2,000,000 people who could fit the definition of a worker.[43] This figure was considerably larger by the mid-1920s. Further, there were large numbers of artisans in the cities who could have been considered reasonable fodder for the growing Communist movement.

But while the CCP met with great success at the beginning in organizing the workers, its political progress generally was considerably slower. So the CCP turned to the KMT led by Sun Yat Sen. The CCP was under the very strong influence of the Comintern, the organizer of the 'world revolution' which was committed to a surprisingly orthodox Marxist interpretation of the Chinese situation. It believed that it was necessary for the KMT to carry through the bourgeois-democratic revolution, and once this was accomplished the Communists could, when the time was ripe, carry out the socialist revolution. Thus, in 1923 at the Third Party Congress, the CCP agreed that the KMT 'should be regarded as the centre of all revolutionary forces'[44] and that members of the CCP could become members of the KMT without prejudice.

This alliance was not as far-fetched as it now may seem for in the 1920s the KMT was strongly influenced by the Bolshevik revolution in Russia. At a very early stage in his career Sun had advanced a 'rich nation–poor nation' thesis which lumped Russia and China together as two of the exploited nations of the world. He also proposed a type of socialism that he believed would fit into the Chinese framework. He was not, however, a Marxist. Much of his writing reflected the previous Chinese experiences, especially with regard to questions of foreign imperialism and the idea of freedom for the Chinese people. On the latter point, he believed that there was too much freedom and that a long period of disciplined political tutelage was required before the Chinese people were ready for notions such as democracy. His heavy emphasis on indoctrination was not unlike the emphasis placed on political education by the earlier dynasties.[45]

The early period of cooperation with the KMT worked reasonably well. Although the CCP was not wholly behind the idea, it did accept the general requirement that it obey the directives of the Comintern. So the CCP acted as a group within the KMT where they were permitted one-sixth of the seats on the executive. The CCP did well organizing in the cities and the KMT was acting in the countryside—although elements in the CCP did have an interest in what was happening among peasant groups as well as what was occurring among the workers.

In 1925 numerous events happened which had profound reverberations throughout China. In mid-May a worker was killed in the international settlement in Shanghai by a Japanese foreman and this led to an industrial dispute. It should be noted that within the international settlement it was the native Chinese who were treated as 'second-class' citizens. On 30 May, when students began demonstrating in Shanghai, a British soldier fired into the crowd and many demonstrators were killed in the battle which followed. Then in Canton in late June, Chinese military cadets attacked the British and French concessions in that city, and some fifty cadets were killed. Widespread xenophobia followed, and out of this the forces leading the KMT revolution were able to gather strength and embark on a military campaign throughout the country.

But during this period Sun died, and a dispute concerning the leadership of the movement began between the left and right wings of the KMT. Chiang Kai Shek had originally aligned himself with the left, but the great sources of financial support came from the right, the group comprised largely of the landlords. With the growing campaign of the KMT to unify the country, the peasants supported the revolution, but the KMT cooperated with the landlords in order to maintain the financial support it believed necessary to keep the operation going. The right wing of the KMT put pressure on Chiang to end the alliance with the CCP and tension between the KMT and CCP continued to grow. Meanwhile the great northern campaign, the final phase of the revolutionary movement, was moving ahead with growing success. Thus, although there was tension between the CCP and KMT, the Comintern still argued that the CCP should continue its period of cooperation despite some CCP misgivings.

As Chiang and his armies approached the city of Shanghai, the workers' organizations, under the leadership of the Communists, began to prepare the way for the victorious national army. But when Chiang and his army entered Shanghai in April 1927, thousands of workers were arrested, many of the leaders were executed, and the CCP was outlawed by the KMT. Since the period of cooperation was finished, the remaining CCP leadership was faced with the prospect of picking up the pieces of the April disaster.

But with the Shanghai massacre and destruction of the workers' organizations the CCP faced a very difficult doctrinal position. The party had accepted the thesis that the KMT was to lead the national revolution, but that revolution was now at an end. So it was time to begin the socialist-dominated revolution which was to be led by the Communists who represented the proletariat. But there was no idea about how this revolution could take place given the unavailability of the working class to the Communists after the workers' organizations were decimated. The movement would have to go into the countryside to exploit peasant dissatisfaction that was widespread as a result of KMT cooperation with the landlords. The real problem was how this could be rationalized in terms of the traditional Marxist-Leninist idea of revolution.

The Peasants as a Revolutionary Class

As suggested, some leaders of the CCP were anxious about the CCP-KMT arrangement from the beginning. Mao was among those doubtful about the usefulness of the alliance between the parties.[46] Above all, Mao had a very early interest in the importance of the peasantry as a revolutionary force. Even before the events of 1927 Mao was among those CCP activists urging greater activity among the peasants. Some Communists within the KMT had already been actively engaged in the countryside organizing and working with the peasants.[47] For the first time the peasantry was being considered for the much larger role it was to pursue in the future.

In 1926 Mao published a work which dealt with the question of potential allies in the revolution[48] and identified five classes in China: (1) the landlord class and the managerial class; (2)

the middle bourgeoisie; (3) the petty bourgeoisie; (4) the semi-proletariat; and (5) the proletariat. He recognized that the proletariat, while very small, was the leading revolutionary group and was at the centre of any revolutionary movement. There were two reasons for its pre-eminence. First, members of this class were strategically located in cities and were, therefore, well-concentrated should the right moment for open revolt suddenly arise. Second, as a result of their economic deprivation they had little to lose in the fight for a better life. But while they made very good fighters and could be relied upon to give a good account of themselves, they were small in numbers and could not hope to carry out the revolution on their own. So the proletariat had to look for allies.

Mao immediately ruled out the landlord and managerial (comprador) class as allies of the proletariat: 'The big land-lord and big comprador classes in particular always side with imperialism and constitute an extreme counter-revolutionary group'.[49] A possibility existed within the middle bourgeoisie; some members of this class would eventually become allies of the revolutionary classes while others would go over to the enemy. The middle bourgeoisie also represented poor pickings for the revolutionary movement because as the revolution gathered steam, the middle bourgeoisie would fall apart.

The petty bourgeoisie represented a class of people that had real revolutionary potential. Dividing them into three sections, the right wing consisted of those who aspired to the middle bourgeoisie. The second section was also in reasonable economic condition but had realised which way the world was moving and understood that they were up against the higher classes. The third section consisted of those whose standard of living was falling. They found their condition virtually intolerable and sought the revolutionary movement. But as the revolution gained momentum all three sections could join.

But the most probable revolutionary ally for the proletariat was the group that Mao called the semi-proletariat.[50] He described five groups under this heading: (1) the semi-owner peasants; (2) the poor peasants; (3) the small handicraftsmen; (4) the shop assistants; and (5) the pedlars. The most interesting were, however, the first two groups who could be further sub-divided into upper, middle and lower peasants. Of these the revolutionary potential was on a continuum running from highest potential among the lowest peasants to lowest potential among the highest peasants. Effectively, all Mao really said was that those who are the most exploited in the community are those who will be most prone to revolt against those who appear to be doing the exploiting. Now this discovery does not really seem to be particularly earth-shaking. However, Mao was the first of the Marxist theorists who recognized the genuinely revolutionary potential of the peasant and this was a deviation of great magnitude from what must be considered the orthodox Marxist view. It was a position that was not universally accepted by the party activists and caused great consternation in the leadership. Since Mao was not to become the leader of the party until 1935, there was conflict throughout the period between 1927–35 within the party over this question.

It was when Mao visited Hunan province that he 'discovered' the great potential of the peasant. In reporting on the activity of the peasant he prophesied

'In a very short time, in China's central, southern and northern provinces, several hundred million peasants will rise like a mighty storm, like a hurricane, a force so swift and violent that no power, however great, will be able to hold it back'.[51]

He described how the peasants had organized and then acted to overturn the landlords. Here he was striking out at the KMT 'allies' who were in league with the landlords and who supported them in return for financial aid. Thus, the KMT had become the exploiters, rather than being allied with the agitated peasant groups.

But Mao did not deviate from the Marxian definition of revolution. As described earlier, the Marxian definition of revolution is based on the movement from one epoch to another, or the overturning of one class by another. Mao simply moved the location of the revolution. 'A rural revolution is a revolution by which the peasantry overthrows the power of the feudal land-lord class.'[52] He perceived of the poor peasants as the vanguard of this revolutionary movement, the group that would motivate the others to join the movement.

The most significant feature of Mao's recognition of the peasantry, especially the poor peasantry, as a revolutionary class is the point that their revolutionary potential had developed without the aid of teachers and agitators. The peasants had perceived for themselves that they were exploited and mistreated.

They had come to the revolutionary movement themselves, not because leaders had swept them along. Mao demonstrated a great faith in the masses at this juncture, a faith that reveals itself in all of his revolutionary theory. It is much more mass-orientated than what may be found in the Leninist idea of revolution, and the faith in the revolutionary potential of the masses is the dominant theme that is found in all of the works of Mao from the beginning of his career. It is a theme that has never altered.

Revolutionary Strategy

In 1943, Mao is reported to have said in a speech which explained the dissolution of the Communist International, 'Revolutionary movements can be neither exported nor imported. Despite the fact that aid was accorded by the Communist International, the birth and development of the Chinese Communist Party resulted from the fact that China herself had a conscious working class'.[53] Earlier, Mao had described the errors that revolutionaries had made. One error was to adopt the manuals of revolutionary warfare used by the Soviets indiscriminately, regardless of whether they were applicable to the Chinese situation. A second error, and perhaps a more grievous one, was the tendency to imitate successes of the past even though such successes were no longer possible using the same tactics. Third, and related to both of the previous errors, was the desire of the Chinese movement to emulate the Soviet experience. Mao wrote that such people

'do not see that their laws and manuals embody the specific characteristics of the civil war and the Red Army in the Soviet Union, and that if we copy and apply them without allowing any change, we shall also be "cutting the feet to fit the shoes" and be defeated. Their argument is: since our war, like the war in the Soviet Union, is a revolutionary war, and since the Soviet Union won victory, how then can there be any alternative but to follow the Soviet example? They fail to see that while we should set special store by the war experience of the Soviet Union, because it is the most recent experience of revolutionary war and was acquired under the guidance of Lenin and Stalin, we should likewise cherish the experience of China's revolutionary war, because there are many factors that are specific to the Chinese Revolution and the Chinese Red Army'.[54]

It is not at all difficult to understand why Mao took this particular line. The coalition with the KMT had been imposed on the CCP by the Comintern although it had the acquiescence of the CCP Central Committee. Nevertheless, it was an arrangement that came about as a result of an analysis by outside sources rather than by those most immediately concerned with the situation. The Maoist strategy grew out of the tragedy in Shanghai, for from that time on the orthodox strategy which was based on the availability of the working class, became obsolete. All of the assumptions that had been made were demonstrated to be wrong and the CCP was effectively starting from the beginning again.

But the vital point that Mao raised is that despite the general applicability of the revolutionary theory to countries with roughly the same objective situation, the strategy that had to be adopted had to be based on the particular situation as it was developing in any particular country. That the Marxian analysis was adequate in explaining the social situation in countries as disparate as the Soviet Union and China was not doubted by Mao at all. He fully accepted, as we have seen, the significance of classes in society and how revolution was nothing more or less than a reordering of the class relations. What Marxian analysis did not provide was an indication of the means by which the revolution was to be brought about, and here is where Mao has made his greatest contribution. As one commentator has suggested, 'No other Communist leader has written so much and so well on the tactics of rural warfare. No other Communist leader has been so influential in making rural-based revolution a supreme law unto itself'.[55]

The military formula is a relatively straightforward account of the need to hit the enemy where he is weakest and of the necessity of remaining patient in the face of adversity. While the revolution will occur and will eventually succeed, the military necessity is to make life as easy as possible until the opportune time arrives to take the offensive. It means that a war must be largely defensive but, if possible, it must be a war of harassment as well. The enemy will become demoralized and the revolutionary army will gain strength and support. With its growing strength a growing boldness will develop as well. Once this happens, the corner will have been turned and the eventual victory assured.

Essentially, Mao argued that there was a need to study the

laws of war and how these laws might be used to meet the particular situation. In moving from the general to the particular the student of revolution first needed to master the notion of what wars are, then to understand what revolutionary war is within the context of war. Finally he had to determine (according to the audience Mao was addressing in 1936) how China's revolutionary war fitted into the more general context of revolutionary war and war. In the tradition of the Chinese master-teacher, Mao wrote:

'The only way to study the laws governing a war situation as a whole is to do some hard thinking. For what pertains to the situation as a whole is not visible to the eye, and we can understand it only by hard thinking; there is no other way. But because the situation as a whole is made up of parts, people with experience of the parts, experience of campaigns and tactics, can understand matters of a higher order provided they are willing to think hard'.[56]

The thinkers must consider all of the problems that relate to the barriers standing in the way of the ultimate victory of the revolution. Above all, Mao stressed the view that flexibility must be the watchword of the revolutionary movement. Tactics must be adapted to the particular situation; nothing was to be gained —in fact, all could be lost—by using tactics that were successful elsewhere and which had evolved from rather different situations without first examining such tactics critically. So in order to understand which tactics must be utilized, the particular situation of China had to be understood.

Mao suggested that there were four principal characteristics of the Chinese revolutionary war. First, he described China as a 'vast, semi-colonial country which is unevenly developed politically and economically and which has gone through the revolution of 1924–7'.[57] This is a significant feature for with the poorly developed state of capitalism, the proletariat was rather small—remember the Marxian proposition that the extent of the proletariat varies in direct proportion to the variation in the size of capital. Because of this smallness of the proletariat the peasantry became the revolutionary fodder. Further, China was a country under the partial imperialist domination not of one country, but of many. Thus, the imperialist powers had used China as a type of battleground, guarding their own interests, and the Chinese had to deal with these competing powers.

The second and third characteristics were directly related to one another. On one hand the enemy was big and powerful while on the other the Chinese Red Army was small and weak. This was of vital importance for the Maoist line because it represented one of the most important ways in which the Chinese revolutionary situation differed from the Russian case. No internal enemy confronted the Bolsheviks in the same way that the KMT confronted the CCP. Additionally, the intervention in Russia between 1919 and 1921 by the Western Allies was considerably different from the effects of the Japanese invasion of China. This was to figure prominently in the ultimate success of the Red Army.

The final characteristic of the Chinese revolutionary war was the combination of the CCP leadership and the agrarian revolution. Mao saw the importance of this combination because the agrarian revolution demonstrated that there was a large body that stood opposed to the KMT and was willing to give itself to the revolution. The Communist Party leadership was important because it was a unified leadership when contrasted to the KMT, and it had a clear purpose and goal. As Mao said, 'small as it is, the Red Army has great fighting capacity, because its members, led by the Communist Party, are born of the agrarian revolution and are fighting for their own interests, and because its commanders and fighters are politically united'.[58]

From an understanding of these conditions Mao argued that the Red Army and the movement would have to go on the defensive for a fairly long period of time. In fact, before going on to the counter-offensive several conditions would have to be met. He listed six conditions in all :

1 The population actively supports the Red Army,
2 The terrain is favourable for operations,
3 All the main forces of the Red Army are concentrated,
4 The enemy's weak spots have been discovered,
5 The enemy has been reduced to a tired and demoralized state,
6 The enemy has been induced to make mistakes.[59]

For Mao the first condition was the most important. So much depended upon the support of the populace that all else could be lost without it, and the army must rely on the help given to it by the local people. This condition is one of the most clearly generalizable in the revolutionary situation. It is certainly one of the clearest features of the Viet Nam war as evidenced by the counter-guerrilla operation utilized by the United States and South Viet Namese forces. If the population could not be considered loyal, move that population to another location where it could be contained. The difficulties encountered by Che Guevara in Bolivia and his eventual death may have reflected a lack of support from the general population. This may also be a reflection of the problems inherent in 'exporting' revolution.

The Maoist view toward the revolutionary war remained relatively stable until its conclusion. While the Red Army finally did go over to the offensive in 1946 and achieved victory in 1949, the tactics that Mao devised were adhered to and demonstrated to be correct in the circumstances. Most important was the reliance upon a willing and supportive population. This thesis is integral in all of Mao's writings and is central to his notion of an ongoing revolution in society, for when the opposing forces are defeated, the revolution is not over. The exploitive forces are turned out, but 'the ultimate aim for which all Communists strive is to bring about a socialist and Communist society'.[60] This can be accomplished only through the constant involvement of the masses in the process. The notion of the continuing revolution is contained in the Maoist idea of the mass line.

The Mass Line

The theory of revolution propounded by Mao does not end with the successful conclusion of the democratic revolution. Instead, it must be continued until the socialist revolution is realized. But this revolutionary process, as well as the antecedent democratic revolution, may be accomplished only with the active participation of the masses. Such participation should not imply that there exists a huge body of people who are there to be manipulated by the leadership. The vision of a conscious revolutionary peasantry that Mao formed when investigating the peasant movement in Hunan never altered: The 'startling' finding that Mao made was not that the peasants had been brought to the revolutionary boil by the party agitators, but that the peasants had spontaneously come to support the growing idea of revolution through their own perception that they were being exploited by the ruling class, the landlords. As early as 1934, Mao 'advocated work to persuade the workers and peasants that we represent their interests, that our life and theirs are intimately interwoven'.[61]

This is not to suggest that Mao was in any way denigrating the role of leadership. In a sense he was elevating it because he demanded from the leaders that they be sensitive to the ideas that the masses had. Since the masses were 'living through' the revolution, and the revolutionary situation was continually changing, the leadership would have to keep in touch with the masses. Thus, 'if the knowledge of revolutionaries does not change rapidly in accordance with the changed situation, they will be unable to lead the revolution to victory'.[62]

According to the sympathetic view toward the development of Mao's thought, Mao had sensed that the debacle of 1927 resulted from an estrangement between party and mass. The leadership ought to have been prepared for the problems that were going to happen. Above all, the leaders ought not create artificial barriers in thought or behaviour that would cut them off from the masses or revolutionary mass base. Critically, Mao clearly set the responsibility for the elimination of such barriers on the leadership of the party. As early as 1934 he was urging the party to set to the work of persuading the workers and the peasants of the need for cooperation. The key phrase here is 'persuade'; the party was not to coerce the peasants.

The concept of the mass line suggests that there is a continual movement toward Communism. This is in keeping with the standard Marxian idea that one stage gives way to a new stage. But the new stage already exists in the minds of the masses. It is, however, scattered and fragmented; therefore, the party leadership must bring the ideas together and return them to the masses. It is also a very sensible technique for anticipating the problems that might arise among the masses. As Lewis states:

'The mass line method of leadership prescribes techniques to maximize participation and enthusiasm of the Chinese people and to dissipate their possible antagonism toward party officials. To achieve the greatest motivation of the population with the least hostility has necessitated a wide variety of propaganda, training and guiding techniques such as debates, rallies, small group studies and campaigns of emulation and self-reform'.[63]

The method of the mass line which was set out in 1943 includes four progressive stages; perception, summarization, authorization and implementation.[64] In the perception stage cadres operate within the worker-peasant masses studying the scattered and unsystematic views. In this manner they identify problems and attempt to coordinate the different views. Thus, they can determine areas of strength and weaknesses of party operations. In the summarization stage the cadres sum up the various views in a coherent whole. In the authorization stage the highest authority in the area examines and sends back authoritative directives. And in the implementation stage the general directives are sent back through the apparatus to be explained and popularized among the masses, and the masses then adopt the directives as their own. The process occurs in the following manner:

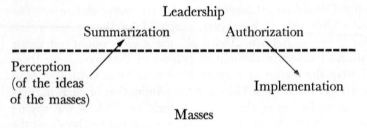

The notion of the mass line rests on four assumptions. First, all progress must inevitably depend upon the action of the masses. Secondly, people know what they want, so the leaders must go to the masses in order to learn from the masses. Third, any action by the masses requires that it must be taken by themselves. And fourth, latent in the masses is a boundless creative power and this power makes revolutions.

Whether the mass line is an effective method of continuing the revolutionary process is an open question. Townsend, for example, found that it was a useful technique from the standpoint of organizational success and 'it has also contributed heavily to the development of national political community in China and very modestly to exposure of political elites to popular opinions and demands . . .'.[65] But Townsend has rather serious reservations about the future prospects of the Maoist revolutionary ideal. Whether a second generation of CCP leaders—and the masses—can be fired by the same ideals that grew out of the traumatic revolutionary years is an open question. Revolutionary goals have a tendency to disappear as the revolutionary era becomes a part of the dimmer past. The Maoist notion of the mass line is devoted to keeping the revolution going, and the Great Proletarian Cultural Revolution may have been part of this process.[66] Since the Maoist group was afraid that the revolutionary fervour was dying, the cultural revolution attempted to revive the revolution and revolutionary goals.

So whether one views the mass line as it is accepted in the Maoist sense as a method of keeping the masses involved in the revolution, or in the more cynical way that includes the mass line in the category of ways to control the population, it is very much a part of Mao's theory of revolution. From the earliest days of his career, Mao saw in the masses a revolutionary consciousness that must be tapped if the movement was to succeed. Mao said, 'the harder the struggle, the greater the need for Communists to link their leadership closely with the demands of the vast masses . . .'.[67] Each time there was a setback in the revolution Mao embarked on campaigns to involve the masses more directly with the leaders. In this respect, his theory of revolution remained virtually unchanged for nearly fifty years.

Summary of Maoism

Despite the deification of Mao that has occurred during the past few years he will not be remembered by those outside China as one of the great philosophers in the Marxist-Leninist tradition. His works do not have the same theoretical merit as the works of Lenin, Luxemburg, and Lukacs, among others. His essays in the late 1930s which were attempts to rectify his weaknesses as a philosopher are not inspiring and do not really add to his stature.[68] But Mao's contribution as a theorist of revolution is probably unequalled by any twentieth century thinker including Lenin, for no one has had as much influence outside his own environment as Mao has had. What Mao wrote has had relevance for numerous underdeveloped systems. Revolutions from Cuba to Indo-China have been related to the Marxian idea of what revolution is and how it happens. In this application of a model developed originally with industrial societies in mind, Mao added an entirely new dimension to Marxian analysis that permitted the model to be applied to the pre-industrial society.

At the core of Maoist thought, there is but one factor that insures that the revolutionary movement will eventually succeed. That factor is the support of the masses. But it is a support that stems from the understanding that the masses themselves have that in the past they have been exploited by the ruling groups, and here, for the first time, a revolutionary movement and leadership is really concerned for those who are involved in the movement. Thus, the basic proposition that revolutionary movements can survive and win only when the masses are favourable to it whether in the industrial or pre-industrial society is the real Maoist contribution to the theory of revolution that he derived from the model Marx had left for him.

Conclusion: Contemporary Marxism

The Marxian model of revolution has proved to be a vital and useful approach to the analysis of revolutionary situations. But although we have suggested that the Marxian theory may be seen to be invalid or, at least, not yet validated, many of the Marxian propositions survived for a considerable period of time. We have seen that one of the most important propositions was that which involved the proletariat in the revolutionary struggle and recognized the proletariat as not only a revolutionary class but *the* revolutionary class. Lenin's theory of revolution was based upon the role that the proletariat was to play in each stage of the revolution. Even Mao, who was operating in what had become a society virtually without a proletariat after the Shanghai massacre of 1927, accepted the role of the proletariat as the vanguard of the revolution. While Mao recognized the revolutionary potential of the peasantry, he was able to justify this seeming departure from Marxian analysis by referring to types of peasants as 'semi-proletariat', as did Lenin. Thus they had the attributes of the proletariat which helped to explain their revolutionary proclivities. Neither Lenin nor Mao would deny the revolutionary potential of the proletariat if that proletariat was available at all. They altered, however, some traditional views of Marxism in their reliance upon the party in the revolutionary movement. Both Lenin and Mao stressed the need to 'guide' the revolution and the revolutionary class, until all class enemies were destroyed, although Mao was more concerned than Lenin with the leader-mass connection.

More recent theorists who are classed in the Marxian tradition because of an acceptance of the Marxian model of revolution have gone considerably further than Lenin or Mao in dealing with Marxian propositions. They have effectively rejected all of the propositions that Marx included in his theory. Those who figure in this later 'generation' of Marxists are theorists and philosophers like Herbert Marcuse, Frantz Fanon and Régis Debray.[69] Each has made a major contribution to revolutionary analysis generally and to Marxian analysis in particular. What these theorists share is the rejection of the proletariat as a revolutionary class. Instead, they have each argued that other groups will be responsible for making the revolution. The proletariat no longer has the inclination, much less the will, to overthrow the bourgeoisie.

As we have seen, Marcuse rejects the working class as a group that has revolutionary potential. Mobilization of the population has occurred in the advanced industrial societies which has tended to mitigate against the type of conflict that Marx foresaw in society. There is a general agreement on major issues which has brought former 'opposites' together. Marcuse maintains that 'this unification of opposites bears upon the very possibilities of social change where it embraces those strata on whose back the system progresses—that is, the very classes whose existence once embodied the opposition to the system as a whole'.[70] For Marcuse the possibility for social change is likely to be found in 'the substratum of the outcasts and outsiders, the exploited and persecuted of other races and other colours, the unemployed and the unemployable'.[71] The basic scheme of Marxian analysis is still present. One class exploits and one class is exploited. The alteration comes in the composition of the classes.

Fanon also rejected the working class as a revolutionary class and, in doing so, went considerably further than Mao in ascribing the peasantry a revolutionary potential. He maintained that when the urban revolutionaries went into the countryside

'These men discover a coherent people who go on living, as it were, statically, but who keep their moral values and their devotion to the nation intact. They discover a people that is generous, ready to sacrifice themselves completely, an impatient people with a stony pride. It is understandable that the meeting between these militants with the police on their track and these mettlesome masses of people, who are rebels by instinct, can produce an explosive mixture of unusual potentiality'.[72]

Fanon perceived that the working classes of the newly independent African states would not make demands upon the government, for the workers realized that they 'are in fact the most favoured section of the population, and represent the most comfortably off fraction of the people'.[73] Fanon does have some support with regard to his view of the non-existence of revolutionary potential in the proletariat: 'The conclusion seems inescapable that, whether or not Fanon was correct in identifying the African peasantry as a revolutionary class, contemporary Africa offers no other'.[74]

While both Debray and Fanon rejected the working class as a revolutionary class, Debray was less inclined to accept the possibility of spontaneity of the revolutionary movement than Fanon. But unlike the earlier Marxists who believed in the need for the party to guide the revolutionary movement, Debray has argued that the guerrilla movement would precede the development of the revolutionary party, a complete reversal of the Maoist view. The possibility that the proletariat would be the vanguard of the revolution was rejected, for by living in the urban environment the worker was corrupted by his surroundings. Utilizing the Cuban revolution as his 'ideal type', Debray has written that 'the mountain proletarianizes the bourgeois and peasant elements, and the city can bourgeoisify the proletarians'.[75]

More recently, however, the working-class-as-a-revolutionary-class proposition has been regaining much of its lost popularity. The great impetus for rethinking what was thought by many to be a non-viable proposition was the period between March and June, 1968, in France. This period of unrest, now known as the May Revolution, brought a broad front of workers and students together who were opposed to the Gaullist regime. This revolt, which nearly brought down the government, involved universities being closed down by the students and factories being occupied by the workers, particularly younger workers. While the strike momentum was gaining strength the government appeared helpless, but eventually the revolt was brought to an end. Two alternative explanations have emerged from Marxists which explain the failure of the revolt. Neither explanation questions the revolutionary potential of the working class.

On the one hand the 'traditional' Marxists have argued that while theorists such as Marcuse have been proved wrong, the time was not ripe for a revolution to succeed. One commentator has noted that 'the majority of wage and salary workers still supported the reformist parties or even those of the bourgeoisie'.[76] Thus, according to this view, the party and the trade unions are capable of leading the revolution : the subjective situation has yet to be met. On the other hand, Daniel Cohn-Bendit, the student activist who sprang into prominence during this period, has argued that the working class had the ability to bring about the revolution. It was, however, betrayed by the party which practises a type of bureaucratic authoritarianism that has its roots in the Leninist theory of the revolutionary party. Cohn-Bendit argues that in his view 'the militant acts as an agent of the people and no longer as their leader',[77] for in leadership are the seeds of authoritarianism.

Thus, we appear to have come full circle : from working-class-as-a-revolutionary class back to working-class-as-a-revolutionary class. Still, there exists considerable disagreement among Marxian theorists concerning the correctness of the early propositions. Whatever the outcome of this particular dispute, all Marxists accept the Marxian model of revolutionary change. The idea of two classes conditioned by the economic scheme of things standing in opposition to each other has been the most widely applied model of social and revolutionary change. As we shall see, the other models and theories of revolutionary change, i.e., the non-Marxian, are very largely attempts to establish alternative explanations of how and why revolutions come about.

Notes and References

1 Shlomo Avineri, *The Social and Political Thought of Karl Marx*, London, 1968, p. 151.

2 Karl Marx and Frederick Engels, 'Preface to the Russian Edition of 1882', *Manifesto of the Communist Party*, from *Selected Works* : Vol. I, p. 23.

3 *Ibid.*, p. 24.

4 *Ibid.* See also Avineri, *The Social and Political Thought of Karl Marx*, p. 153.

5 George Lichtheim, *Marxism: An Historical and Critical Study*, New York, 1961, pp. 327–8.

6 Isaac Deutscher, *The Unfinished Revolution: Russia 1917–1967*, London, 1967, p. 15.

7 See, for example, Adam B. Ulam, *Lenin and the Bolsheviks*, London, 1966; Ulam suggests that Lenin may have been strongly affected by the death of his brother, at least subconsciously. For a more detailed psychological approach which does not attribute a great deal to this incident see E. V. Wolfenstein, *The Revolutionary Personality: Lenin, Trotsky, Gandhi*, Princeton, 1967. See also Chapter 8.

8 V. I. Lenin, 'Letters on tactics', from *Selected Works*, 6, London, 1936, p. 33.

9 George Lukacs, *Lenin: A Study on the Unity of his Thought*, trans. Nicholas Jacobs, London, 1970, first published, 1924, p. 11.

10 V. I. Lenin, *The Two Tactics of Social Democracy in the Democratic Revolution*, from *Selected Works*, 3, pp. 39–133.

11 *Ibid.*, p. 77.

12 *Ibid.*, p. 82.

13 *Ibid.*

14 *Ibid.*, p. 86.

15 Leon Trotsky, *The Permanent Revolution and Results and Prospects*, London, 1962, p. 194.

16 *Ibid.*, p. 195.

17 *Ibid.*

18 V. I. Lenin, 'The tasks of the proletariat in our revolution', from *Selected Works*, 6, pp. 45–76; and 'Letters on tactics'.

19 *Ibid.*, p. 35.

20 V. I. Lenin, 'The tasks of the proletariat in the present revolution (April 1917): the April Theses', from *Lenin on Politics and Revolution*, ed. by James E. Connor, New York, 1968, p. 159. See also *Selected Works*, pp. 21–6.

21 Marx and Engels, *Manifesto of the Communist Party*, p. 46.

22 Herbert Marcuse, *One Dimensional Man*, London, 1964.

23 *Ibid.*, p. 32.

24 V. I. Lenin, *What is to be Done?*, trans. by S. V. and Patricia Utechin, London, 1970. First published in Great Britain, 1963, p. 80.

25 *Ibid.*, p. 94.

26 *Ibid.*, p. 99.

27 *Ibid.*, p. 109.

28 *Ibid.*, p. 123.

29 *Ibid.*, p. 156.

30 *Ibid.*, p. 165.

31 *Ibid.*, pp. 169–70.

32 Rosa Luxemburg, 'The role of organization in revolutionary

activity', from *Rosa Luxemburg: Selected Political Writings*, ed. and introduced by Robert Looker, London, 1972, p. 99.

33 *Ibid.*

34 Paul Frölich, *Rosa Luxemburg: Her Life and Work*, trans. by Edward Fitzgerald, New York, 1969. First published 1940, p. 108.

35 Luxemburg, 'The role of organization in revolutionary activity', p. 104.

36 See Lenin's description of the tendency of imperialism to split the workers in *Imperialism, the Highest Stage of Capitalism*, Moscow, 1970, pp. 102–3.

37 A. James Gregor, *A Survey of Marxism*, New York, 1965, p. 251.

38 Stuart R. Schram, *Mao Tse-Tung*, Harmondsworth, Middlesex, 1966, p. 223.

39 Samuel Huntington, *Political Order in Changing Societies*, New Haven, 1968, Chapter 5.

40 See Samuel Huntington, 'The bases of accommodation', *Foreign Affairs*, *46*, 1968, pp. 642–56.

41 For a discussion of Mao's debt to Lenin, for example, see Stuart Schram, *The Political Thought of Mao Tse-Tung*, Harmondsworth, Middlesex, 1969, first published 1963, pp. 134–38. Mao did not 'invent' the peasant for the Marxists; the peasant has existed since the beginning. See, for example, Frederick Engels, *The German Revolutions*, ed. by Leonard Krieger, Chicago, 1967. But the role that the peasant was to play in revolutionary warfare was indeed first developed in the Maoist vision of revolution. Mao effectively turned the peasant into a practical, revolutionary fighter.

42 Mao Tse-Tung, 'A single spark can start a prairie fire', from *Selected Works of Mao Tse-Tung*, Vol. 1, Peking, 1967, p. 127.

43 Jacques Guillermaz, *A History of the Chinese Communist Party 1921–1949*, trans. by Anne Destenay, London, 1972, p. 40.

44 Wolfgang Franke, *A Century of Chinese Revolution 1851–1949*, trans. by Stanley Rudman, Oxford, 1970.

45 Barrington Moore, *Social Origins of Dictatorship and Democracy*, Harmondsworth, Middlesex, 1969. First published 1966, pp. 201–27.

46 See Arthur Cohen, *The Communism of Mao Tse-Tung*, Chicago, 1964, pp. 29–53.

47 Stuart Schram, *Mao Tse-Tung*, Harmondsworth, Middlesex, 1966.

48 Mao Tse-Tung, 'Analysis of the classes in Chinese society', *Selected Works of Mao Tse-Tung*, Vol. 1, Peking, 1967, pp. 13–22.

49 *Ibid.*, p. 13–4.

50 See Lenin's views on the semi-proletariat. 'Tasks of the proletariat in our revolution', pp. 59–61.

51 Mao Tse-Tung, 'Report on an investigation of the peasant movement in Hunan', *Selected Works of Mao Tse-Tung, 1,* p. 23.

52 *Ibid.*, p. 28.

53 Stuart Schram, *The Political Thought of Mao Tse-Tung*, Harmondsworth, Middlesex, 1969, p. 421.

54 Mao Tse-Tung, 'Problems of strategy in China's revolutionary war', *Selected Works of Mao Tse-Tung, 1,* p. 181.

55 Cohen, *The Communism of Mao Tse-Tung*, p. 73.

56 Mao Tse-Tung, 'Problems of strategy in China's revolutionary war', p. 185.

57 *Ibid.*, p. 196.

58 *Ibid.*, p. 198.

59 *Ibid.*, pp. 215–6.

60 Mao Tse-Tung, 'The Chinese revolution and the Chinese Communist Party', *Selected Works of Mao Tse-Tung, 2,* p. 331.

61 John Wilson Lewis, *Leadership in Communist China*, Ithaca, New York, 1963, p. 22.

62 Mao Tse-Tung, 'On practice', *Selected Works of Mao Tse-Tung, 1,* pp. 295–310.

63 John W. Lewis, *Leadership in Communist China*, p. 71.

64 See Mao Tse-Tung, 'Some questions concerning methods of leadership', *Selected Works of Mao Tse-Tung, 3,* pp. 117–22.

65 James R. Townsend, *Political Participation in Communist China*, Berkeley, 1967, p. 198.

66 There are numerous works dealing with the cultural revolution. Among them are Joan Robinson, *The Cultural Revolution in China*, Harmondsworth, Middlesex, 1969; *China after the Cultural Revolution* (A Selection from *The Bulletin of the Atomic Scientists*),

New York, 1970; Robert J. Lifton, *Revolutionary Immortality: Mao Tse-Tung and the Cultural Revolution*, Harmondsworth, Middlesex, 1969; and Tai Sung An, *Mao Tse-Tung's Cultural Revolution*, New York, 1972. These works are only a small selection of what is available but they represent a fair cross-section of the views that scholars have taken to the events in China during the cultural revolution.

67 Mao Tse-Tung, 'Some questions concerning methods of leadership', *Selected Works of Mao Tse-Tung, 3*, p. 122.

68 See Mao Tse-Tung, 'On practice', and 'On contradiction', both from *Selected Works of Mao Tse-Tung, 1*, pp. 295–310 and pp. 311–47.

69 Marcuse is a German philosopher who left his native country when the Nazis came to power. Because of his sharp break with many of the traditional Marxian propositions, he has been one of the most controversial figures in contemporary philosophy. A very useful introduction to his work is Alisdair MacLintyre, *Marcuse*, London, 1970. Fanon was a physician whose work took him to Algeria. While there he became a supporter of the revolutionary movement that eventually led to the French withdrawal from that country. Fanon became one of the most widely read anti-colonialists. Debray is a French philosopher who spent considerable time in Cuba after Castro came to power. While investigating the guerrilla movement in Bolivia (led by Che Guevara) for a Mexican newspaper, he was arrested by the Bolivian authorities and spent several years in prison.

70 Marcuse, *One Dimensional Man*, p. 19.

71 *Ibid.*, p. 256.

72 Frantz Fanon, *The Wretched of the Earth*, trans. by Constance Farrington, Harmondsworth, Middlesex, 1967. First published 1961, p. 101.

73 *Ibid.*, p. 97.

74 David Caute, *Fanon*, London, 1970, p. 75.

75 Régis Debray, *Revolution in the Revolution?*, trans. by Bolkye Ortiz, Harmondsworth, Middlesex, 1968, p. 75.

76 Jack Woddis, *New Theories of Revolution*, London, 1972, p. 362.

77 Gabriel Cohn-Bendit and Daniel Cohn-Bendit, *Obsolete Communism: The Left-Wing Alternative*, trans. by Arnold Pomeruus, Harmondsworth, Middlesex, 1968, p. 250.

Chapter 6
The Functionalist Approach to Revolution

Marxist sociology is concerned largely with an explanation of social change as revolutionary change. Within this tradition all revolutionary change is seen as structural change for it involves the most meaningful alteration in the relations of the classes in a society. Much of what might be termed non-Marxist social science is devoted to an explicit refutation of these premises of Marxist sociology. First, not all structure change comes in the form of an alteration of the classes and the class relations in society. As Dahrendorf has argued, 'In principle a theory of class illuminates only a small segment of the wide field which can be described by the vague concept of structure change. We can neither expect nor, above all, assume that a theory of class will cast a glimmer of its light on other aspects of structure change as well'.[1]

Second, the dominant theme with regard to social change in much of non-Marxian sociology is that while social change is a common—indeed, an endemic—feature of life, it is by no means inevitable that social change must always be in the form of a revolution, especially as Marx defined it, an alteration in the relation of the classes. Instead, revolutionary change is but one form of social change and probably an exceptional form at that. Furthermore, 'by no means all challenges to established power distributions or forms of government are class-oriented, or directly concerned with relative social position, except in the definitional sense that a challenge to power is aimed at somehow changing the exercise of power'.[2] Revolution, then, while suggesting radical social alteration, may take a number of forms. Class alteration may be one form, but other changes are certainly possible.

This non-Marxian tradition in sociology does not maintain that all societies are basically stable and that social change is a rare occurrence or process. Nor does it suggest that social conflict is not frequent; it simply rejects the notion that conflict is the main feature of all societies. Instead, this tradition would be inclined toward the view that civil societies are essentially consensual by nature and that the elements of such societies are 'shared systems of belief, sentiment and values; and culturally standardized criteria of technical, aesthetic and moral evaluation'.[3] Or, if the view is taken that conflict is endemic in society, then such conflict as there is tends to evolve into consensual conflict, a condition in which groups and individuals may still do battle with one another, but they do battle according to reasonably well-defined 'rules of the game' that are accepted by most of the members of society within which battles are taking place. That some groups win and some groups lose does not inevitably lead to a revolution. The losers do not rise up against the victors in order to right what they would consider the wrong that has been done to them. The losing group, instead, recovers to contest the battle another day. It reassesses its strategy so that it will be able to avoid the errors that might have been responsible for the defeat. This is, in effect, the ethos that underpins electoral strategy in democratic societies. If a political party loses an election, it accepts the defeat and fights the next election.

There are, at least, two schools that we may identify within this tradition, and each has made a contribution to our understanding of revolutionary change. First, the model of revolutionary change developed by Chalmers Johnson stems from the 'functionalist' view of society, one of the major approaches in the study of sociology. Second, there are the notions of revolution that flow from the pluralist view of society. These ideas are expressed most aptly in the works that have been written by Hannah Arendt and William Kornhauser and are referred to as theories of mass society. Both the functionalist and mass society schools tend to reflect strong ideological commitments to ideas of democracy, and these ideas come through the works rather clearly. In this chapter we shall look at the functionalist approach and its usefulness in the analysis of revolutionary change. The next chapter will focus on the theory of mass society.

The Functionalist Notion of Revolution

The most important and widely cited contributions to an understanding of revolutionary change that emanate from the functionalist school are those of Chalmers Johnson, but these works have not been universally well received. One rather scathing review of Johnson's second book has declared that 'this is one of those rare works which leaves this reader, at least, with a sense of having totally wasted his time. The author combines to an unusual degree the qualities of superficiality, banality, and pretentiousness'.[4] But whether one holds this dismissive attitude or adopts a more favourable view of Johnson's work, it is necessary to make an analysis of the model that he has developed for at least two reasons. First, it is one of the few recent examples that we have of an attempt to develop a useful framework within which the questions of how and why revolutions occur may be examined. Second, and perhaps of greatest significance to us, Johnson's work represents a major effort to utilize the writings of Talcott Parsons for the purpose of analysing radical social change.[5] Parsons' work has had a profound influence not only in his own field of sociology but in the other social sciences as well, particularly political science where many scholars owe Parsons an enormous intellectual debt.[6]

Studies containing critical analyses of Parsons' work range from wildly sympathetic to very strongly hostile.[7] From the standpoint of political science, Parsons is particularly important because, as Runciman suggests, 'the fact remains . . . that functionalism is the only current alternative to Marxism as the basis for some kind of general theory in political science',[8] and it is Parsons who may be considered the primary exponent of this 'theory'.

As a major alternative to Marxian sociology Parsons developed a very different view of what society is. As we have seen, society for Marx was conflictual because of its inbuilt contradictions, i.e. the division of society into classes which reflect the mode of production. Even a 'peaceful' society is founded upon the coercive power of the dominating class over the dominated class, or the ability of one class to hold another class in a type of bondage through force and/or the imposition of a particular set of values.

Society, for Parsons, also has a conflictual potential that may or may not be realized, but this conflict stems not from the fact that one class has the goods and power and one class does not. Instead, the potentiality of conflict is due to the general scarcity of valuable or valued goods in any society. Conflict arises because of the competition for those goods:

'By virtue of the primordial fact that the objects—social and non-social—which are instrumentally useful or intrinsically valuable are scarce in relation to the amount required for full gratification of the need dispositions of every actor, there arises the problem of allocation: the problem of who is to do what, and the manner and conditions under which it is to be done. This is the fundamental problem which arises from the interaction of two or more actors'.[9]

Parsons, then, does not ask the question, 'how does humanity move to a classless and, hence, conflict-free existence?' He is instead concerned with how conflict is contained and how, given the chronic scarcity of goods in society, people manage to survive together. He answers his own question by 'postulating interlocking "interests" in need gratification which are, at the same time partly defined by, and integrated with, mutually held criteria of evaluation'.[10] In other words, men are able to work out ways of living with one another with conflict held to a bare minimum because over a very long period of time they have been able to solve the problems that recur with solutions that have generally come to be agreeable to most members of the society. Thus, over generations, behavioural patterns are such that members of a community expect others to act in certain socially accepted ways, and this predictable behaviour is accepted as normal while any deviation from these predictable ways is conceived as being not normal within the context of that society and the 'rules' it has developed. These 'rules' may persist over many generations and can be very difficult to alter.

Parsons has identified four structural categories in developing his own functional paradigm of societies and what makes them cohere: values, norms, collectivities and roles.[11] While each of these is important and will be discussed, for the purpose of understanding Johnson's model of revolution, one needs an understanding first of all of what values are. While the term connotes a variety of meanings in different contexts, these meanings tend to be related and an understanding of one makes the slight variation in the term of no particular consequence in understanding what it means in a different context. A particularly useful definition of values is provided by Kluckhohn who states:

'Values define the limits of permissible cost of impulse satisfaction in accord with the whole array of hierarchical enduring

goals of the personality and sociocultural system for order, the
need for respecting the interests of others and of the group as
a whole in social living'.[12]

In this context values are more than simple definitions of the
limits of what one may or may not do. They also define the
types of things that one might even think of doing as well as
those things one would not consider at all. In this sense, Smelser
calls values 'the most general component of social action . . .
values state in general terms the desirable end states which act
as a guide to human endeavour'.[13] Values here are not goals, but
they define what the goals of a community ought to be and
preclude discussion of potential goals which do not fit with the
general value system. More than this, values are also responsible
for the sense of community that people in society have. Johnson,
for example, calls them 'the definitional symbols which, when
shared, establish the conscious solidarity that characterizes men
joined together in a normal community'.[14]

But values may be defined in ways other than as the
definitional constraints of a community, as Johnson makes clear.
Values also serve as explanations of events as well as explanations
for the particular environment of a society. An example of values
as explanations relates to the religious outlook of the community.
If, in medieval times, a man who was thought by the community
to be 'evil' in the context of their particular religious values
suddenly was struck dead by lightning in front of the church,
the particular event could be easily explained as divine retri-
bution, or as God punishing one who transgressed the holy law.
In so far as the social system is concerned, the situation in which
the peasant found himself with regard to land ownership in
India or in relation to the dominant family in the particular
locale as in China might be explained by the caste or clan
systems of values that were operative in those two societies
respectively. Although it may be considered doubtful that these
were the values to which the peasants adhered willingly given
the tradition of so many peasant revolts,[15] in the ideal society—
or in the society in balance or equilibrium—the values would be
adequate to explain whatever inequalities or social differences
might be found in the particular communities. And so long as
there were no particular pressures in a country like China, in
terms of sudden population growth or as a result of natural
disasters such as droughts or floods that placed too great a strain

on the existing system to provide enough land for the population or to grow enough food, then the values were adequate to keep the social situation reasonably stable.

Norms differ from values in that values are general while norms tend to define the specific rules of the community. Norms 'have regulatory significance for social processes and relationships but do not embody "principles" which are applicable beyond *social organization* . . . . In more advanced societies, the structural focus of norms is the legal system'.[16] In a sense the norms make the values operative while, in turn, the norms are 'legitimized by values but operate at a lower level of generality with respect to expected concrete collective and role performance'.[17] The operative word here is 'concrete' for norms refer to those rules which govern actual situations in the day-to-day life of the individual.

The term 'roles' may have several meanings. On the individual level and in simplest terms, roles might refer to the various parts that the person 'plays' in his everyday life. Hence, an eighteen year old male person might be, at various times in one day, a student, son, musician, football player and vacation-time postman. With regard to society, 'roles serve to guide the choices and the actions of their incumbents by specifying rights, duties or obligations, sanctions, facilities, and so forth'.[18] It is the composite aggregation of roles that forms various structures. Thus, the political structure of a community may be comprised of the sum of various roles such as Prime Minister, President or Members of Parliament.

A collectivity, for Parsons, is punctuated by solidarity which 'is characterized by the institutionalization of shared value-orientations'.[19] This means that to speak of any category such as blondes, or males, or dogs, does not make a collectivity. The such as the United Kingdom (a collectivity) is a democracy (the groups such as Americans or Englishmen, members of a boating club or football club. Thus an individual may belong to a number of collectivities and fill roles which are associated with each.

In putting the four concepts, values, norms, roles and collectivities, together, Parsons would 'use the term *values* for the shared normative component, and the term . . . *norm* for the component that is specific to a given role . . .'.[20] If a society such as the United Kingdom (a collectivity) is a democracy (the organizing value), the individual who is a member of parliament (the role) will give up his seat (the norm) when the parliament is dissolved in order to hold an election.

According to the functionalist view, a particular social system will have difficulties when the values cannot account for changes in the environment or, conversely, when changes in the values mean that the environment itself comes to be seen as wrongly organized. The reason why any question of values or value-environmental relationship is so important is that values, as they have been described, tend to subsume norms and roles as well as being the reasons for the continued existence of the collectivity.[21] When such values can no longer explain the environment, then the social system will enter a period of great difficulty. Examples of the value-environment distortion are manifold. The young Russian peasant who had grown up in a small, rural community at the turn of the twentieth century had a particular orientation to a small community environment. In this society, life centred around the extended family and the type of farming work that was done; the dominant values would be strongly influenced by the religious teaching in the environment. If this individual went to one of the new industrial centres such as St Petersburg or Moscow for the opportunity of accumulating money he would have been thrust into a new environment which could hardly compare to the social milieu he had left behind. Since this process was occurring on a rather large scale, the person applying the functionalist model to the Russian case could suggest that the new group of workers were a potential collectivity, which would eventually seek to alter the environment as a new set of values developed. This represents a different explanation from that which a Marxist would give. The Marxist would argue that the new form of dehumanizing work and life style in which the worker was forced to engage would lead to class consciousness which is more than just a common awareness of misery. It is an understanding on the part of the worker that the basic problem is one of exploitation and this understanding would lead eventually to revolution.

The functionalist would argue that the new environment would require a new set of values, and once the values were adjusted and/or the environment altered, either through evolution or revolution, the system would once again return to balance or equilibrium, the situation in which values and environment are synchronized. The type of work the individual did might or might not have an impact upon the individual's outlook. What is important in this view is that through the process of change there is no inevitable movement to a dictatorship of the proletariat or a communist society. Instead, society would probably be organized with statuses and roles that would be redefined in terms of the new values, which now more satisfactorily explained the environment.

Another example of value and environmental dyssynchronization may be found in the situation that confronted German soldiers, and other members of the populace, at the end of World War I. The values that were operationalized in the position of the Kaiser and the authoritarian social structure that had existed in Imperial Germany were said to be widely held.[22] Even the previously dissident element in the population, the Social Democratic Party, had voted generally to support German policy during the war. Yet overnight the environment altered considerably and the German citizen was presented with a new republic in place of a monarchy, a lost war in place of the widely held expectation of victory, and the possibility of being governed by sections of the society, particularly the Social Democrats, which had not actually governed before nor, indeed, been thought fit to govern by the majority of citizens.

Thus, the people in Germany were presented with two alternative possibilities. They could either accept the changes that had occurred suddenly and alter the value system in order to cope with the new environment or they could work to restore the environment that reflected the values that had guided the community before the war. Given the eventual disaster that befell the Weimar Republic, one may conclude that the values could not be altered rapidly or radically enough to cope with the new and unfamiliar situation. The economic disaster of the early 1920s and the occupation of the Ruhr by the Allies did not help to build confidence in the regime. A number of commentators have concluded that it was not the democratic constitution that was at fault for the eventual failure of the Republic. Instead, it was the inability of the politicians to graft a democratic constitution on to what had too recently been a basically authoritarian social system.[23] All of the events that damaged the credibility of the government seemed to have reinforced a desire for at least some aspects of the older, authoritarian, but more familiar and comfortable environment.

The way in which Chalmers Johnson attempts to use the Parsonian approach to guide the development of a model of revolutionary change is found in two books, *Revolution and the Social System* and *Revolutionary Change*. Although the conception of revolution that is depicted in the model is basically the same in both analyses, the model is refined considerably in the second. Further, the first is largely an attempt to construct a taxonomy of revolution which clarifies his definition of what a revolution is. The latter work concentrates more fully on the model itself with special interest in the question of legitimacy and elite intransigence. In the remainder of this section, the model will be described. Some of the strengths and weaknesses of the model will be suggested with special emphasis on the definitional problems and the importance of elite intransigence.

The Model

A revolutionary situation may be said to exist when values and the environment of a particular society are no longer synchronized. Given this notion, Johnson argues that 'revolutions must be studied in the context of the social systems in which they occur'.[24] This is required because the values and the environment may be considered peculiar to the particular social system. Because of the need to understand the situation in which the dyssynchronization is occurring, Johnson says that 'the sociology of functional societies comes logically before the sociology of revolution'.[25] Thus, to understand why a particular society is suddenly threatened by revolution, some familiarity with the previously 'stable state' of that society is also required just as it is necessary to understand generally how societies 'function' properly before being able to determine what factors are responsible for their malfunctioning.

Within the society that has in the past been functioning 'properly', i.e. where a revolutionary or violent situation has not presented itself, certain pressures may build up which may be categorized in a fourfold 'sources of change' typology.[26] These sources of change are identified as '(1) exogenous value-changing sources; (2) endogenous value-changing sources; (3) exogenous environment-changing sources; and (4) endogenous environment-changing sources'.[27] Exogenous value-changing sources might refer to the introduction of Marxism to China in the period just prior to 1921 when the Communist Party was founded, or to the foreign education of eventual leaders. Social background studies of revolutionary elites almost inevitably consider whether the leaders did spend any substantial time either studying or working abroad. Johnson identifies 'internal innovators' as possible sources of endogenous value-changing sources,[28] but here he recognizes the difficulty in placing the sources of change in particular categories because how a man becomes an internal innovator without some access to ideas that are outside his environment seem problematical at best. Exogenous environment-changing sources could be in the form of a foreign invasion or the introduction of new irrigation techniques that have first been applied successfully elsewhere. Endogenous environment-changing sources might be the sudden expansion of the population which puts pressure upon the food or land supply.

Once these types of problems are brought to bear upon the social system, the various parts of the system may be able to adapt to the changes. Population pressures may be met by birth control procedures, more equitable land distribution, or by expansion in the industrial sphere thus providing new jobs for the extra population which in turn provides more markets for the goods. Potential elites and their new ideas may be accommodated or co-opted into the elite so that their career paths will not be blocked by the incumbent elite.[29] The critical point to be understood is that if the system can adapt to the changes, the problem no longer exists and the system is back, once again, in 'equilibrium'. However, should the system be unable to cope with the various pressures, and those pressures become widespread, a condition of 'multiple dysfunction' may be said to exist; this condition, Johnson maintains, may be compared with the state of a body suffering from various illnesses.

The condition of multiple dysfunction which exists because of the pressures of the sources of change, must be met by the political elite of the society which has basically one of two alternatives. It may either choose to accommodate the pressure for change or it may resist it. If it accommodates the pressure, and does so successfully, the social tensions are eased, even though its own position may be made more difficult. If it chooses to resist it must utilize more and more force to maintain its position. This use of force is known as power deflation.[30] If the elite is unable to put an end for the demand or pressure for change then the continued use of force is perceived to be illegitimate by the populace. The lower level of legitimacy is referred to as the loss of authority.[31] Taken together, power deflation and loss of authority which are both symbols of elite intransigence, may be seen as the necessary conditions of revolution. The sufficient condition, identified by Johnson as the X factor or the accelerator, will most likely be the failure of the intransigent elite to maintain the support of the means of coercion, generally the army.

Given these categories, Johnson is able to suggest the following additive formula which may be taken as his model of revolution:

$$\text{Multiple dysfunction} + \text{Elite intransigence} + \text{X} = \text{Revolution}$$

Johnson has expanded the model considerably in his second work but this expansion is actually a refinement of the basic model above. In analysing the model several considerations need to be made. First, Johnson's conception of what a revolution is is never clearly stated, so we must determine what revolution is within the context of Johnson's work. Second, is the model that Johnson developed a causal model in the sense that the term has been described earlier? Third, how useful are concepts such as elite intransigence, power deflation and loss of authority in analysing why a revolution occurs? Finally, we must focus on the problem of utilizing a model of revolutionary change which is related to a theory of social persistence.

Definitional Problems

It is not original to suggest that many problems concerning the implications and basic assumptions of particular models and theories are simply problems of definition. Yet the model that Johnson has produced is a good example of this difficulty as his work lacks clarity in the definitional sense. It is particularly fitting that we should focus on this problem first because Johnson is himself disdainful of definitional imprecision. He criticizes Arendt, for example, because of 'the extreme imprecision and narrowness of Arendt's idea of freedom used to *define* revolution'.[32] Arendt has argued that critical 'to an understanding of revolutions in the modern age is that the idea of freedom and the experience of a new beginning should coincide'.[33] Here Arendt is referring to the impact of the ideological component on those who are involved in the revolution.

Johnson argues that 'the constructing of definitions at the outset is a sterile and often tautological balancing of many different impressions'.[34] Nevertheless, he chooses to utilize as a starting point for his own work a definition by Neumann which conceives of revolution as 'a sweeping, fundamental change in political organization, social structure, economic property control and the predominant myth of a social order, thus indicating a major break in the continuity of development'.[35] This definition keeps within the framework of the 'great revolution' school that was identified earlier. Neumann believed that revolutions are 'the dynamic element of world affairs',[36] and saw such elements in the context of occurrences such as the Russian and the Chinese revolutions which have had a profound effect in other countries.

There are two significant points implicit in the type of definition that Neumann used. First, Neumann was not writing about a simple rising up of a dissatisfied populace; his definition goes much further in suggesting that one may measure a revolution only in terms of the amount of change in the society in which the revolution has occurred. By specifying the types of changes as well as the areas of change, Neumann argued that a change of government personnel is not a revolution in itself; it is simply a change in government personnel through means other than an election or whatever the accepted form of change happens to have been. The second point which follows suggests that the attempt at a seizure of power must be successful to be considered a revolution. Thus, such a seizure of power is defined as a revolution only when the takeover is accompanied by alteration of aspects of society specified by Neumann. The changes that Neumann suggested as part of a revolution may only be brought about by a successful overthrow of the previous regime and are unlikely to result from the self-liquidating tendencies of the old regime.

Although Johnson begins with Neumann's definition, the conception of revolution that he actually utilizes differs enough for us to conclude that the two writers are not discussing the same phenomenon at all. In order to present the Johnson definition we have two tasks. First, we must see how Johnson connects the definition of revolution with his conception of violence. Second, we must examine his taxonomy of revolution which, when clearly confronted, indicates that he has a radically different conception of revolution than indicated by his use of the Neumann definition as the starting point.

Revolution, for Johnson, 'is not the same thing as social

change; it is a form of social change'.[37] What distinguishes revolution from other forms of social change is that revolutionary change is always violent. Johnson never deviates from this viewpoint. In *Revolution and the Social System* he states that revolutionary changes 'that are not initiated by violent alteration of the system are instances of some other form of social change'.[38] In the later work he rather contemptuously dismisses the notion of the non-violent revolution by suggesting that 'despite all evidence to the contrary, some scholars of revolution persist in refusing to accept the idea that an irreducible element of any revolution is the resort to, or acceptance of, violence'.[39] We have already seen the difficulty Johnson has with the rather tortured conception of violence as behaviour that disorientates others. In this sense, violence is seen as deliberately antisocial behaviour. What is of importance is that even the apparent presentation of a definition that effectively means social change accompanied by violent action is not really an accurate description of the definition which he eventually uses. This is made clear by the use of the term 'revolution' in his typology, in which the definition of revolution is not radical change through violence. It seems, in fact, that his definition of revolution is not related to the question of social change at all: it is only the attempt to overthrow the government through violent means.

Johnson's typology of revolution could have been a valuable contribution to the analysis of the phenomenon. Typology construction is a difficult but potentially rewarding task for it permits the researcher to bring a degree of order to what appears to be the chaos of the real world. The constructed type has been defined as 'a purposive, planned selection, abstraction, combination, and (sometimes) accentuation of a set of criteria with empirical referents that serves as a basis for comparison of empirical cases'.[40] By placing cases into various cells, or categories, the researcher is able to focus more clearly on the factors that make the type distinctive as well as what makes the various categories belong to one general type. Typologies assist in theorizing because the researcher is able to make predictions of outcomes based on what he has understood through his constructed types. But typologizing is not the most fruitful of exercises if the researcher is not certain what it is that he is actually fitting into his classificatory scheme, and this would appear to be Johnson's major error. His general type includes categories that we might not have considered revolutions at all given his earlier use of the

Neumann definition and his own suggestion that revolution is a type of social change.

Johnson identifies six types of revolution. There are the jacquerie, the millenarian rebellion, the anarchistic rebellion, the Jacobin Communist revolution, the conspiratorial coup d'état, and the militarized mass insurrection. He distinguishes among the six on the basis of four criteria: '(1) targets of revolutionary activity; (2) identity of the revolutionaries (masses, elites-leading-masses, and elites); (3) revolutionary goals or "ideology"; and (4) whether or not the revolution is spontaneous or calculated'.[41] Thus, the militarized mass insurrection, the type of revolution that is of greatest interest to Johnson, is characterized by (1) the desire on the part of the revolutionaries to replace the existing regime,[42] (2) the fact that there is a mass movement which is led by an elite, (3) the adherence of the revolutionaries to a particular revolutionary ideology—Marxism-Leninism in the case of the Chinese Communist movement which is the primary example of the type and (4) the following of a calculated and carefully worked out strategy in order to achieve success. Jacqueries, on the other hand, 'aim at the government, have legitimist goals, are made by the masses (jacquerie leaders are usually peasant figures, local priests, or rural secret societies), and are normally spontaneous'.[43]

We need not criticize Johnson for his usage of these four criteria. By applying them it may be argued that Johnson has adequately distinguished among six types of revolution and that these are all the types known to man. We may even accept the rationale that led Johnson to select these six types. What is disquieting is that three of the six types, the jacquerie, the millenarian rebellion and the anarchistic rebellion, are rebellions, i.e. in Johnson's own terms, unsuccessful attempts at the overthrow of the existing government. Johnson has included them as types of revolution even if they do not involve success in overthrowing the previous regime or government. This represents a considerably different point of view than the one expressed by Neumann, for Neumann's definition rested on the degree of change that occurred after a seizure of power. In Johnson's typology, three of the six types are likely to result in no change at all. Once each rebellion is defeated the existing system may return to its original state.

Ultimately, then, Johnson is left with a rather paradoxical situation. According to a careful analysis of his own taxonomy and utilizing his own terminology, a revolution has occurred when values and environment are 'resynchronized' after a period of dyssynchronization, even if the revolutionaries have failed in their attempt to dislodge a particular ruling elite. Taking this view to its logical conclusion, no change needs to have occurred at all. All that needs to have happened is a rising, whether successful or unsuccessful, and a rising and radical social change are not the same phenomenon. A rising may lead to social change or it may not, but Johnson appears to ignore this point. If he defines revolution as both a type of violence and as a type of social change—as he does—then it is implicit that the rising succeed, yet in both of the works involved he does not say that at all. Instead, three of his six types entail unsuccessful risings and, therefore, the possibility of no change. Surely, this makes the concept of revolution that Johnson proposes less exclusive and, therefore, less useful than it would have been had he held Neumann's original definition. Thus, Johnson's model is not a model of revolutionary change if revolution implies social change. It is a model dealing with the attempted overthrow of an existing regime or government, which to most theorists of revolution is a distinct phenomenon, quite different from revolution itself.

The Causal Model

The second question that we need to ask is whether this is indeed a model in the sense that we have utilized the term. Does the model enable the researcher to see the relationships of the different variables so that theories may be derived from it? Johnson appears to have some reservations about the utility of the model for such a task. He begins a chapter dealing with the measurement of disequilibrium with the statement that 'it is intrinsically impossible to construct a statistical measure that will predict the occurrence of a revolution'.[44] One is not entirely certain what Johnson means here, since it would have been assumed that the attempt to develop indices of disequilibrium was aimed precisely at predicting revolutions. When used with the model such indices should aid the researcher in making predictions about when and why the revolutions will occur, which, after all, is what theorizing is about.

Johnson certainly uses the language of causal models in his analysis. When he posits the combination of multiple dysfunction and elite intransigence involving power deflation and the loss of authority, he is suggesting the necessary conditions for revolutions. When speaking of the 'accelerator' he is suggesting that this is 'the event which triggers revolution in a society that is disequilibrated and that has a discredited base of authority'.[45] Thus, what causes people to act is the perception on their part that the governing elite is not capable of maintaining the monopoly of force. If Johnson's concept of revolution is correct, then he has set up a proper causal model from which it should be possible to test hypotheses and derive theories.

If we assume that his definition of revolution is the attempted overthrow of a government or a regime, Johnson is suggesting that the sufficient condition is the moment when the revolutionary thinks that he has a chance of success. Yet having argued that prediction is not really possible, we are not certain when that point is. Johnson cautions us that 'systems analysts of revolution are all too often guilty of arguing that disequilibrium is a prerequisite for revolution but that a system is known to be disequilibrated only because a revolution has occurred'.[46] This he tells us is a tautology, and of course it is. But if Johnson is unable to predict the point at which an outcome is possible (or probable) on the basis of his own structured information, i.e. information that is filtered through the model, then he, too, can do no more than tell us that the revolution occurred because the system *was* 'disequilibrated' enough and the revolutionaries thought that the time was right.

As we have suggested earlier, a proper causal model must be structured as an 'if → then' sequence. It cannot be structured as 'then → if'. In other words, such a model must be able to aid the researcher to predict a particular event or series of events before those events occur. It is not an adequate model from the standpoint of theorizing if it merely structures the information in a descriptive sequence without actually explaining what 'amount' or 'value' of a particular variable is required before the revolutionary event will (or is most likely to) occur.

All that Johnson seems to have done is provided us with a 'sequence' model. This does not mean that the model is not potentially useful. Indeed, models may also be used to describe, and if a model of revolution has been able to set up a sequence of what must occur prior to a revolution then it is of considerable value even if it is not a causal model and one from which we are able to derive theories. But, as we shall see, it is even questionable whether Johnson's particular time sequence is an accurate 'picture' of all revolutionary change.

Legitimacy and Elite Intransigence

Perhaps the most interesting part of Johnson's model is that which examines the notions of legitimacy and elite intransigence. He deals with elite intransigence in both works but refines the concept considerably when in the second book he ties it to the question of legitimacy. Even so, the basic contribution that the elite makes to the revolutionary situation is put quite succinctly in the earlier work. Johnson tells us that 'it takes two to make a revolution, and one of these two is always the status quo elite'.[47] Thus, if the elite is unresponsive to the pressures that do build up in a community then a revolution will be likely to occur. Further, and this is a most significant assertion, 'if the elite is not intransigent, simple change will occur, dysfunction will be relieved, and no revolution will take place'.[48] Three assumptions must be seen to flow from this remark. First, the elite is seen to have full control over the means of coercion in the state at least until the army deserts. Second, we must assume that the elite knows what the proper solution ought to be since 'intransigence' suggests 'pig-headedness' in the light of evidence about what the proper course of action ought to be. Third, and most important, Johnson seems to be saying that regardless of the social situation, an intelligent, thoughtful elite always has the ability to head off a revolution. The implication of this idea is clearly that the maintenance, or loss, of legitimacy is dependent upon the actions of the ruling elite. In order to understand what this means, we must first consider what legitimacy is, for this concept is, for the functionalist, the key to the explanation of how and why revolutions occur.

Apter has provided a particularly interesting notion of what legitimacy is. He maintains that

> '. . . legitimacy is related to a set of conceptions held by significant members of the polity about the rightness of a political pattern, which, in turn, provides the patterns with a set of properties. Legitimacy is thus a behavioural term referring to a set of limits on governmental action. It is with reference to legitimacy that right conduct in office is defined. When legitimacy is withdrawn, government is weakened'.[49]

Within the context of Apter's definition of what constitutes legitimacy, three reasons emerge as explanations of its loss. First, some of the significant members of the polity may choose to withdraw support from the government. Such was the case when the army decision not to support the Diem regime in South Viet Nam led to the overthrow of the regime through a coup in 1963, and a long series of military regimes. It was immaterial whether the population concurred. The second possibility involves the rise of a new, politically aware group which is not recognized by the political system as having political relevance. For years, the Social Democrats in Germany were not included in any aspects of the decision process; to exclude them the regime deliberately developed social welfare programmes that would demonstrate the lack of any justification for the Social Democratic Party. This situation also occurred in the Soviet Union when the Kulaks resisted government plans to reorganize agricultural production. By the time this resistance developed, however, the regime was sufficiently strong to deal with the problem. National group activities reflected in Basque, Breton, Welsh and Scottish nationalist agitation for the development of regional autonomy is another example. A third way for the loss of legitimacy to occur is for the political system to close itself off and to drive away formerly politically significant members of the polity. Clearly, the KMT decision to outlaw the Communist Party in China in 1927 had the effect of driving the CCP into the countryside which was the base from which the CCP eventually gained control of the state.

Apter's conception of legitimacy raises three important problems. On the surface the idea of a politically significant element in the polity seems clear enough. Were we examining the situation in South Africa, it could be argued that the black and coloured populations of that state would be considered politically insignificant since it would not matter whether those populations were actually supporting the regime. Yet, ironically, much of what the regime in South Africa has had to do during the past years has been to keep those insignificant populations 'in their place' through a combination of coercion and conciliation. Second, the lack of legitimacy in Apter's terms may not lead to a weakening of the government at all. To the contrary, freed from the constraints of a perceived moral order, the government may be able to act in way that the highly 'legitimized' regime might shrink from doing. Third, Apter's idea of legitimacy is very difficult to operationalize. It is a conception that, at best, provides us with a tautological series of explanations. If a regime collapses, it is because the politically significant part of the population has withdrawn support. The way that we know it was the politically significant part of the population that withdrew support is because the regime collapsed. How else are we to understand which portion of the population is politically significant?

Since legitimacy is an underlying feature of Johnson's model we need to understand what it is in the scheme that he presents. As we saw earlier, values have two related meanings, first, as explanations of the environment, and, second, as 'standards of appropriate actions'. For Johnson, 'the most important function of the value system in a society is to authorize the use of force'.[51] This legitimate use of force comes about because 'the state is the institutionalization of authority, which is a special form of power'.[52] Authority, then, is legitimized power. Coercion is legitimate in the Johnson model provided the populace continues to recognize the right of the government to expend, or use, power. According to this view, if the elite is intransigent and continues to 'spend' power without replenishing the supply of power—and it may be able to replenish its supply by making changes to re-synchronize values and environment—then the continued use of power will not be seen as legitimate and the regime will be faced with loss of authority. Within this framework the loss of authority is dependent upon what Johnson has called power deflation, the overuse of force for non-legitimate actions.

Johnson seems to be arguing that the retention of legitimacy depends upon the action of the elite, first in meeting the types of problem that arise in society, and, second, by confronting whatever dissident groups that might arise as well. Further, Johnson appears to be saying that there is an inverse relationship between authority and the use of force: the more force a political system is required to utilize in order to maintain its position, the more likely it is to lose legitimacy in the eyes of the populace.

Two criticisms of Johnson's notion of legitimacy are relevant. First, the increased use of force may not lead to the loss of authority at all. Instead, the increasing use of force by a regime may actually be 'functional' in that it leads to the eventual establishment of legitimacy. Johnson does accept the probability that a regime may maintain itself without moral sanction provided it still maintains the monopoly of coercion. He suggests that the result of this is a 'police state',[53] and he points particularly to South Africa in this instance. Yet, what Johnson does not take into account is the possibility that the overwhelming use of force by a particular body such as the army might lead eventually to the establishment of legitimacy. Spain might well be an example of this but only time will demonstrate whether that will be the case. Surely this is the philosophy of much of counter-insurgency. If you 'buy time' by bolstering the regime, sooner or later the populace will come around to supporting the regime. Again, Johnson is not unaware of the possibility of the means of coercion remaining in the hands of the elite, but the possibility of coercion leading to greater authority is not considered.

Second, according to the way that the model is constructed, power deflation and loss of authority are seen as 'causes' of revolution. In other words, revolution is the dependent variable and the two necessary 'causes' are the independent variables which are utilized to explain why a revolution occurs. But given that Johnson really defines revolution as an insurrection, or a rising whether successful or unsuccessful, such a rising by a marginal group or small dissident group may in fact lead to power deflation and loss of authority rather than the reverse sequence. The sudden act of destructiveness by a guerrilla group may have a heavy impact upon the fortunes of an elite group. Smelser in a work that begins with the same view of society as does Johnson has dealt with this possibility.[54] He reverses the order of the model so that the precipitating factor may precede the rise of a counter-elite and the action of the 'legitimate' elite. Thus, a revolutionary situation may exist prior to the advent of the group that will eventually seize power.

What separates Johnson's approach from Smelser's is that Johnson, as we have seen, suggests that a reasonable elite can 'head off' the revolution. The implication is that the elite has an unlimited range of options from which to choose in defusing the situation at virtually all stages of the process. Smelser, on the other hand, suggests that the elite may be playing a role throughout the movement toward a revolution, but that by the time the revolutionary outbreak has occurred, the elite may not have within its own power the ability to prevent the outcome. In fact, Smelser's major thesis is that the number of possible outcomes decreases as the revolutionary situation nears its conclusion.

This discussion is not intended to suggest that Johnson's view of how a revolution occurs is nonsense, for it is not. Instead, the sequence that Johnson assumes to be correct may not be the only possible sequence of events. Dunn's earlier admonition that 'there can be no revolutions, however abortive, except where the previous regime, whether by its weakness or by its viciousness, has lost the right to rule',[55] seems to be open to criticism precisely because, as with Johnson's view, we are dealing with an empirical question. That a regime no longer has the support of the populace is not necessarily the only answer to the question, 'why was the regime overthrown?', or, indeed, 'why has a rising occurred?'.

The Problem of Bias

A charge that is frequently directed against the functionalist bias in sociology is that, because of the particular concern with the moral community and what makes a particular society cohere, it tends to ignore problems of social change or how and why social change occurs, and may actually be taking a value position that does not really permit it to accept the propriety of change other than within the already existing framework. Change other than that which is morally sanctioned is not seen as being 'right' or 'good'. The two charges are related, obviously, and if the functionalist formula fails on the first count it is likely to fail on the second. In so far as the first problem is concerned, Cohen has maintained that if the functionalists 'really do have a theory of social persistence they must also have a theory of change'.[56] Social change, in this sense, could be examined as the reverse side of the coin. But Cohen goes on to say that 'the truth of the matter is that if functionalists have not produced adequate theories of social change this is largely because they have not produced adequate theories of social persistence'.[57] The functionalists have tended to suggest the requisite functions that enable a social order to persist, but they have failed to present an adequate explanation of why such functions are necessary. It has simply been assumed that they are necessary when, from a theoretical standpoint, this must be demonstrated empirically.

Mills argued that the functionalists' concern with the value system has led to a lack of interest in questions of power, especially with regard to economic and political institutions.[58] He charged that Parsons had accepted 'the American myth' which seemed to argue for social persistence rather than questions of social change. But while suggesting the possibility that the American myth is only a myth with little grounding in fact he says that 'the continuity of the American political system is quite unique having been threatened by internal violence only once in its history; this fact may be among those that have misled Parsons in his image of The Normative Structure of Value-Orientation'.[59]

The jump from arguing that persistence of social systems is more common than uncommon to a position that radical social change of a revolutionary nature is wrong is not so great as might be imagined. If, as was argued at the outset of this chapter, the 'functionalist' school sees revolutionary change as uncommon, it follows that the word 'abnormal' may soon begin to replace 'uncommon' since normality is conceived in the form of an unchanging system state. And if the functionalist is arguing that such change is uncommon he is conflicting directly with the Marxian conception which holds that societies are inevitably revolutionary.

In analysing Johnson's arguments, one is left with the uncomfortable feeling that he is arguing such change is not only avoidable, but that it is desirable to avoid revolutionary change entirely. The first point he raises in his second work is that 'the Western concept of revolution is . . . tied to a vision of political organisation in which revolt is unnecessary and therefore unjustifiable'.[60] The term 'unnecessary' is interesting in this context, for Johnson seems to be arguing that if it is 'necessary' (for whatever reasons remains unclear throughout his work) then it is justifiable. Yet later he argues—and once again in direct contrast with the Marxian view—that 'society is a form of human interaction that transcends violence, of which one form is revolution. Revolutions are in this sense antisocial, testifying to the existence of extraordinary dissatisfaction among people with a particular form of society. They do not occur randomly, and they need not occur at all. Revolution can be rationally contemplated only in a society that is undergoing radical structural change and that is in need of still further change'.[61] Ignoring the last point—which seems to suggest that Johnson is positing a definition of revolution that is different than the one we have derived—it is certainly unclear what Johnson has in mind when he says that revolutions are antisocial. If they are 'testifying to the existence of extraordinary dissatisfaction' then are such movements really antisocial? At what point in time does the predominant value system—or that which ostensibly orientates behaviour—cease being the one that is held by the elite and become the value system adhered to by the revolutionary group? If the values are no longer synchronized with the environment then how can the revolutionary be engaging in violent or antisocial action? The obverse of what Johnson argues might well be true. The revolution may be an eminently social activity which is designed to allow the popularly accepted value system to be implemented in concrete form by the counter-elite. If we assume that Johnson's notion is valid, then any activity on the part of the Communist Government on the Chinese mainland prior to the United Nations' reconsideration of the Chinese question would be looked upon as antisocial and violent since the Communists represented a revolutionary movement. This is the unfortunate implication of Johnson's argument.

In fairness to Johnson, it may be argued, as we have seen, that he places a certain blame on the old elite. He argued in *Revolution and the Social System* that 'social violence is the appropriate response to intransigent resistance; it occurs because known methods of non-violent change are blocked by the ruling elite. That is to say, revolution is politics continued at the level of a violent physical showdown'.[62] Here he appears to be saying that violence is not antisocial at all. In fact, violence is 'appropriate' to use Johnson's own word. It is merely politics, which one may assume to be normal but continued at a different level. It is, nevertheless, politics. Yet later in dealing with the notion of the role of the social scientist in the analysis of revolutionary change, Johnson argues that the social scientist needs to examine potentially revolutionary situations to prevent them from developing further. He argues that 'in the case of diagnoses of societal disequilibria that might lead to revolution, the social scientist can only hope that his worst fears will not be realized and that political actors will bring about processual change instead of revolution'.[63]

When arguing for the development of an index of disequilibrium he maintains that such an index 'would provide a means of warning a legitimate elite of the possibility of revolution, thereby alerting it to the need for both policies of social change and military counter-insurgency preparations'.[64] It is indeed difficult to envisage the truly legitimate elite having to face such problems of insurgency unless we assume that such insurgency is externally caused, and the elite is unable to meet such a threat. In any event, Johnson is asking the social scientist to play a rather different role than 'objective analyst' of what is happening in the world.

Thus, it is difficult to escape from the view that Johnson holds to a particular moral position that determines his view that revolution is avoidable, violent, antisocial, and wrong. More than this, Johnson seems to be saying that reasonable men could work out reasonable solutions. The problem to be confronted is that reasonableness defined in terms of values may vary between the alternative value structures. What Johnson is saying is that reasonableness ought properly be defined by the ruling elite, for if revolutions are antisocial, then it logically follows that the revolutionary leadership is unreasonable.

Conclusion

A careful analysis of Johnson's model of revolutionary change suggests that what the functionalists are saying is that if a society is having difficulties of such a degree that the social values are unable to account for major environmental changes (or vice versa), and the political elite are unwilling to make the necessary alterations in order to bring the values and the environment back into harmony, then a revolution is likely to occur. In this respect, Johnson's model is certainly no fleshier than Aristotle's or Marx's and suggests only a sequence of events that ostensibly leads to revolutionary change. Yet this functionalist model of revolution is not satisfactory for a number of reasons.

As we have seen, it suffers from very serious definitional problems for 'revolution' really refers to any attempt to overthrow an existing government. The sequence of events that the model suggests must occur in the revolutionary process seem inadequate from the empirical standpoint; other sequences seem possible. Further, the approach suffers from a particular bias that appears to refer to revolutionary activity as abnormal or deviant behaviour. This particular view allows the functionalist to suggest that revolutions are always avoidable, a proposition that is at best doubtful and at worst ludicrous. Thus, it errs in the direction of inevitability in much the same way that the Marxian tradition does, although the results of each sequence are quite different.

But the most damning criticism of the functionalist model is twofold. First, the model is rather trivial. It is highly probable that if something is wrong somewhere in a particular society and the army, or means of coercion in the hands of the elite suddenly abandons that elite, a rising of some sort will occur. Second, and this criticism flows from the first, the model really does not help us to understand why a revolution occurs—we are not able to derive theories from it. It suggests so many possible combinations and variables that it effectively becomes not particularly useful at all.

For Marx, it was clear. Alienation leads to class consciousness, or social awareness, and revolution follows. The notion of alienation suggests a combination of variables which, while potentially broad, rules out a great number of variables as well. For Johnson, multiple dysfunction occurs. How and why this happens is never very clear, and we must live with the possibility that any social trauma at any time might lead to a revolution. So much for the possibility of prediction.

What one is forced to conclude is that the functionalist model of revolutionary change as developed by Chalmers Johnson is interesting only in so far as it is a contemporary attempt to provide an alternative to the Marxian model and theory of revolution. It provides a set of categories, as does the mother theory, structural-functionalism, which is very broad and not particularly well thought out. As such, it is inadequate as an aid in understanding why revolution, even as defined by Johnson, occur.

Notes and References

1 Ralf Dahrendorf, *Class and Class Conflict in Industrial Society*, Stanford, California, 1959, p. 129.

2 Wilbert Moore, *Social Change*, Englewood Cliffs, New Jersey, 1963, p. 85.

3 Percy Cohen, *Modern Social Theory*, London, 1968, p. 98.

4 Pierre van den Berghe, 'Review of Johnson's *Revolutionary Change*', *American Sociological Review*, 32, 1967, p. 681.

5 See also Neil Smelser, *Theory of Collective Behaviour*, London, 1962.

6 See for example Gabriel A. Almond and James S. Coleman (eds), *The Politics of Developing Areas*, Princeton, 1960, and Gabriel A. Almond and G. Bingham Powell, Jr, *Comparative Politics: A Developmental Approach*, Boston, 1966, as two of the most important works flowing from the Parsonian tradition.

7 See, for example, C. Wright Mills, *The Sociological Imagination*, Harmondsworth, Middlesex, 1970, first published 1959. Mills presents a particularly negative view of Parsons' work(s). For a sympathetic treatment see William C. Mitchell, *Sociological*

Analysis and Politics: The Theories of Talcott Parsons, Englewood, Cliffs, New Jersey, 1967.

8 W. G. Runciman, *Social Science and Political Theory*, Cambridge, 1965.

9 Talcott Parsons and Edward Shils, 'Values, motives and systems of action', from *Toward a General Theory of Action*, ed. by Talcott Parsons and Edward Shils, New York, 1965.

10 Robin M. Williams, Jr, 'The sociological theory of Talcott Parsons', from *The Social Theories of Talcott Parsons*, ed. by Max Black, Englewood Cliffs, New Jersey, 1961, p. 72.

11 Talcott Parsons, *Societies: Evolutionary and Comparative Perspectives*, Englewood Cliffs, New Jersey, 1966.

12 Clyde Kluckhohn, 'Values and value-orientations in the theory of action : an exploration in definition and classification', from Parsons and Shils, *Toward a General Theory of Action*, p. 399.

13 Smelser, *The Theory of Collective Behaviour*, p. 25.

14 Chalmers Johnson, *Revolutionary Change*, Boston, 1966, p. 42.

15 Barrington Moore, *Social Origins of Dictatorship and Democracy*, Harmondsworth, Middlesex, 1969. First published 1966, p. 213.

16 Parsons, *Societies . . .*, p. 18.

17 Talcott Parsons, 'An outline of the social system', from *Theories of Society*, ed. by Talcott Parsons, Edward Shils, Kaspar Naegele, and Jesse R. Pitts, New York, 1965, p. 43.

18 Mitchell, *Sociological Analysis and Politics*, p. 100.

19 Parsons and Shils, 'Values . . .', from Parsons and Shils, *Toward a General Theory of Action*, p. 193.

20 Parsons, 'An outline of the social system', from *Theories of Society*, p. 42.

21 See Smelser, *The Theory of Collective Behaviour*, particularly Chapters 1, 2 and 10.

22 Ralf Dahrendorf, *Society and Democracy in Germany*, Garden City, New York, first published 1967.

23 See above. See also A. J. Nicholls, *Weimar and the Rise of Hitler*, London, and F. L. Carsten, *The Rise of Fascism*, London, 1967.

24 Johnson, *Revolutionary Change*, p. 3.

25 *Ibid.*

26 *Ibid.*, p. 64.

27 *Ibid.*

28 *Ibid.*, p. 68.

29 Talcott Parsons, *The Social System*, New York, 1951, pp. 523–4.

30 Johnson, *Revolutionary Change*, p. 91.

31 *Ibid.*

32 Johnson, *Revolutionary Change*, p. 118.

33 Hannah Arendt, *On Revolution*, New York, 1965, pp. 21–2.

34 Chalmers Johnson, *Revolution and the Social System*, Stanford, 1964, p. 2.

35 Sigmund Neumann, 'The international civil war', *World Politics*, *1*, 1948–9. Also *Ibid.*, p. 2.

36 *Ibid.*, p. 344.

37 Johnson, *Revolutionary Change*, p. 5.

38 Johnson, *Revolution and the Social System*, p. 6.

39 Johnson, *Revolutionary Change*, p. 7.

40 John McKinney, *Constructive Typology and Social Theory*, New York, 1966, p. 3.

41 Johnson, *Revolution and the Social System*, pp. 27–8.

42 Johnson utilizes Easton's definition of a regime which is 'the constitutional order' of a society. See David Easton, *A Systems Analysis of Political Life*, New York, 1965, pp. 190–211.

43 Johnson, *Revolution and the Social System*, p. 34.

44 Johnson, *Revolutionary Change*, p. 119.

45 *Ibid.*, p. 99.

46 *Ibid.*, p. 120.

47 Johnson, *Revolution and the Social System*, p. 6.

48 *Ibid.*, p. 7.

49 David Apter, *The Politics of Modernisation*, Chicago, 1965, p. 236.

50 Johnson, *Revolutionary Change*, p. 21.

51 *Ibid.*, p. 26.

52 *Ibid.*, p. 30.

53 *Ibid.*, p. 91.

54 See Smelser, *The Theory of Collective Behaviour*. Smelser's work does not actually deal only with the phenomenon of revolution.

55 John Dunn, *Modern Revolutions*, London, 1972, p. 246.

56 Cohen, *Modern Social Theory*, p. 50.

57 *Ibid.*, p. 58.

58 Mills, p. 45.

59 Mills, pp. 46–7.

60 Johnson, *Revolutionary Change*, p. 3.

61 *Ibid.*, pp. 59–60.

62 Johnson, *Revolution and the Social System*, p. 6.

63 Johnson, *Revolutionary Change*, p. 167.

64 *Ibid.*, p. 120.

Chapter 7
The Theory of Mass Society

The theory of mass society is one of the more important and influential theories of revolution. Yet strictly speaking, this theory is less a theory of revolution than it is a theory of social stability. In much the same way that the fuctionalist notion of revolution is derived from an attempted explanation of why societies cohere and continue to 'function' over a long period of time, mass society theory attempts to explain the advent of the revolutionary mass movement which may arise when the traditional barriers to such a phenomenon suddenly break down. The revolutionary mass movement is perceived as a phenomenon of the twentieth century, and may be understood as the outgrowth of certain features of contemporary society such as industrialization and the development of rapid communications which brings members of a society together in closer proximity to one another.[1] Closely related to the mass society theory is the concept of totalitarianism which is frequently seen as the end result of the successfully mounted mass movement.[2] Certain types of revolutionary mass movements are referred to as totalitarian movements.

To appreciate the implications of mass society theory several points must be understood. First, it is a theory that was developed in the wake of the Nazis coming to power in Germany in 1933. The rise and success of the Nazis came as a profound shock to the Western world for it was difficult to understand how an industrially advanced, highly cultured and literate, and democratic society that Germany ostensibly was should deliver itself to the self described rabble that led the Nazi movement. The Nazi movement was also interesting because, as Horowitz has suggested :

'Fascism is the only authentic mass movement unique to the twentieth century that has proven successful. The socialist movement never really developed beyond an elite cadre and rarely, if ever, strayed from party politics of a relatively orthodox variety. In part, this was due to the democratic traditions of socialism, and in part to a disbelief in the

146

capacity of the masses to rule equitably. It is true that the Soviet Revolution was a mass movement, but its successes were due, in the main, to disillusionment over the defeat of Russian national ambitions in World War I; it too, in the form of Leninism, had to accommodate the national question; and it had to take into profound consideration economic rather than political interests. Nonetheless, it can be stated that throughout Europe, fascism represented a unique combination of mass sentiment and elitist manipulation that enabled the existing capitalist social structure to survive, if not always flourish'.[3]

Whether only the Fascists have mounted successful mass movements is an open question. Surely the Communist movement in China could be cited as just such a successful movement although the socialist roots generally are in the nineteenth century. Nevertheless, the image one has of the Nazi following and the understanding that the following was widespread and sincere is perhaps more widely accepted today than it was at the end of World War II. We now know that the Nazis probably enjoyed enormous popularity within Germany.

A second feature of mass society theory is its acceptance of a particular definition of democracy. It is a theory founded on the pluralist philosophy which has been derived from James Madison, discussed and popularized by de Tocqueville in the years before the Civil War in the United States, and widely accepted as a reasonable explanation of American democracy, the prototype of pluralist democracy. While Madison's ideas have been updated by many writers, a basic acceptance of pluralism as stable democracy is both explicit and implicit in the writings of the mass society theorists and the theory cannot be properly understood without specific reference to the tenets of pluralist democracy.

A third feature of mass society theory is that empirical analysis has not really permitted us to reject the theory finally as being invalid. The kinds of assumptions and propositions that are part of the theory have been subjected to a number of interpretations which have not yielded the types of results that permit a clear and emphatic denial of the theory. As we shall see, even recently the conflict about its correctness has been reopened so that we are not fully capable of discarding the theory. Although it will be argued that the theory seems to be invalid, enough questions remain to make us hesitate before finally rejecting it.

Pluralist Democracy

Because of the significance of the idea of pluralist democracy to mass society theory, it is essential to have some idea of what pluralist democracy is. To do this, we shall examine how it has evolved in the context of the United States, the 'model' of this particular type of democracy. While, in a sense, the notion of pluralism may be assumed to be historically specific to the United States, theorists like Arendt and Kornhauser have applied its basic assumptions elsewhere, arguing that the factors that promote social stability in one society may be effective in other societies as well, and the absence of those factors is likely to lead to instability.

The origins of the contemporary notion of pluralist democracy may be found in the writings of James Madison, the fourth President of the United States. After the constitution of the new United States was adopted following extensive debate, it was submitted to the individual states for ratification. Madison, along with Alexander Hamilton and John Jay, wrote a series of articles urging the ratification of the proposed constitution.[4] These articles now form what is called *The Federalist Papers*, and several of them written by Madison deal specifically with the republican principle and federalism. These works are now taken as an early statement of the pluralist view of democracy.

Madison believed that all societies are punctuated by conflict, largely due to such factors as the unequal distribution of property. Within societies there are varieties of groups which compete with each other in order to gain what benefits there are to be gained in the society. These groups, or 'factions' as Madison called them, are defined as 'a number of citizens, whether amounting to a majority or minority of the whole, who are united and actuated by some common impulse of passion, or of interest, adverse to the rights of other citizens, or to the permanent and aggregate interests of the community.[5] There are two ways of removing the causes of faction; the first by destroying liberty and the second by seeing that all citizens have the same opinion. But for Madison the first solution 'was worse than the disease'.[6] Liberty, he believed, is essential to the political life of the state. The second solution would not be practicable because of the 'diversity in the faculties of men'.[7] One could not expect all people to be guided entirely by the same hopes and outlooks.

Thus, for Madison, 'the latent causes of faction are . . . sown in the nature of man'[8] which is one of the basic premises of pluralism. There are differences among men and different interests that may never be resolved and as long as civilization persists, the divergencies are going to be found to exist. This view differs sharply from the Marxist view which would hold that the different interests do not result from factors found in the nature of man at all. Instead, certain factors of the society are responsible for man behaving in the manner that he does. Remove the causes—the particular mode of production and the structural arrangements that result—and the problem of 'faction' disappears as well.

Madison believed that the basic social problem was the management of the types of conflict that would be bound to exist in society. His solution was a combination of republicanism and federalism which would permit the conflicts to continue, but with carefully constructed constraints preventing the possibility of permanent victors in the disputes. Republicanism, a form of representative government, would shield the decision process from excessive behaviour on the part of the populace, one of the dangers in a direct democracy, yet it would allow for popular participation through the selection of representatives. Further, by dividing the government into departments and agencies, demands from one of these parts would counter the demands made by the other part. The further division of the governing process through federalism was aided by the size of the United States, a point de Tocqueville raised years later. Size was a virtue because if the sphere of society was extended, it would 'take in a greater variety of parties and interests'.[9] Thus, it would be 'less probable that a majority of the whole will have a common motive to invade the rights of other citizens; or if such a common motive exists, it will be more difficult for all who feel it to discover their own strength, and to act in unison with each other'.[10]

This benevolent combination of federalism and republicanism was most eloquently described in *Federalist Paper* 51, where Madison argued that the government of the United States had attained divided power. Such power had been surrendered voluntarily by the people of the new republic to the various agencies, departments and governments that had been created. Madison anticipated that the 'different governments will control each other, at the same time that each will be controlled by itself'.[11]

He argued further in what may be understood as the classical exposition of pluralism that the people had to guard not only against the possible oppression of rulers but also against the injustice of one part of the society toward another. Arguing that 'different interests necessarily exist in different classes of society',[12] he believed that if a majority were united, then the rights of minorities would be insecure. There were two solutions to this problem, the first being called an aristocratic solution in which the chief authority of the state would guard against such a likelihood. But in this solution the authority could favour the majority or the minority to the detriment of others. The other solution was the one that was ultimately adopted for the United States:

> 'Whilst all authority in it will be derived from and dependent on the society, the society itself will be broken into so many parts, interests and classes of citizens, that the rights of individuals, or of the minority, will be in little danger from interested combinations of the majority. In a free government the security for civil rights must be the same as that for religious rights. It consists in the one case in the multiplicity of interests, and in the multiplicity of sects. The degree of security in both cases will depend on the number of interests and sects; and this may be presumed to depend on the extent of country and number of people comprehended'.[13]

The existence of no permanent, enduring majority would permit a just society to flourish. All would have a potential voice in the decisions that ultimately affected them, and no one group would be able to dominate to the detriment of others.

Whether the precepts of pluralism became firmly rooted in the American tradition could only be considered as an empirical question. De Tocqueville, visiting the United States in 1831, assessed the success of the Madisonian formula and began his analysis with an assumption that is crucial to the mass society theory. He argued that 'social power, superior to all others, must always be placed somewhere; but . . . liberty is endangered when this power finds no obstacle which can retard its course, and give it time to moderate its own vehemence'.[14] Thus, between the rulers and the ruled there is a need for a buffer of some sort so that the superior power cannot be used without restraint, a view which reflected, for de Tocqueville, a fear of the excesses of the French Revolution. What is of particular interest is that de Tocqueville perceived that superior power could be rooted in the leadership or in the masses. He believed that majority rule was a potential problem in the United States and argued prophetically that 'If ever the free institutions of America are destroyed, that event may be attributed to the omnipotence of the majority, which may at some future time urge the minorities to have recourse to physical force'.[15] De Tocqueville foresaw the tendency of the majority to believe in the 'rightness' of a course of action and the tendency for a lack of tolerance of dissenting opinion once that course of action had been determined.

But de Tocqueville thought that the United States was probably safe from the excesses of majority rule for several reasons. First, there was no centralized administration, and any attempt to impose despotism from above would be fraught with difficulties as a direct result of lack of such machinery. Second, he saw that the American movement toward a system of law had rendered the legal profession which dominated that system 'hostile to the revolutionary spirit and the unreflecting passions of the multitude'.[16] Combined with the jury system, the average citizen of the United States was 'socialized' into a society in which the laws dominated, and respect for the tradition of the judicial underpinning of the state enabled its effective functioning.

In terms of its size, the United States was fortunate since there was room and resources for everyone. But, de Tocqueville suggested, other societies were large and not heavily populated, yet they had succumbed to the problems of instability and the failure to develop democracy. The United States had avoided this by putting together laws which insured the rights of citizens and an adherence to those arrangements which, at the time, appeared to be working.[17]

Critical to de Tocqueville's analysis as well as to Madison's was the appreciation that a particular type of 'social engineering' which had been unused anywhere else in the world, might prove amenable to a continuation of stable democratic society. Neither man was blind to the dangers of such engineering; a careful analysis of de Tocqueville's work provides ample evidence that he foresaw many of the problems that might exist for the United States in the future, but for the time being, the particular 'formula' was seen to be working.

Contemporary analysts have been able to update these earlier notions of pluralism by depicting how the Madisonian formula has actually evolved and changed in the context of the American political system. The most original and consistently interesting of the pluralist thinkers has been Robert Dahl who has suggested the following 'axiom' of pluralism in the United States, as practised in ideal circumstances:

> 'Instead of a single centre of sovereign power there must be multiple centres of power, none of which is or can be wholly sovereign. Although the only legitimate sovereign is the people, in the perspective of American pluralism even the people ought never to be an absolute sovereign; consequently no part of the people, such as a majority, ought to be absolutely sovereign.[18]

Much of what Dahl has written has been directed toward seeking answers to the same types of questions that de Tocqueville posed. It has led him also to a substantial revision of the Madisonian formula, which Dahl has maintained, does not actually solve the basic contradiction which seems to have been built into the Madisonian system. The contradiction arises between the question of equal rights and minority protection for if everyone has equal rights and the majority rules how do you have minority protection? Dahl has argued that the society that has emerged in the United States is one in which majorities rarely rule on policy matters although the values that constrain rulers as well as populace emanate from the 'majority'. But, if majority rule, in the sense of government policy-making is largely a myth, so too is the possibility of majority rule in terms of oppressive legislation. Minorities operating in such a system are protected by the basic values of the community which prevent an oppressive majority from forming. Additionally, the constitutional rules tend to define which groups do have an advantage or a disadvantage in the competitive system for Dahl argues 'in no society do people ever enter a political contest equally . . .,'[19] a modification of the Madisonian thesis. This argument leads Dahl to his major thesis: 'A central guiding thread of American constitutional development has been the evolution of a political system in which all the active and legitimate groups in the population can make themselves heard at some crucial stage in the process of decision'.[20]

The critical words in the formula are 'active' and 'legitimate'. A group that is unconcerned with a particular problem or set of problems will not affect outcomes. The basic premise which

Dahl has is that not all issues are of interest to all groups.[21] Only when a group is affected will it wish to participate in the decision process and whether that group is able to participate in the decision process depends on the particular values of the society itself. What is of vital importance in Dahl's view of democracy as it has evolved in the United States is that he recognizes that not all citizens are treated equally and that the constraints of the system are not equally applied. But 'majorities' are rarely if ever mobilized on an enduring and permanent basis, and 'the making of governmental decisions is not a majestic march of great majorities united upon certain matters of basic policy. It is the steady appeasement of relatively small groups'.[22] Majorities are unlikely to feel the intense interest in particular issues which might activate affected minorities.

Others, besides Dahl, have updated the original notion of pluralist democracy. Schattschneider, for example, has included the role played by leaders in the decision process. He has taken into account the size of the United States and the population, factors which point to the improbability of all citizens participating in the decision process. He has argued that democracy 'is a competitive political system in which competing leaders and organizations define the alternatives of public policy in such a way that the public can participate in the decision-making process'.[23] He has relied upon the concept of group competition not only as a definition of pluralist democracy, but of democracy generally, but he has implied that the role of leadership and organizational activity is to simplify the alternatives so that the interested public is better able to make the types of choices that it does.

The pluralist notion of democracy is founded upon a belief in group competition. It is not now based upon a principle of perfect equality nor is it dependent upon a situation in which all citizens participate actively in the decision process. What is vital is that groups have the opportunity to act when they are affected by particular issues, and they are shielded in some way from the actions of a wilfully oppressive elite group by a combination of moral and constitutional restraints. It is this assumption that lies at the heart of the theory of mass society and may be seen in Arendt's argument that 'democratic freedom may be based on the equality of citizens before the law; yet they acquire their meaning and function organically only where the citizens belong to and are represented by groups or form a social and political hierarchy'.[24] The theory of mass society is an attempt to explain why this hierarchy breaks down and what happens when it does.

The Theory of Mass Society

The theory of mass society is clearly derived from the pluralist model of society that has just been described. Kornhauser has maintained that 'the preservation of critical values (especially freedom) requires the social insulation of those segments of society that embody them'.[25] Social insulation is achieved through group adherence which, at the same time, shield elites and non-elites from one another. Mass society occurs when, for some reason, the group allegiances seem to have broken down. When such allegiances break down a situation remains 'in which elites are readily accessible to influence by non-elites and non-elites are readily available for elites'.[26] From this we may understand the major proposition of Kornhauser's work : 'A high rate of mass behaviour may be expected when both elites and non-elites lack social insulation, that is when elites are accessible to direct intervention by non-elites, and when non-elites are available for direct mobilization by elites'.[27] Here, the key word is mobilization for it is the underlying belief of mass society theorists that the breakdown of the intermediate groups may lead to the development of the totalitarian movement which can develop only in the mass society.

Kornhauser has identified two sources of criticism of mass society, the aristocratic and the democratic. Since the democratic criticism is directly related to the rise of the Nazis, the particular example that will be used, we shall concentrate only on that criticism. It is fitting also because the democratic criticism of mass society is the basis of Arendt's analysis as well.[28] The democratic criticism of the existence of mass society leading to totalitarianism is based on the notion that 'the decisive social process' is 'the loss of insulation of non-elites and the rise of elites bent on total mobilization of a population'.[29]

There are three major terms implied in the democratic criticism of mass society. First, a growing 'atomization' of the individual occurs as he loses his group attachments. Because of this he feels a loss of community with his fellow human beings. Second, as a result of his atomization there is an individual readiness to embrace new ideologies which is actually a quest for community to replace the lost community. Third, there is a rise of totalitarianism, or a pseudo-community, in which there is total domination of the society by an elite group. The individual adheres to the totalitarian movement initially because it offers him security.

Arendt believes that the basic connection to the class structure had protected the late nineteenth and early twentieth century from the rise of the mass movement. But by the time the First World War had ended and the Weimar Republic was founded, the old ties that had bound the members of society together were virtually destroyed. Once this had happened, groups like the Nazis were able to capitalize on the situation that presented itself. Arendt argues that :

'The truth is that the masses grew out of the fragments of a highly atomized society whose competitive structure and con-comitant loneliness of the individual had been held in check only through membership in a class. The chief characteristic of the mass man is not brutality and backwardness, but his isolation and lack of normal relationships. Coming from the class-ridden society of the nation-state, whose cracks had been cemented with nationalistic sentiment, it is only natural that these masses, in the first helplessness of their new experience, have tended toward an especially violent nationalism, to which mass leaders have yielded against their own instincts and purposes for demagogic reasons'.[30]

Ultimately, for Arendt, it was 'social atomization and extreme individualization that preceded the mass movement'.[31] Without the breakdown of the traditional ties and the atomization of the individual, the mass movement would not have been possible.

Kornhauser suggests that mass behaviour is a form of collective behaviour which exhibits four characteristics. First, the focus of attention tends to be remote from personal experience and daily life. In the period of Weimar this may have been reflected in the public attitude toward the Treaty of Versailles or the Allied occupation of the Ruhr. Abel has argued that various groups came to focus on different problems, but they shared one feature in common—'almost all blamed the government for their troubles and turned their attacks against it'.[32] In China, the foreign action against the native Chinese in Shanghai and Canton may have caused the public to take action against the foreigners. Second, the mode of response to the remote objects tends to be direct as shown in the incidence of strikes, riots, and street fights. During the late 1920s and into the 1930s, politics in Germany was extended to the streets with the paramilitary organs of Nazi, Socialist and Communist Parties fighting each other regularly. Third, mass behaviour tends to be highly unstable, readily shifting its focus of attention and intensity of response. Mass apathy may also be present. During the period between 1930 and 1933 the Nazi fortunes rose, but also fell. Indeed, by the time Hitler was invited to form a government, it had appeared as if the Nazis had already peaked in terms of the popular support that they enjoyed. Fourth, when mass behaviour becomes organized around a programme and acquires a certain continuity in purpose and effort, it takes on the character of a mass movement. Thus, the action of the atomized and lonely individuals in associating themselves with the new movement or new group is what gives the movement its fodder.[33]

Those that join the mass movements tend to be drawn from all social classes in the society. Kornhauser has argued that:

'in particular it is the socially uprooted and unattached members of all classes who support these movements first and in the greatest numbers. This implies that *unattached intellectuals, marginal members of the middle class, isolated industrial and farm workers* have been the major social types in totalitarian movements'.[34]

It is when these individuals feel classless and unattached that they become swept up into the movement.

Thus, in order to examine the theory to test its validity we must explore three facets of it. First, does the concept of marginality contribute to an understanding of the origins of the mass movement? We may be able to determine who came into the mass movement at the beginning of its existence and establish whether they were 'marginal' individuals. Second, were atomized individuals those who joined the mass movement or are such mass movements really an extension of class allegiances? Finally, it is worth examining how the basic biases that are obvious in the pluralist model distort the image that is drawn of the mass society.

Marginality

As we have seen, for the non-Marxist sociologist and political scientist, the revolutionary act is not simple to explain. If a society is conceived in terms of a community of shared values, it is exceedingly difficult to come to grips with the situation in which a particular segment of the community has taken up arms against the authority structure. The question why a segment of the community acts this way is pertinent when referring either to the composition of the revolutionary elite or to the composition of the mass that feeds the revolution. The question of the composition of the mass will be examined in the next section. The problem now is to examine the significance of Kornhauser's suggestion that the individuals who comprise the revolutionary leadership, or those first attracted by the 'mass movement', are 'marginal' members of the society. Is it possible to identify the revolutionary elite by reference to particular qualities that separate its members from the general population? Further, what is the significance of the differences that may be found to exist between the revolutionary elite and the elite group that it aims to replace?

In the contemporary analysis of political elites, political scientists and sociologists have concentrated on the social background characteristics of elite groups. If for no other reasons,[35] the study of the social background characteristics of the leadership may be helpful in understanding what it is that a society values in its leaders. As a result of such studies some social scientists have suggested that these individuals may be considered marginal men and women. To suggest that an individual is marginal is to say that he has certain background attributes that make him different from the bulk of the population. Thus, Trotsky, who was a Jew, would be considered marginal in the context of Russian society. There would be no particular problem in being a member of a marginal group if the individual had no aspirations for membership in the majority group. 'The marginal man appears only when the group conflict emerges as a personal problem.'[36] When he tries to move from his own group to the majority group then his marginal status becomes significant.[37]

Moskos has suggested 'that an initial radical revolutionary elite is characterized by a membership which is intellectual, Western exposed, and marginal in its ethnicity, and that the second generation of the radical revolutionary elite witnesses a rise in heartland born, less educated and non-Western exposed individuals'.[38] This 'hypothesis' is of much greater relevance to the newly independent countries of Africa and Asia than the industrial societies in which revolutions have been virtually non-existent. In the former countries, the revolutionary leaders are likely to be considerably better educated than the rest of the population and often very well-travelled given the opportunity for education outside of the country. One of the main aspects of elites of developing systems that would be examined is travel experiences of the members of that body. Such experiences could be most influential in the eventual revolutionary posture of the individual.

Moskos is suggesting that it is the original revolutionary group which is likely to demonstrate the trait of marginality. In his own study of the Albanian political elite which focused on the transition from pre-Communist to Communist rule, he suggested that:

'Persons may be marginal when they belong to distinct and minority religious groups. In a rural and isolated society, ethnic groups with relatively greater exposure to the world community tend to be marginal. In a society largely illiterate, advanced education can be a marginal trait'.[39]

Marginality, then, is defined in terms of the community itself. Further, if the concept is to be useful then the individual must be considered marginal prior to his becoming a revolutionary; he is not marginal because he is a revolutionary. It is an open question whether marginality is a cause of revolutionary behaviour, but it is implicit in the idea that it is a cause and must, therefore, precede revolutionary behaviour.

Using this concept, Hitler would be described as a marginal man because he was Austrian rather than German by birth. In the dominant Protestant community of which Hitler was eventually the leader, Hitler was born a Catholic. Educationally, he had not attained the standard of achievement that the leaders of pre-Nazi Germany had. Additionally, he was of petit bourgeois background at a time when leaders tended to be upper and upper middle class. Most important, he aspired to mainstream status, i.e., he always thought of himself as a German. Another example of marginality is contained in the background of Eamon de Valera, one of the leaders of the Irish revolutionary movement. He was born abroad and is only half-Irish, his father having been Cuban. This may have been a factor in the strong commitment De Valera displayed to the cultural revival in Ireland which brought so many of the young people to the eventual revolutionary movement.

Generally, if we examine several cases in which revolutions

have occurred, the shift from the initial revolutionary group make-up to the group that succeeds it does not seem particularly pronounced. In an analysis of the Irish elite, for example, it was found that there was little evidence of 'marginality' on the part of the initial revolutionary group and few differences between the initial revolutionary group and the group that succeeded it.[40] In the case of China, however, at first glance, several of the characteristics to which Moskos refers seem to have been present.[41] If the Kuomintang represented the initial radical revolutionary elite and the Communists the second generation elite in China, then the indication that the Kuomintang leadership tended to come from the larger coastal cities and be children of merchants and businessmen while the Communists were the products of the countryside would be adequate evidence to consider the hypothesis confirmed. This finding would seem to indicate that because the bulk of the Chinese population was comprised of peasants and agrarian interests when the Kuomintang first became involved in the movement toward revolution, the Kuomintang leadership would have to be considered marginal. Because the Communists were mainly comprised of peasant-background members, they would be thought of as less marginal than the Kuomintang because they shared background characteristics that were like the general population.

This particular notion of marginality seems questionable, however, on two counts. First, both elite groups seem to have been as well-travelled and as well-educated as each other. There were differences in the locations of their educations; nevertheless, the levels attained were similar. What is really different, then, is the locations from which the leaders came. But this difference, in terms of the Chinese case seems reasonable. It would be indeed strange if the first revolutionary elite group did not come from the urban areas which are those locations particularly exposed to the ferment of ideas which generally precede a revolutionary movement. Thus, what this notion of marginality is really masking is the tradition that ideas begin in the urban areas and permeate the hinterlands. This may be a more adequate explanation of the time lag that separates the two groups.

Second, what Moskos seems to be arguing is that the marginality of the first elite generation may be defined with reference to the second elite generation. In other words, if the second generation differs substantially from the first generation then the first generation is marginal. But this explanation also seems inadequate. Perhaps a more satisfactory explanation of the differences between the two generation is the different skills that are found between the two groups. Here it would be argued that different groups are required to carry out different tasks, and the tasks depend upon the particular stages of the revolution. Thus, a revolutionary environment giving way to a post-revolutionary environment is likely to involve 'the general trend in which power passes from high-status agitators to lower-status administrators'.[42] The revolutionary generation is likely to be comprised of individuals with particular skills to mobilize and inflame a potentially revolutionary mass. The second generation may be better able to manage the day-to-day problems of economic growth and development that new regime are likely to face.

Either or both of these arguments would appear to be more adequate than Moskos' discussion of marginality. But Moskos is not the only scholar to have considered the possibility that revolutionaries are marginal members of the community. A somewhat different approach to the question is found in work that has been done by Lerner, Pool and Schueller. They began with the premise that 'a man who deviates from a substantial number of variety of predominant attributes in his society may be regarded as a "marginal man" '.[43] While this does not appear to deviate from the viewpoint expressed by Moskos, the approach used to analyse marginality was different. In order to examine the concept of marginality as it is applied in the German case, the authors compiled a list of thirteen attributes, and if the individual in question had any of these attributes, regardless if in others there were no differences, then he was considered to be marginal.[44] Through the use of these attributes the authors concluded that among the various groups that they were considering the Nazis were indeed a marginal group.

There are difficulties, however, with the list of attributes that Lerner *et al* utilize. Although they define marginality in terms of the dominant community at large, the list of attributes 'were selected as deviations from the stereotype of the ideally preferred background and career of a nationalist elite German'.[45] The stereotype was developed by taking a composite picture of the previous elite group. But the attributes of a general populace are most likely to be substantially different from the attributes of the previous elite group. In fact, it is highly likely that the revolutionary group is considerably closer to the general populace than is the previous elite. One cannot infer marginality of the second elite group with reference to the previous elite; marginality may only be inferred through comparison with the population.

Further, if one infers marginality from the differences between elite group A and elite group B, another problem arises. If revolution is defined in terms of an alteration of the social structure, then it is true by definition that the new elite group is comprised of a different type of elite than the previous group. After all, this is what the revolution entails; could it be a revolution if it did not include such differences? A group that deposed an aristocratic ruling group would be most unlikely to come from that social formation although a few members of that new group could be deviant members of that previous group.

The concept of marginality when applied to the elite group has not been particularly successful in the few cases that have been analysed, but this should not imply that the concept is not useful or wrong. What does seem to be a problem is that its application thus far has been unsatisfactory. First, when examined with reference to the change from the initial revolutionary elite to the second generation it fails to take into account the possibility that what appears as marginality is only a range of differences in the particular skill groups that are present. Second, inferring marginality by comparing the pre-revolutionary elite with the revolutionary elite assumes that the pre-revolutionary group is not marginal. But, in fact, it may be the case that the pre-revolutionary group is marginal. A revolution may be responsible for bringing in a less marginal group which is more like the general population than was the previous elite group. Third, any elite group is 'marginal' when compared with the mass. There are always attributes in the elite which makes it the elite and separates it from the mass. It may be in the form of education, occupation, or travel experiences, but an elite will always differ from the mass whether the elite group in question is a revolutionary elite, a post-revolutionary elite, or a non-revolutionary elite.

Finally, the concept of marginality seems to be largely derived from the early attempts to explain where the early Nazis came from. Much of the literature from that period suggests that the earliest participants in the movement, from the elite group to the first followers, were largely those individuals who were unable to adjust to the new circumstances following the end of World War I. But the inability to adjust or to accept the Weimar Republic is not the same as being marginal in terms of background attributes. Nor is it proper to assume that those who had the greatest difficulty in adjusting to the new life situation were only those who were marginal.

The Mass Movement

The major problem in examining the roots and growth of the mass movement, or totalitarian movement, is attempting to determine what group or groups join these movements and what factors are responsible for the groups or individuals joining. Two particular viewpoints have emerged. The first represents the view taken by the mass society theorists and is best stated by Hannah Arendt :

> 'Totalitarian movements are possible wherever there are masses who for one reason or another have acquired the appetite for political organization. Masses are not held together by a consciousness of common interest and they lack that specific class articulateness which is expressed in determined, limited, and obtainable goals. The term masses applies only where we deal with people who either because of sheer numbers, or indifference, or a combination of both, cannot be integrated into any organization based on common interest, into political parties or municipal governments or professional organizations or trade unions. Potentially, they exist in every country and form the majority of those large numbers of neutral, politically indifferent people who never join a party and hardly ever go to the polls'.[46]

Kornhauser holds basically the same view : 'People who are atomized readily become mobilized. Since totalitarianism is a state of total mobilization, mass society is highly vulnerable to totalitarian movements and regimes'.[47]

The expressed attitude of the mass society theorists is that, with the breakdown of the class system, the traditional allegiances to the political parties disappear as well. The parties, ironically, tend to become more strident and more avowedly tied to the lines that they traditionally hold despite the fact that the classes are actually breaking down. With specific reference to Germany, Arendt stated :

'They had lost, moreover, without being aware of it, those neutral supporters who had never been interested in politics because they felt that parties existed to take care of their interests. So that the first signs of the breakdown of the Continental party system were not the desertion of old party members, but the failure to recruit members from the younger generation, and the loss of the silent consent and support of the unorganized masses who suddenly shed this apathy and went wherever they saw an opportunity to voice this new violent opposition'.[48]

In 1928, the Nazis had won some 800,000 votes. By 1930, their vote had increased to nearly 6,500,000 and in the election of 1932 they won nearly 14,000,000 votes. For the mass society theorists the large proportion of individuals that had previously been non-voters were among the first to support the Nazis: 'the radicalization of the electorate originated among the previous non-participants in party politics, who probably come from various social groups . . .'.[49] The clear implication of this statement is that those new voters tended to be the individuals who, despite coming from a particular group or class, were able to go against their groups or class allegiance and vote for the organization that represented the mass movement. The only type of individual likely to do this would be that individual freed from the group or class loyalty: the 'atomized' individual.

The alternative viewpoint does not conceive of the mass movement as one which derives its support from the atomized members of former groups or classes. Instead, it postulates that what occurred in Germany was not a breakdown of class ties, but a strengthening of those ties with the Nazi mass movement gaining most of its support from the middle class members of society who had previously voted for groups such as the liberal parties. Thus, 'the main mass support came, . . . from the middle layers of society'.[50] This view is suggested more strongly by Geiger who argued, 'A class denies with indignation being a class and leads a bitter class struggle against the idea and reality of the class struggle'.[51]

The reasons for the middle class drift to the mass movement was suggested as early as 1933 by Lasswell:

'In so far as Hitlerism is a desperation reaction of the lower middle classes, it continues a movement which began during the closing years of the nineteenth century. Materially speaking, it is not necessary to assume that the small shopkeepers, teachers, preachers, lawyers, doctors, farmers and craftsmen were worse off at the end than they had been in the middle of the century. Psychologically speaking, however, the lower middle class was increasingly overshadowed by the workers and the upper bourgeoisie, whose unions, cartels and parties took the centre of the stage. The psychological impoverishment of the lower middle class precipitated emotional insecurities within the personalities of its members, thus fertilizing the ground for the various movement of mass protest through which the middle classes might revenge themselves'.[52]

According to this view, the members of the middle classes, feeling that they were being threatened both from the wealthier and higher status and the poorer and lower status members of the community, struck out against both groups.

The German case is obviously a particular one, but the concepts that are applied there ought to be applicable elsewhere. Lipset has suggested that generally the mass movement could develop in any system, and will be composed of those members of the strata that are for some reason suffering the greatest tensions. Thus, 'the real question to answer is : what strata are most "displaced" in each country?'[53] For Lipset, 'a low level of sophistication and a high degree of insecurity predispose an individual toward an extremist view of politics'.[54] Thus, not all members of a particular stratum will participate in, or be swept into, the mass movement. In the German case, only particular types of individuals within the middle class would join in the Nazi movement or vote for the party. They would represent the more 'authoritarian segments' of the middle class, and would tend to be of rural or small town rather than urban background, have lower levels of education than comparable members of the middle class and be self-employed rather than workers or professional people. In the latter case, the self-employed would, ostensibly, be more vulnerable to changing economic circumstances and, therefore, more afraid of the kinds of pressures and tensions that developed in Germany than their non-entrepreneurial and better educated middle class counterparts.[55]

Fortunately, a fairly large body of literature about voting patterns exists with specific reference to the rise of the Nazi party. The conclusions reached in these works, however, are not always compatible and authors using similar data but different analytical techniques have tended to bolster both the mass society and the class movement arguments although the majority of findings are more supportive of the class analysis. These studies tend to be of two types. The first includes case studies of particular regions of Germany, either with reference to changes in the voting trends or detailed examinations of changes in the various aspects of social life within the particular area. The second type of study focuses on the voting patterns of Germany generally without specific reference to the type of change that is occurring in one or more individual regions. As stated, the studies tend to support the class thesis in so far as one is able to interpret such studies with any real degree of clarity and confidence. Still, there have been some recent and important contradictions of the class theme which we must also examine.

Two very early studies of electoral behaviour in pre-Nazi Germany tend to support Lipset's thesis about where the individual who voted for the Nazis was drawn from. Pollack examined four Reichstag elections as well as the two Presidential elections in which Hitler was a candidate and found little evidence to suggest that it was the marginal or alienated voter who was responsible for the great upsurge of Nazi support. When turnout increased substantially, the Nazis gained in some districts and lost in others.[56] Pollack found that in the period between 1930 and 1933, 'many of the urban industrial areas showed a greater electoral interest than did the agricultural areas. At the same time, the increased popular vote in the large cities as a rule was cast against Hitler, while the agricultural areas regularly showed a strong interest in him'.[57] The implications of this finding suggests that the new voters were as strongly committed to the old class ties as were the earlier voters. Further, if one assumes that communists, as represented by the Communist Party (KPD), were more committed to the success of the proletariat than the more traditional Social Democratic Party (SPD) then these new voters may actually have been demonstrating greater class loyalty than the previous voters, but one must accept this interpretation with the same caution as the others, for as Pollack pointed out, there are some districts in which this easy interpretation seems to be confounded by other factors, particularly religious and border issues.[58]

The increase of support for the KPD should not be taken as merely another indication of general support for the Left.

The SPD, or establishment socialists, supported the continued existence of the Weimar Republic, for which they were responsible, while the KPD advocated a socialist republic. Thus, a vote for the KPD could well be interpreted as a vote to overthrow the Republic in the interests of the proletariat while support for the SPD was at the very least status-quo-oriented and, at most, directed toward greater social justice within the existing framework.

Heberle examined the rise of the Nazi vote in one particular region of Germany, Schleswig-Holstein. The region was of particular interest because Nazi support there was more extensive than in other parts of Germany. In this region the Nazi share of the vote in Reichstag elections went from four per cent in 1928 to fifty-one per cent in 1932. In rural communities the Nazis received nearly two-thirds of the votes cast in 1932. In his analysis, Heberle argued that at the beginning of the Nazi movement in 1920 the party was urban-centred, and its first supporters tended to come from all classes.[59] But, following the unsuccessful Beer Hall Putsch in November 1923, and Hitler's imprisonment, the real growth of the Nazi support occurred in the rural regions.

Schleswig-Holstein provided a particularly interesting laboratory since it contained many of the elements in microcosm that were to be found in macroscopic Germany. Further, as a border region, it was perhaps more susceptible to the strong nationalist appeal of the Nazis because of the sensitivity to the problem caused by the cession of territory at the end of World War I. All such border regions, particularly those near Poland, tended to support the nationalist movements more decisively than did the other regions of Germany.

Heberle identified three major groups in the region and referred to them as 'the main channels of political currents . . .'.[60] The three groups were (1) the large landowning classes and wealthy farmers and the bourgeoisie who tended to vote for the Conservatives, (2) the urban and rural middle class which included small farmers and some agricultural labourers and which moved from liberalism to Nazism, and (3) the working class, both urban and rural, who tended toward the SPD and later the KPD. In his major hypothesis Heberle concluded 'that the classes particularly susceptible for Nazism were neither the rural nobility and big farmers nor the rural proletariat, but rather the small farm proprietors, very much the rural equivalent of the lower middle class or petty bourgeoisie which formed the backbone of the NSDAP in the cities'.[61]

Allen's analysis of the rise of the Nazis in 'Thalburg' further reinforces this image of the middle class movement toward the Nazis as well as the working class' continued adherence to the Social Democrats or to the KPD. Allen, however, does not suggest that there was a conscious middle class movement which led to the Nazi success. Rather,

'It was the depression, or more accurately, the fear of its continued effects, that contributed most heavily to the radicalization of Thalburg's people. This was not because the town was so deeply hurt by the depression. The only group directly affected were the workers; they were the ones who lost their jobs, stood idle on the corners, and existed on the dole. Yet paradoxically the workers remained steadfast in support of the status quo while the middle class, only marginally first by the economic constriction, turned to revolution'.[62]

That such fear on the part of members of the middle class existed is amply demonstrated by Allen who concluded that 'the most important factor in the victory of Nazism was the active division of the town along class lines'.[63] He found that there was an 'atomization' of the population, but this occurred after the Nazis came to power. The Nazis deliberately destroyed the social fabric of the local society by doing away with the social clubs, the main 'reinforcers' of the social awareness, and replacing them with Nazi organizations. which were better able to mobilize the population for the Nazis.

What Allen is suggesting is a critical departure from mass society theory. Those who explain the rise of the Nazis by reference to the atomization of the populace would argue that this was the culmination of a long historical process of the decline of the classes. The Nazi seizure of power was merely the final result of this process. Allen is saying that the class structure had not broken down at all; instead, the classes had become polarized with the middle class supporting the Nazis and the working class supporting the Socialists. Thus advocates of mass society theory argue that the Nazis came to power as a result of the atomization of society while Allen is arguing that the Nazis brought about the atomization of the society, and that they 'atomized' the society to facilitate their rule.[64]

The evidence thus far would appear to be conclusive in the

direction of the Nazis as a middle class movement rather than a movement which drew 'the disaffected and apolitical from all strata'.[65] Recently, however, O'Lessker has challenged Lipset's thesis by suggesting that the critical time at which the Nazis made their electoral breakthrough was the 1930 Reichstag election. He accepts Lipset's notion that the Nazis gained mostly from the disaffected middle class in the 1932 election, but given the more sophisticated statistical techniques that O'Lessker uses he argues that 'one can hardly escape the conclusion that it was a combination of new voters and defecting Nationalists that transformed the Nazi party into a true mass movement in September, 1930'.[66] O'Lessker strengthens this point by suggesting that in the second election in 1932 when turnout dropped substantially it was predominantly the Nazis who suffered a loss in votes. Further, he argues, if his analysis is applied to the Left, the KPD growth demonstrates a pattern similar to the Nazis. This point is significant because it once again suggests the 'massness' of extremist politics, if that is what the Nazis and Communists represented, rather than the 'classness' of such movements, at least in the initial stages.

O'Lessker's conclusions have been criticized on two counts. A first criticism is related to the method used and suggests that had he used an even more advanced technique than he did, he may have reached a conclusion similar to Lipset's.[67] A second criticism emerges from Shiveley's investigation of voting in Weimar. Shively attempted to determine the strength and persistence of party identification in Weimar Germany and found that there was 'evidence that party identification in the sense of learned and enduring attachments to parties was not a factor in Weimar elections'.[68] But if party loyalty was not strong, class or group loyalty did seem to be strong. He suggested 'that Weimar voting depended on voters' sense of the social group to which they belonged (proletarian or Catholic or Protestant bourgeoisie), and of the political party or parties appropriate to that group'.[69]

Shively is arguing that voters who did not have particularly strong party loyalty did have group loyalty and could move from party to party within the context of the particular group or class. Thus, when a voter moved from his original party to the Nazis it was in support for the particular class rather than a reflection of the collapse of that class. In so far as new voters were concerned, the increase in turnout benefited not only the

Nazis but other parties as well. Shively's conclusion directly contradicts Arendt and Kornhauser who, as we have seen, argued that the Nazis derived their basic support from those atomized individuals who were freed from class ties. If Shively's conclusions, taken with those of Pollack, Heberle and Allen are correct, then the 'theory' of mass society is merely a hypothesis that has been demonstrated to be wrong. Class allegiances seem to have become stronger rather than weaker in this period, and the Nazis and Communists were the main beneficiaries.

But we cannot discard the theory on the basis of electoral analyses. While on the surface the evidence seems strong that what occurred in Germany were class rather than mass movements, what we lack is the kind of evidence that tells us what individuals were actually thinking. One cannot infer individual behavioural patterns or attitudes on the basis of aggregate analysis. Further, and this is a limitation of any aggregate analysis, while the aggregate figures may indicate shifts of voting blocs, the researcher cannot be absolutely confident that those blocs are made up of voters from the bloc he thinks they are coming from. If three parties, A, B and C, each receive 33 per cent of the vote in election 1, and in election 2 Party A receives 50 per cent, B 33 per cent and C only 17 per cent, it is by no means certain that Party A's increase came from Party C. A large number of A's votes may have come from B with C's votes going to both A and B. Thus, what seems a simple pattern of movement may be considerably more volatile when analysed through other methods such as interviewing. Unfortunately, such analyses are not available to us with regard to Weimar Germany, and the conclusions that we have reached are merely tentative.

Conclusion

While we have examined the basic assumptions upon which the theory of mass society is based, we have not discussed some of the weaknesses of the pluralist notion of democracy. So pervasive has the concept of pluralist democracy been that social scientists who have been schooled within its basic framework have tended to accept its basic tenets uncritically. Mills criticized this tendency by suggesting that instead of accepting the principles of pluralist democracy as the actual condition of society, social scientists ought 'to go beyond a mere enumeration of all the facts that might conceivably be involved and weigh each of them in such a way as to understand how they fit together, how they form a model of what it is you are trying to understand'.[70] If the researcher is continually positing the multiplicity of groups in a society he may well be ignoring areas of leadership cohesion simply because such cohesion is unexpected. Further, there is a tendency to ignore the importance of certain key veto groups, unseen by the researcher and public which may, in fact, be the key decision makers. Certainly Dahl, whose critique and up-dating of pluralism was discussed earlier, has been criticized precisely for his failure to confront the issue of unseen, yet influential, actors.[71]

Mills' most widely read work was concerned with the growing tendency of what might have been the pluralist society to become a society in which a more cohesive elite dominated. He suggested in much the way that Dahl did—although they reached different conclusions—that 'as historical conditions change, so do the meanings and political consequences of the mechanics of power'.[72] As a society becomes more complex, the forms of social relation-ships that may have punctuated that society in simpler times may give way to new arrangements in which groups no longer compete and in which an elite dominates a mass. Mills was not necessarily criticizing the mass society theorists in this respect; he was only suggesting that the type of pluralism that they have assumed flourishes in the United States is no longer a reality in the advanced industrial society. Certain features of modern life such as mass communications serve to break down traditional social relationships.

Gusfield has criticized the notion of pluralism from a some-what different standpoint. He has argued that pluralism is but one form of democratic organization and, perhaps, not the best form for several reasons. The pluralist thinkers have tended to argue that membership in a group or intermediate organization is functional for national attachments. Such membership in groups maintains social stability. That stability is no longer possible once those organizations or groups are destroyed. But, Gusfield argues,

'It is *not* true that attachment to intermediate structures insures attachment to the larger national instituions and structures. As a society undergoes change, it is likely that specific groups will be adversely affected by economic or social change. Similarly, some groups may develop new aspirations and objectives. In both cases they may come to feel that the existent political order is insufficient to command their allegiance. A shifting balance of forces is, however, not the same phenomenon as the breakup of an associational structure, the shattering of a class, or the decline of primary group support. It is even reasonable to maintain that an external threat to a group promotes its sense of solidarity and aids in the development of group identity and organization'.[73]

Thus, when the troubles of the 1920s and 1930s were most pronounced in Germany, the members of the populace adhered not to the state or nation, but rather to the particular group or class to which individuals belonged. Even when they assumed that by voting for the Nazis or Communists they were upholding German 'ideals', they were supporting ideals that were class rather than mass related.

Gusfield goes on to argue that mass society may actually be functional for a greater sense of social solidarity and stability in a society because 'in so far as mass societies create homogenous experience for a population, there is an increased possibility of consensus on substantive issues'.[74] We have already commented on the Maoist notion of the mass line and the possibility that political involvement is very widespread in China. This would suggest that a social hierarchy actually gets in the way of the legitimate wishes and demands of the population; if democracy is participation by the mass, then pluralism might not be fully compatible with democracy at all for it interferes with the transmission of the legitimate demands of the people to the leaders.

We need carry this discussion no further for the basic purpose was to suggest that, just as the Marxists begin with a particular view of the world that may or may not be correct, the mass society theorists begin with a basic set of assumptions which are accepted by them as valid and correct. But such assumptions may be, and have been, criticized. Pluralism is not the only philosophy of participatory democracy.

But even if the pluralist notion of society is accepted as a correct assessment of how a stable democracy persists, it is, as has been shown, very difficult to justify the assertion that it is the breakdown of group or class ties that lead to the growth of the revolutionary mass movement. On the contrary, there is a strong and convincing body of evidence that the one case which mass society theorists utilize as the primary example of what happens when group attachments break down is not such an example at all. Instead, group and class loyalties became so strong that movements developed from these 'intermediate' structures that were so powerful and so persistent that the ostensibly democratic political system which allowed them to grow could not survive. And the traditional social structure which had made the democratic political system so frail also perished in the final days of the Nazi era.

Notes and References

1 For a discussion of the revolutionary mass movement, see Robert Tucker, *The Soviet Political Mind*, New York, 1963.

2 Among the better known works which deal with totalitarianism are C. J. Friedrich and Z. K. Brzezinski, *Totalitarian Dictatorship and Autocracy*, Cambridge, Massachusetts, 1956; Hans Buchheim, *Totalitarian Rule: Its Nature and Characteristics*, 1968; and C. J. Friedrich (ed.), *Totalitarianism*, New York, 1954.

3 Irving Louis Horowitz, *Foundations of Political Sociology*, New York, 1972, p. 239.

4 Madison was one of the major figures at the convention that drafted the Constitution of the United States. He later had a distinguished political career during which he was Secretary of State and later President. Hamilton, an advocate of strong, central government, later served in George Washington's administration and was the first Secretary of the Treasury. Jay became the first Chief Justice of the United States, but is not well-remembered for that. His most important task was the settlement of various disputes that still remained with Great Britain following the Treaty of Peace between Britain and the United States.

5 James Madison, 'The Federalist No. 10', from *The Federalist*, by Alexander Hamilton, John Jay and James Madison, New York, 1941, p. 54.

6 *Ibid.*, p. 55.

7 *Ibid.*

8 *Ibid.*

9 *Ibid.*, p. 61.

10 *Ibid.*

11 James Madison, 'The Federalist No. 51', p. 339.

12 *Ibid.*

13 *Ibid.*, pp. 339–40.

14 Alexis de Tocqueville, *Democracy in America*, edited and abridged by Richard D. Heffner, New York, 1956, p. 115.

15 *Ibid.*, p. 121.

16 *Ibid.*, p. 123.

17 *Ibid.*, pp. 123–7.

18 Robert A. Dahl, *Pluralist Democracy in the United States: Conflict and Consent*, Chicago, 1967, p. 24.

19 Robert Dahl, *A Preface to Democratic Theory*, Chicago, 1956, Phoenix Edition, 1963, p. 137.

20 *Ibid.*

21 See footnote 7, Chapter 2.

22 Robert Dahl, *A Preface to Democratic Theory*, p. 146.

23 E. E. Schattschneider, *The Semi-Sovereign People*, New York, 1960, p. 141. See also T. R. Dye and H. Zeigler, *The Irony of Democracy*, Belmont, California, 1970.

24 Hannah Arendt, *The Origins of Totalitarianism*, New York, 1958. First published 1951, pp. 312–3.

25 William Kornhauser, *The Politics of Mass Society*, New York, 1959, p. 22.

26 *Ibid.*, p. 32.

27 *Ibid.*, p. 43.

28 *Ibid.*, p. 22.

29 *Ibid.*

30 Arendt, *The Origins of Totalitarianism*, p. 317.

31 *Ibid.*

32 Theodore Abel, 'The why of the Hitler Movement', from *Anger, Violence and Politics: Theories and Research*, edited by Ivo K. Fierabend, Rosalind L. Fierabend, and T. R. Gurr, Englewood Cliffs, New Jersey, 1972, p. 284.

33 Kornhauser, *The Politics of Mass Society*, p. 43.

34 *Ibid.*, p. 182.

35 For a discussion of the relationship between social background characteristics and attitudes see Lewis Edinger and Donald Searing, 'Social background in elite analysis : a methodological inquiry', *American Political Science Review*, 61, 1967, pp. 428–45.

36 A. W. Green, 'Re-examination of the marginal man concept', *Social Forces*, 26, December, 1947, p. 167.

37 See Milton Goldberg, 'A qualification of the marginal man theory', *American Sociological Review*, 6, 1941, pp. 52–8.

38 Charles Moskos, 'From monarchy to communism : the social transformation of the Albanian elite', from *Social Change in Developing Areas*, ed. by Herbert R. Barringer, George Blanksten and Raymond W. Mack, Cambridge, Massachusetts, 1963, p. 215.

39 *Ibid.*, p. 214.

40 See A. S. Cohan, *The Irish Political Elite*, Dublin, 1972.

41 See Robert C. North with Ithiel de Sola Pool, 'Kuomintang and Chinese Communist elites', from *World Revolutionary Elites*, ed. by Harold Lasswell and Daniel Lerner, Cambridge, Massachusetts, 1966, pp. 319–455.

42 William B. Quandt, *Revolution and Political Leadership: Algeria, 1954–1968*, Cambridge, Massachusetts, 1969, p. 159.

43 Daniel Lerner with Ithiel de Sola Pool and George K. Schueller, 'The Nazi elite', from *World Revolutionary Elites*, p. 288.

44 *Ibid.*, p. 305.

45 *Ibid.*

46 Arendt, *The Origins of Totalitarianism*, p. 315.

47 Kornhauser, *The Politics of Mass Society*, p. 33.

48 Arendt, *The Origins of Totalitarianism*, p. 315.

49 See Reinhard Bendix, 'Social stratification and political power', from *Class, Status and Power*, ed. by Reinhard Bendix and S. M. Lipset, Glencoe, 1956, p. 605. Quoted in S. M. Lipset, *Political Man*, London, 1969. First published 1959.

50 Rudolf Heberle, *From Democracy to Nazism*, Baton Rouge, Louisiana, 1945, p. 121.

51 Theodore Geiger, quoted in Ralf Dahrendorf, *Society and Democracy in Germany*, Garden City, New Jersey, 1969. First published 1967, p. 117.

52 Harold Lasswell, 'The psychology of Hitlerism', *Political Quarterly*, IV, 1933, pp. 373–4. Quoted also in Lipset, *Political Man*, pp. 135–6, Lasswell also says :

'It is worthy of comment that the lower middle classes, stung from political passivity into political action, have been able to furnish their own crusading leadership. Hitler, the self-made, semi-intellectual, son of a small customs official in the service of the Habsburgs, stirs his own class to an unwonted spurt of political aggressiveness. Other social groups, like the wage earners, have so often been led by men who were social renegades from the older social strata that this self-sufficiency of the bourgeoisie inspires respectful interest'; pp. 383–4.

53 S. M. Lipset, *Political Man*, p. 139.

54 *Ibid.*, p. 140.

55 *Ibid.*

56 James K. Pollock, 'An areal study of the German electorate, 1930–1933', *American Political Science Review*, 38, 1944, p. 93.

57 *Ibid.*, p. 140.

58 *Ibid.*

59 Heberle, *From Democracy to Nazism*, p. 10.

60 *Ibid.*, p. 41.

61 *Ibid.*, p. 112.

62 William Sheridan Allen, *The Nazi Seizure of Power*, 1966, p. 24.

63 *Ibid.*, p. 274.

64 Dealing with the rise of Stalin, Arendt takes a similar view. 'The means by which Stalin changed the Russian one-party dictatorship into a totalitarian regime and the revolutionary Communist parties all over the world into totalitarian movements was the liquidation of factions, the abolition of inner-party democracy and the transformation of national Communist parties into Moscow-directed branches of the Comintern', Hannah Arendt, *The Origins of Totalitarianism*, p. 379. For a most interesting analysis of Arendt's work see Margaret Canovan, *The Political Thought of Hannah Arendt*, London, 1974.

65 Karl O'Lessker, 'Who voted for Hitler? A new look at the class basis of Nazism', *American Journal of Sociology*, 74, p. 63.

66 *Ibid.*, p. 67.

67 Allan Schnaiberg, 'A critique of Karl O'Lessker's "Who voted for Hitler?"', *American Journal of Sociology*, 74, pp. 732–5.

68 W. Phillips Shively, 'Voting stability and the nature of party attachments in the Weimar Republic', *American Political Science Review*, 66, 1972, p. 1220.

69 *Ibid.*, p. 1222.

70 C. Wright Mills, *The Power Elite*, London, 1956, p. 245.

71 Peter Bachrach and Morton Baratz, 'Two faces of power', *American Political Science Review*, 56, December 1962, pp. 947–52; and 'Decisions and non-decisions: an analytical framework', *American Political Science Review*, 57, September 1963, pp. 632–42.

72 Mills, *The Power Elite*, p. 265.

73 Joseph R. Gusfield, 'Mass society and extremist politics', *American Sociological Review*, 27 (1), 1962, p. 26.

74 *Ibid.*, p. 28.

Chapter 8
Psychological Approaches to Revolution

The theories and models of revolution that have been discussed so far may be placed in the sociological category; each has focused on the factors in society which are responsible for initiating the revolutionary process. Even the theory of mass society which is largely concerned with the process of the atomization of the individual begins with an assumption that it is the breakdown of the traditional social fabric which leads to atomization. All these approaches see the revolutionary act of the individual or group within society as the dependent variable, explained, determined, or caused by general or certain specifically identified social conditions. The societal factors judged to be important may vary from theorist to theorist, but in all cases the theorists focus on these factors and assume that the revolutionary act follows from the occurrence of societal conditions.

Another category of theories and models is concerned with the individual and the perceptions of that individual about the social situation, or the particular personality of an individual, which might cause him to rebel or to become an active revolutionary. While recognizing that revolutionary acts do not occur in a vacuum, the theorists that we would place in this category are not as concerned with the actual social conditions prior to the revolutionary situation as they are with the perceptions that members of the populace have of the social situation and how these individuals respond to the perceived social situation.

The general category of psychological approaches may be further divided into four sub-categories: (1) studies that deal with the background of individual revolutionaries; (2) theories which are concerned with the 'repression of instincts'; (3) the theory of rising expectations; and (4) the theory of relative deprivation.

Studies of individual revolutionaries vary considerably. They range from simple historical biographies to very sophisticated and ambitious psychoanalytic analyses. All, whether of the simple or more sophisticated variety, are concerned to explain why individuals become revolutionary leaders. As such, they are different from any of the other theories that we have examined (with the exception of one aspect of the work which deals with marginality), for all of the theories discussed previously have been concerned with mass rather than elite behaviour.

Once finished with the revolutionary personality we shall return to the question of mass behaviour. The first of the works with which we shall be concerned in this category deals with what may be referred to as 'the repression of instincts' and is typified by the work of Pitirim Sorokin who wrote his major work on revolution in the 1920s.

The second category of psychological theories concerned with mass behaviour is the theory of rising expectations. Originally propounded by de Tocqueville in his study of the French Revolution, it enjoyed a rebirth during the 1930s with the work of Crane Brinton and has more recently been utilized in an analysis of revolution by James Davies.

But by far the most important of the psychological theories is the theory of relative deprivation, an approach whose main exponent is Ted Gurr. It is an outgrowth and modification of the theory of rising expectations and is much less of a theory of revolution than it is one of collective violence. Our interest, however, is whether it is able to provide us with reasons why people rise up against an existing regime.

Studies of Individual Leaders

Conquest tells us that during the years of Stalin's rule in the Soviet Union it was not the particular economic and social factors of the period that were responsible for the way in which that country was ruled. 'On the contrary, the central factor was ideas in the mind of the ruler impelling him to action very often against the natural trend of such forces.'[1] In a study by Lifton, the cultural revolution in China is viewed as the outgrowth of Mao's inner need for immortality which, while unobtainable biologically, is possible if his ideas and thoughts are continued in the aftermath of the revolution that bears both his name and imprint. Generalizing from the Chinese case, Lifton argues that to the leader, 'his revolutionary "works" are all-important, and only to the extent that he can perceive them as enduring can he achieve a measure of acceptance of his own eventual death'.[2] Thus, major periods in the histories of the two countries that Stalin and Mao led are explained not in terms of the particular environmental or social factors of the time spans that are in question, but in relation to the psychological make-up of the leaders and different needs that they may have had.

The two assessments of revolutionary leaders are part of a widely held viewpoint in political science that suggests :

> 'The personality characteristics of leaders and of men who aspire to leadership—in so far as they are relevant to their successes and failures, their relationship to their social environment, and their decision-making activities, would seem to demand the particular attention of those who claim that the struggle for power over public policy-making is the prime concern of political science'.[3]

Thus, one of the ways, perhaps the primary way, that we may come to understand how and why particular policies are developed may be through an appreciation of the characteristics and personality traits of the leaders who devise those policies. Particularizing this view to deal with the study of revolutions, the way in which we may be able to understand why different revolutions take on certain characteristics is by understanding the factors that motivate the leaders of those revolutionary movements which may be certain personality traits developed in very early childhood.

Most studies of revolutionary leaders are descriptive accounts of the events that may have led to the individual joining or initiating a movement dedicated to the overthrow of the existing regime. Implicit in such studies is the assumption that the events selected by the researcher are, in some ways, part of a coherent picture which helps to explain the life pattern of that individual. Extended to the study of elites generally, numerous analyses of the social background of leaders have appeared with the underlying premise that if we understand the significant background features of an elite group we will be able to predict their attitudinal and behavioural patterns. Although such a view has received some severe buffeting in recent years,[4] a continued faith in social background for the prediction of attitudes persists.[5] As we found when dealing with the question of marginality as an explanation of possible revolutionary behaviour, the evidence is not overwhelmingly convincing when subjected to careful analysis. Yet the persistence of social scientists in pursuing the concept of marginality with regard to revolutionary elites should be noted.[6]

In addition to the 'regular' biographies of political and revolutionary leaders and group analyses of elite formations there are the more sophisticated studies which are part of, or borrow heavily from, psychology in order to explain why leaders behave as they do. These studies may be devoted to an explanation of behaviour which could be construed as irrational by observers who are unaware of the particular personality factors that may explain such behaviour.[7] The works may be attempts at explaining tendencies in individuals to behave in certain ways because of early life experiences that these individuals had. The analysis of childhood, therefore, is vital in this type of approach because 'every adult, whether he is a follower or a leader, a member of a mass or of an *elite*, was once a child'.[8] When he is a child he develops his 'conscience', or 'dependence on himself',[9] that permits him to cope with the varied problems he may have to face. Each stage of development is vital, and each crisis he confronts requires that he calls up the sum of his development to that point. Thus, how he copes with a problem today is largely dependent upon many of his experiences in the days before.

Revolutionary behaviour, according to this approach, is not a chance occurrence. The person who is prone to such behaviour and who rises to leadership in the revolutionary movement is not suddenly filled with a sense of the world's injustice when he encounters privation and hunger for the first time. Instead, the sight of such unhappiness triggers a propensity or disposition that already exists. Without such a propensity he may view the ills of the world with some or no disquiet, but he is unlikely to become a revolutionary. The basic hypothesis that is suggested by this analysis is

'The less an individual is dedicated to radical social change and a total displacement of the ruling class, the less he will be likely to embody the psychological attributes of the revolutionary personality. The more he is inclined to the use of peaceful or traditionally legitimate political means, the less likely he will be to have a revolutionary psychology'.[10]

So the question, 'Why does a person become a revolutionary?' may only be answered in terms of those psychological factors or types of experiences which predispose the individual to revolutionary behaviour. To explore this possibility we shall examine some occurrences in Lenin's and Hitler's lives which are thought by some of their biographers to have contributed to their revolutionary zeal. With reference to these factors we shall assess how useful such information is.

By virtually all accounts, Lenin's childhood was ideal. He came from a reasonably well-to-do family that apparently gloried in intellectual achievement. Lenin's father was a school inspector who had gone to university at a time when someone with his particular background had little opportunity of doing so. The father was, apparently, a supporter, or at least a non-questioner, of the regime, but toward the end of his life he was probably badly affected by proposed changes in the educational system.[11] Still, the family environment was a happy one with an accomplished father and a devoted and intelligent mother. All this suggests a very stable background, but, as one biographer suggests, this circumstance should be borne in mind 'because it must have contributed to the character of the future revolutionary, to the self-confidence, inner balance and fullness of his personality'.[12]

There are, from the outset, suggestions of a reserve and self-control on the part of the young Lenin. He did not, for example, begin walking until he was three, and if psychological explanations are accepted,[13] rather than any physiological condition which may have impeded walking, such late-walking might suggest a basic mistrust of the world, or great caution. 'This mistrust, assuming it existed, was not so great as to impair Lenin's grasp of reality. But it did result in a certain perception of reality which, in the context of revolutionary politics, had important consequences'.[14] There are numerous allusions to this mistrust of the world as well as his caution in his many dealings. But does one attribute the type of revolutionary party that Lenin advocated and eventually developed to a cautious outlook that may also have been reflected in his late walking, or is it a manifestation of his incisive understanding of the Russian society in which political organizations were easily infiltrated by the secret police?

In any event, certain occurrences do seem to have had a great impact upon his life although these occurrences are interpreted rather differently by various sources. The first of these was the death of his father in 1886 when Lenin was fifteen years old. If one accepts a psychological explanation, then the death of

Lenin's father at this particular juncture in his life could have had a vital impact upon his later behavioural pattern. Erikson has suggested the importance of the Oedipus Complex with regard to Luther—'the ambivalent interplay of rivalry with the father, admiration for him, and fear of him which puts such a heavy burden of guilt and inferiority on all spontaneous initiative and on all fantasy'.[15] While in Luther's case, the problem was a rather pronounced one, the argument would be made that the adolescent male must go through the Oedipal phase. In Lenin's case the argument would be advanced that 'when his father died . . . Lenin was beset by great feelings of guilt, as a result of the adolescent reactivation of the Oedipal struggle. Lenin was in the midst of working out his aggressive feelings towards his father when suddenly his father died'.[16] Thus, the particular conflicts to which Lenin may have been subjected at this point remained unresolved.

The second occurrence of major importance in the young Lenin's life was the execution of his older brother, Alexander, which resulted from Alexander's participation in a plot to assassinate the Tsar. This is a particularly interesting event in Lenin's life because it is exceedingly difficult to separate myth from reality with regard to the relationship that the two young boys had with one another and how Lenin reacted to Alexander's execution.

One commentator suggests that Alexander's 'death was not merely a frightful blow to (Lenin), *since there was a great community of interest between the two brothers*, but it brought the whole family into public disrepute and under police ban'.[17] This is a strange comment, indeed, because most of the sources suggest that there was very little community of interest between the brothers and some indication that Alexander did not have a very high regard for the younger brother.[18] Further, while Alexander was familiar with the works of Marx, he apparently 'had no clear idea what practical application he would make of the reading'.[19] There is virtually no evidence that it was Alexander who introduced the young Lenin to Marx's work.

A second myth refers to Lenin's reaction to his brother's execution. Trotsky's description is perhaps the most interesting:

'Unlike coins, invented stories do not wear down with circulation, but on the contrary, grow bigger. The old Bolshevik Shelgunov tells this story: "When they read the telegram that Alexander was executed, Vladimir Ilyich wiped his brow and said, 'Well then, we will seek a more effective road' ". All the laws of human psychology are here trampled on. Volodya (Lenin) is not thrown into despair upon receiving the dreadful news, does not grieve for the irredeemable loss, but wipes his brow and announces the need to find a "more effective road". To whom were these words addressed? The mother was in Petersburg, Anna was still in prison. Evidently Vladimir imparted his tactical discoveries to the thirteen-year-old Dimitriv and the nine-year-old Maria . . .'.[20]

Maria also reported that his brother reacted in the way that Shelgunov said but this too is discounted. It has also been suggested that Alexander's death 'impressed him strongly with the futility of terroristic acts by individuals against highly placed persons as a policy for achieving fundamental social changes. It made him grasp more clearly than before the view that in any social system power rests in the hands of the class that is economically strong, and that a real movement for liberation must work, not by attacks on individual tyrants, but by the organization of the workers as a class with the definite aim of seizing economic power'.[21]

Yet this view also is strongly disputed. There can be little doubt that Lenin was strongly affected by the execution of his brother. The death of a sibling under any circumstances is likely to have a traumatic effect on the other children in the family, and the death of Alexander under the particular circumstances may have been even more of a shock as his revolutionary proclivities were probably not known by members of the family other than the older sister Anna. Deutscher described Lenin as a 'drooping, painstricken boy, struggling to contain his feelings within himself'.[22] Yet it is a long jump from griefstricken brother to radical revolutionary and if Alexander's death did trigger in Lenin a desire to 'settle the score' with the autocracy, he 'knew not how to approach the task of revenge'.[23] His conversion to Marxism seems to have come after Alexander's death, possibly as a result of it, but certainly not through a direct introduction by Alexander.

Whether a particular psychological propensity toward revolution existed is an open question. The proponent of the view that Lenin did have such a propensity would argue that 'the death of his father was not enough to make Lenin a revolutionist, nor was the death of his brother; but the two in combination created a mighty impulse towards revolution'.[24] Lenin suffered, according to this view, from guilt, guilt as a result of his unresolved Oedipal complex and guilt associated with the death of an older brother with whom he did not get on particularly well. Once he began to examine some of the works which had an effect on Alexander's life and disposition toward revolution, Lenin moved toward revolution.[25]

Against this view is the one that holds that there is really no evidence that suggests 'maladjustment' as a result of Lenin's early development.

> 'True, the hanging of his older brother . . . when Vladimir was only sixteen, was an event to put iron into his adolescent soul but that only moves the question a little further back : what made brother Alexander into a plotter and a rebel? We shall have to look elsewhere than to the maladjustments of a miserable childhood for the motive forces that drove them to hate feudal barbarism and despotism and to choose revolution as a way of life.'[26]

Here it is the intelligent and thoughtful Lenin that comes to despise the oppression by an autocratic regime of a backward and impoverished people.

If Lenin is difficult to categorize, Hitler is perhaps even more difficult because more than the usual amount of myth surrounds the real man as well as a none-too-sympathetic biographical tradition. Hitler is not now perceived as a good and wise revolutionary leader who brought his country to salvation. Yet this does not make him any less of a revolutionary figure nor is he less interesting. Further, there is a wealth of information about him and most of it is fascinating. Still, it is no easy task to lift from all this documentation the features of his life which are relevant to the eventual direction that he took.

One is sorely tempted to ascribe to Hitler all of the features which suggest psychological maladjustment as the reason for his need to lead. Surely his own written work presents us with a picture of an individual with a difficult childhood, and one in which he clashed regularly with the dominant figure in the home, his father. Hitler wished to be an artist while his father wanted him to have a career in the civil service. As a result the two battled continuously. 'The old man grew embittered, and, much as I loved him, so did I. My father forbade me to nourish the slightest hope of ever being allowed to study art.'[27]

But his father died when the young Hitler was only thirteen, so the pressure to enter the civil service was removed. He was supported throughout the period after his father's death by his mother to whom he was particularly devoted. She eventually allowed him to drop out of the school which might have prepared him for a professional career, and he planned to attend the art academy in Vienna. But he is depicted as a dreamer and a loafer who had little actual artistic talent.[28] The period between the time that he left school and his mother's death were self-described as 'the happiest days of my life'.[29] His mother's death was a great blow to him : 'I had honoured my father, but my mother I had loved'.[30] Out of this type of self-description psychologists could have a field day. But Erikson advises caution:

'Such seemingly naïve coincidence of themes lends itself easily—much too easily—to a psychoanalytic interpretation of the first chapter of *Mein Kampf* as an involuntary confession of Hitler's Oedipus complex. This interpretation would suggest that in Hitler's case the love for his young mother and the hate for his old father assumed morbid proportions, and that it was this conflict which drove him to love and to hate and compelled him to save or destroy peoples who really "stand for" his mother and his father. There have been articles in psychoanalytic literature which claim such simple causality. But it obviously takes much more than an individual complex to make a successful revolutionary. The complex creates the initial fervour; but if it were too strong it would paralyse the revolutionary, not inspire him'.[31]

Other myths characterize Hitler's background, two of which are worth mentioning if only because they have been reported in very distinguished biographies of Hitler. First, it has been suggested that Hitler's morbid concern with venereal diseases in *Mein Kampf* stemmed from the fact that he was syphilitic. If these reports were accurate then 'Hitler's later symptoms—psychological as well as physical—could be those of a man suffering from the tertiary stage of syphilis'.[32] The other possibility is that Hitler was sexually impotent, or at least 'incapable of normal sexual intercourse'.[33] If it were true that Hitler suffered from sexual difficulties then much of his behaviour may be explainable in terms of the particular frustrations that he may have felt.

Recent evidence, however, has indicated that neither of these hypotheses can be confirmed. On the contrary, Hitler did not suffer from venereal disease, and he apparently enjoyed regular relations with women. There is no sound evidence to dispute these findings.[34] Thus, if one wishes to look for the psychological roots of Hitler's behavioural patterns, the childhood experiences may offer several clues—although, as Erikson cautions, one must be very hesitant before plunging ahead with such explanations. Further, the notions concerning Hitler's private life are probably wrong, thus eliminating those factors as potential explanations of his behaviour.

Wolfenstein has attempted to construct a model of revolutionary behaviour which contains many of the factors that have been discussed. First, there is a love-hate relationship that is developed with regard to the father. In a sense, the father provides the masculine figure after whom the son models himself. But the father is also an authority figure who is 'in possession of the most important love object of a person's early life, his mother'.[35] While the Oedipal complex is found in all growing boys it is apparently stronger in the budding revolutionist than other people. Because of the death of the father the conflict is never resolved and the revolutionist 'will try to turn the conflict from an *internal one* into an *external one*, from a conflict within himself to a conflict between himself and others'.[36] Although this is only a starting point, what Wolfenstein is suggesting is that the conflict with the father figure is ultimately transferred to the state and the state, which is the new authority figure, earns the enmity of the revolutionary. Ultimately, each of the revolutionists with whom Wolfenstein dealt 'developed means which allowed him to express hatred of authority without incurring debilitating levels of guilt. Thus at any given intensity of hatred for authority, the higher the level of active guilt, the less violent the form of opposition'.[37] If the individual feels guilty about his hostility then he is unable to transform his dislike for authority figures into active opposition to the state.

Such psychological explanations of the reasons why people become revolutionaries are very interesting, but there are many problems which are attendant upon them. The first and most obvious one is that much of what passes for fact is frequently myth. As we have seen, there is considerable conflict among the biographers of Lenin concerning what effects various occurrences had on his life and the eventual direction he took. His relationship with his brother is unspecified and Lenin rarely mentioned anything about him.[38] Further, it is difficult to determine precisely what Lenin may have learned from his brother about revolution although the evidence indicates that he learned little, if anything at all, while Alexander was alive. Hitler, too, is surrounded by myth, much of it self-generated. His joy that Providence had him born an Austrian to demonstrate the oneness of the German people may have been an attempt to rationalize the fact that he was not born in Germany proper. His relationship with his mother and his father is unclear, although he was apparently closer to his mother than to his father. Even his Vienna days, which may have been the most significant of his formative period, are unmarked by clear indications of what occurred.

It is exceedingly difficult—in fact, it is virtually impossible—to construct an adequate and convincing psychological picture of an individual on such flimsy evidence. Were the evidence stronger, a better case could perhaps be made. But much of what we know about the early lives of such revolutionaries is based upon the recollections of people who are most probably prone to embellish the picture that they have drawn of the revolutionary leader in an attempt to make the person look that much more attractive or, as in the case of Hitler particularly, unattractive. Even if one accepts the merits of a psychological or psychoanalytic approach, the information which comes from acquaintances is no substitute for better information from the original source.

A second problem is also of some importance. It must be clearly understood that the revolutionary personality or individual does not operate in a vacuum. In other words, any theory that purports to explain revolutionary behaviour of the leaders of such a movement is a contingent one, tied to the particular situation that exists. As Gibbs has said, 'there can be no leadership in isolation, it is distinctly a quality of a group situation. There can be no leader without followers. An individual's intellectual quality may be very superior and his individual solution of a group problem may be excellent, but he is not a leader until his solution is communicated, and then not until other people are associated with him in giving expression to his ideas'.[39] We are not at all certain what may happen to the individual with a revolutionary propensity if he finds himself with no revolutionary situation. Does he become a bank robber, an eccentric, or a university lecturer? Further, what happens to all of those people with backgrounds which are similar to revolutionary leaders but who never become revolutionaries? The simplest answer is that we do not know. We cannot explain why Lenin or Hitler became the leader and not some other individual of whom nothing at all is known but who might have all, or many, of the same background characteristics.

One solution to the relative importance of situation as opposed to personality is suggested by Kelvin who has developed two hypotheses:

> 'The greater the degree to which the situation and its problems are defined, the greater will be the influence of that situation, and its problems and demands, in determining the individual who will lead. Conversely, the less structured the situation, the less the possibility to predict its demands, the greater will be the contribution of the individual leader's own personality'.[40]

The implication of these hypotheses is that it is in the revolutionary situation in which the personality of the leader may be of overriding significance in determining the course that the revolution may take. But our understanding of the revolutionary personality and its components is not so advanced as to allow us to explain why such individuals become revolutionaries.

The Repression of Instincts

The 1920s and 1930s were particularly fertile decades for those interested in the study of revolutions. Continual tension marked the era following the First World War as a direct result of the success of the Russian Revolution in turning out the old autocracy and establishing a new order, as well as the rise of nationalist and Fascist movements in many of the countries of Europe. Among the leaders of many of the countries there was a fear of possible Bolshevik-type attacks on the regimes in an attempt to emulate the Russian experience. Whether these 'attacks' were real or imagined, over the twenty-year period Communist movements were unsuccessful and leaders began to accept, if not enjoy, the prospects of 'socialism in one country'.

Just as the more contemporary studies of revolution focus on the Chinese, Algerian and Cuban revolutions, all occurrences which have relevance to contemporary political situations, so the writers in the 1920s and 1930s tended to explore the Russian Revolution which did, after all, advertise itself as the harbinger of the coming World Revolution. The reaction to the Russian Revolution was mixed; many welcomed its promises, but still more feared its consequences. Of the leading theorists of society, none is more interesting on this question than Pitirim Sorokin, the Russian sociologist who left his native country following the Revolution. While others have written very interesting books about the revolutionary process,[41] none has been as influential within the field of sociology as Sorokin, so it is on his work that we shall concentrate in this section.

Two points need to be stressed about Sorokin's analysis of revolution. First, Sorokin was a sociologist rather than a psychologist of revolution. He conceived of social change as being normal within society. In his work, 'the most important aspect of the social system are the *law-norms*',[42] which govern behaviour. When these cease to be adequate, revolution is likely to follow. He saw revolution as 'a comparatively sudden, rapid, and violent change of the obsolete official law of the group, or of the institutions and system of values which it represents'.[43] Such a process involves breaking of the 'official law' to bring about the change, a 'more rapid tempo'[44] than ordinary change, and an attack on a broad front of most of the rules that govern behaviour. Further, it involves a wide participation by the population and always includes some violence whether extensive or not too widespread. Essentially, the basic cause of revolution is a system of values that is no longer integrated. Once this happens, a revolutionary situation may develop, but this lack of integration is, for Sorokin, the 'necessary' cause.

Sorokin's analysis of revolution is placed in the psychological category because he is particularly interested in how certain social forces affect the psychology of the 'individual and how in turn the psychology of the individual comes to affect the re-establishment of social restraints upon the community.

The second point to bear in mind is the strong bias that underlines Sorokin's work. One commentator has remarked that Sorokin has 'addressed himself to the basic problems of the age without being sidetracked by the current cult of "objectivity" '.[45] This is an accurate, if understated, description. Sorokin believed that revolutions were avoidable and unnecessary. Further, revolutions inevitably ended in greater oppression than the oppression that may have started them. It is in understanding the reason for this that we can see the 'psychological' mechanism at work.

At the outset of this book, it was argued that revolutions could be conceived in two ways. The first was basically concerned with the transfer of power and whether it was effected violently or non-violently. The second approach looked at revolution as a process during which certain very pronounced changes took place. The work of Sorokin falls into this latter category.

Sorokin perceived of man as having two aspects. First, there is his individual character. His individual aspects may incline him towards love, hate, peace, violence or a whole host of contradictory moods. Essentially, 'the quantity and quality of man's impulses and reflexes render him, singularly, like a bomb full of different kinds of forces and tendencies capable of bursting and presenting us with a picture of wild disorder'.[46] The second aspect of man is his social being, the fact that man lives in a world with other men, and, as a result, man is not perceived as a wild individual.

Three factors have led man to his now 'normal' or social state. First, the long development of what Sorokin refers to as 'cruel historical schooling'[47] has helped to balance the various instincts and drives and bring such drives into 'coordination' with the environment. Second, social control has evolved through a long traditional growth of laws, morals, religious beliefs, and the like, which have effectively restrained the wild beast from behaving as if he were living in the jungle. Third, man has come to find outlets for his aggressive tendencies other than killing the nearest neighbour or stealing what someone else has; hence, the evolution of athletic competitions and other forms of contests.[48]

The revolutionary period may be roughly defined as the time span during which the social veneer, or overlay, is removed from the populace and the wild beast emerges. Sorokin refers to this extinction of habitual patterns as the 'biologization of the behaviour of the multitude'. According to this view 'with the release of these brakes in the form of religious, moral, legal and other habits declared to be prejudices by revolution, the hereditary reflexes attain full freedom'.[19] It is only when the restraining influences, in whatever form they may come, make their reappearance as they must do inevitably, that we may say that the revolution is over and life is back to 'normal'.

Sorokin took a curiously ambivalent view with regard to the

revolutionary process. He argued that revolution may be seen as a 'perversion' and during the period a number of changes occur in the individual's life pattern. New speech patterns come into practice as evidenced by new phrases and words that were unknown in the pre-revolutionary era. A crass refusal to respect the ownership of property in society comes to the fore and those who are located at the lower end of the social and ownership pyramid call on revolutionary phrases to mask their 'animal greed'[50] in stealing other people's property. He notes the alteration of sexual behaviour ranging from the break-up of 'normal' family life, increased divorces, and general sexual perversion and licentiousness. People are unwilling to work, or to help produce what society needs in order to survive. The various authority relations which were built up over generations break down and the 'perversion of the moral consciousness is gloried'[51] in most of the works of the revolution. Above all, this represents a removal of those factors which 'mediated' between man and his environment. Thus,

'Revolutionary society, up to a certain point, loses its memory, the power to "memorize and reproduce". Suddenly it forgets traditions, beliefs, ideas and is cut away from the past. All historical memories, all the mental luggage of the past, are cut off, as if touched by a magical wand. Society forgets its own likeness, its own name (e.g., in the present name of Russia—the Union of the Soviet Republics—the name "Russia" is absent), its national traditions, its heritage, its historical features'.[52]

But while Sorokin was exhibiting a marked contempt for revolution, he was sensitive to what brings the revolutionary process about. We saw that he viewed revolution as being caused by the inability of values to cope with the environment, as does Johnson. This increasing stress upon the value-environment 'relationship' is always triggered by 'the growth of repression of the main instincts of the majority of society, and the impossibility of obtaining for those instincts the necessary minimum of satisfaction'.[53]

There are, for Sorokin, six general types of repression that may lead to revolution. They are: (1) the repression of the alimentary instincts (hunger); (2) the repression of the instinct of property (would the Marxian tradition admit to such an 'instinct'?); (3) the repression of the instinct of self-preservation; (4) the repression of the sex instinct; (5) the repression of the impulse of freedom; and (6) the repression of the instinct of self-expression. This latter 'repression' is of considerable importance because it is assumed that one of the ways in which an elite group can head off a revolutionary movement is by bringing its potential leaders into the elite. If an elite is thought to be reasonably 'open' then those with leadership qualities will not feel as if they are denied entry into that group.

We need not comment on the empirical validity of such basic 'impulses'. There is no unanimity in the social sciences concerning the meaning of 'instincts' and 'impulses' and whether such phenomena exist. For Sorokin, writing when he did, these were popular 'theories'. Thus, the immediate cause of the revolution could be seen in the repression of those instincts (see diagram). Revolution might develop as a response to repression of one or a few of the instincts, but generally it follows the repression of all of the instincts.

Now, up until this point, Sorokin may be considered a predecessor to people such as Johnson. But once he enters into the discussion of the time span of the revolution itself, which was divided into two periods, he leaves that group. The first period represents the span of time in which the old regime collapses and license reigns. The second period or the counter-revolution is that in which order is restored.

When the old regime is destroyed a type of euphoria reigns within the population. The group which enforced the hated laws and permitted the repression of instincts to continue is gone, and a brief period of optimism follows about the 'future and aspirations of mankind'. But this illusion is soon shattered by the reality of the situation. Without social order the situation deteriorates further rather than improving. The death rate increases and the population suffers to a much greater extent than it did in the past. In addition to the general worsening of the situation, the population becomes exhausted with the fervour and license of the first period. 'The mad expenditure of energy during the first period of revolution has, as its results, the speedy impoverishment of the reserve-fund of energy in the human organism.'[54] Because of this combination of the continued repression of the instincts and exhaustion of the individual, groups are called up who will restore order to society once again. Within this second period, a rebuilding process occurs, 'that of the reintegration, resocialization, and consolidation of psychical processes of the structure of the egos'.[55]

'Causes' of the Beginning of the Revolutionary Process

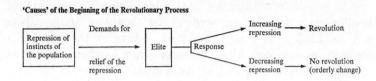

But the return to order always results in a more repressive situation than earlier existed. The previous institutions had not developed accidentally. Society as it had existed 'is the result of centuries of the adjustment of humanity to its environment, and of its individual members to each other; it is the outcome of centuries of efforts, experience and strivings to achieve the best possible forms of social organizations and life'.[56] Since all of that had been torn down, then the rebuilding process is difficult, and the repressive nature of the new order exists precisely because it has replaced a 'genuine' overlay of civilization.

Ultimately, Sorokin admitted, at least implicitly, to his ambivalence. Regimes could be bad, but revolutions, he argued, are worse because 'the cost in human life, suffering and cultural values is so great that it is evident that orderly, evolutionary processes of change are distinctly preferable from every standpoint'.[57]

In many ways, Sorokin's approach to revolution may strike the reader is being naïve. If the strident nature of his major work on the subject was replaced by a more reasoned argument later, the message is still the same : revolutions are bad. But where Sorokin was particularly interesting was in his analysis of the stages of the revolutionary process. His focus on the period after the old regime is overthrown and the psychological 'need' of the members of the populace for a restoration of order is a theme that has not been treated widely in the literature. It is a problem to which we shall return in the concluding chapter.

The Theory of Rising Expectations

It now seems to be part of conventional wisdom that revolutions do not begin when people in society are at the ebb of their existence. Certainly more people have been forced to endure incredibly difficult life-situations than those who have risen in order to destroy that which appears to be oppressing them.

People have lived in appalling conditions for centuries yet most have accepted, at least as evidenced by the relatively low incidence of revolutions, their collective lot and left it to the few to pursue revolutionary ends. One reason for this lack of revolutionary zeal is suggested in the theory of rising expectations which, as now interpreted, advances the idea that 'revolutions are most likely to occur when a prolonged period of objective economic and social development is followed by a short period of sharp reversal'.[58] The 'father' of this theory was de Tocqueville whose contribution to our understanding of pluralism was discussed earlier. But de Tocqueville's 'theory' is somewhat different from the proposition stated above. It may be argued that there are two theories of rising expectations with the first being advanced by de Tocqueville and Brinton while the second theory is a modification of the first by Davies and, more recently, by Tanter and Midlarsky.

The seeds of the theory of rising expectations come out of de Tocqueville's analysis of how and why the French Revolution came about. To de Tocqueville there was much that could appear confusing about the French Revolution. The most puzzling aspect of it was that it occurred during a period in which the French citizens were not suffering from a stagnant or weak economy, nor was political oppression particularly pronounced. If anything, the regime had, over the course of the latter part of the eighteenth century, moved to loosen the types of political restrictions that had been practised earlier. As if to emphasize this and the previous assertion concerning the general economic condition, 'those parts of France in which the improvement in the standard of living was most pronounced were the chief centres of the revolutionary movement'.[59]

Although the first part of the eighteenth century had been stagnant with regard to general growth, 'some thirty or forty years before the Revolution, . . . a change came over the scene'.[60] The economic situation achieved a 'take off' in which people were no longer satisfied with their lot, but were instead determined to improve their situations. Further, with the general growth and development in the standard of living, Frenchmen came to resemble one another to a much greater degree than in the past. Life had come to be directed from Paris. Thus, any explosions there could come to be felt throughout France—and, ultimately, throughout the Western world. Hence, the characterization of revolutions as products of the modern age as a result of wider-ranging communications networks and loyalty to a central notion of nationhood.[61]

What was remarkable about the widely felt increase in prosperity was the presence of archaic laws and customs that could have hindered the general economic growth. The government machinery was inefficient and out-of-date, but de Tocqueville maintained it survived as long as it did because it was able to fulfil two basic functions. First, the government had ceased being despotic but still retained the capability of maintaining order throughout the state. Second, 'the nation possessed an upper class that was the finest, most enlightened of the day and a social system under which every man could get rich if he set his mind to it and kept intact the wealth he had acquired'.[62] Yet despite the increasing prosperity and the government tendency to reduce restrictions, the population was not satisfied or content; instead, it was increasingly hostile to the regime because the regime was seen to be archaic. It was obvious that a revolution was coming. From this, de Tocqueville derived the following theory :

> 'For it is not always when things are going from bad to worse that revolutions break out. On the contrary, it oftener happens that when a people has put up with an oppressive rule over a long period without protest suddenly finds the government relaxing its pressure, it takes up arms against it. Thus the social order overthrown by a revolution is almost always better than the one immediately preceding it, and experience teaches us that, generally speaking, the most perilous moment for a bad government is one when it seeks to mend its ways. Only consummate statecraft can enable a king to save his throne when after a long spell of oppressive rule he sets to improving the lot of his subjects. Patiently endured so long as it seemed beyond redress, a grievance comes to appear intolerable once the possibility of removing it crosses men's minds'.[63]

As the life situation improves, men expect that it will continue to improve. If they perceive that it could decline or that it is likely to be hindered by an obstreperous or inefficient government, then they will take action to remove the potential impediment to progress. If that impediment happens to be the government, then the government must go.

While de Tocqueville was attempting to suggest a 'general

rule' about the incidence of revolutions, using the French Revolution as his case, a 'theory' requires several cases, many if possible, for confirmation. This has been provided by later scholars who have dealt with the question. Crane Brinton, for example, analysed four revolutions, the American, French, Russian and English, and found that the revolutions 'were not born in societies economically retrograde; on the contrary, they took place in societies economically progressive'.[64] Brinton was aware of the condition of many groups within these societies among whom poverty was endemic. But in terms of the early stages and generation of the revolution these poorest and most miserable people do not appear to have been very important. He noted that, within the French and Russian cases, there had always existed periods of famine and starvation which frequently resulted in riots but never in revolutions except in the time periods with which he was most concerned. The revolutions occurred largely because of 'a feeling on the part of some of the chief enterprising groups that their opportunities for getting on in this world are unduly limited by political arrangements'.[65]

Brinton shrank from asserting that this was the sole cause of revolution for many factors need to be taken into account which may also contribute to revolution. Further, Brinton was rather hesitant to push for the validity of his conclusions with regard to a full-fledged revolutionary theory since he was concentrating only on four great revolutions. Nevertheless, his findings with regard to the rising expectations of the population could add to its credibility as a proper theory of why revolutions occur.

Davies, also, has contributed to our understanding of this particular theory although, strictly speaking, Davies is really referring to what factors bring about a rising whereas Brinton's concern was with events triggering a revolutionary process. Davies argues that when people are at the poorest state of existence they are unlikely to revolt. 'Far from making people into revolutionaries, enduring poverty makes for concern with one's solitary self or solitary family, at best a resignation or mute despair at worst.'[66] He cites the numerous studies of the lives of people in concentration and extermination camps in World War II and their generally acquiescing behaviour when faced with the prospect of death.

The formula that Davies develops is known as the 'J-curve' because of the particular shape of the line of 'actual need satisfaction'. Basically, during a period of rising expectation, the *expected* need satisfaction line continues to rise. Running parallel to this, and close to it, is actual *need* satisfaction. As long as people are receiving at least a considerable part of what they are expecting to receive, then they are unlikely to revolt. But if the actual need satisfaction begins to decline while the expectation of satisfaction continues to rise, a wide gap begins to develop between the two. When the gap 'between what people want and what they get'[67] becomes intolerable, they will rise up to destroy whatever it is that is in the way of what they want to get.

Tanter and Midlarsky have generally agreed with the findings of Davies, but they have attempted to modify and refine the theory by arguing that there are various types of revolution, ranging from the palace revolution to the mass revolution. Such revolutions vary according to the degree of mass participation, the duration of the revolution, the level of violence, and the intentions of the insurgents.[68] They argue that 'a revolution generally occurs after a period of instability, and it is suggested . . . that the form of a revolution is dependent on the degree of political instability which exists prior to its occurrence'.[69] That a revolution occurs after a period of instability represents no great contribution to our general understanding of the subject. What they do suggest, however, that is of interest, is a refinement of Davies' notion. They are arguing that the wider the gap between expected and actual need satisfaction the more extensive the revolution is likely to be.[70]

Essentially, Davies and the later work by Tanter and Midlarsky modify the findings of de Tocqueville and Brinton. The earlier hypotheses argue that revolutions tend to occur after an extended period of growth while for Davies and Tanter and Midlarsky revolution is likely to occur after an extended period of growth followed by a sharp decline in the fortunes of a particular system. Both hypotheses are rather different than that which was suggested by Sorokin since in the 'repression of instincts' it may be assumed that people revolt when they believe that they cannot take any more repression rather than when their life situation has been improving over a long period of time. Thus, the question arises over whether one of these 'theories' may be confirmed and the other denied.

Several questions may be raised about either theory of rising expectations. The first and most apparent problem with both sets of psychological theories is their dependence upon aggregate data to explain individual reactions and behaviour. This is a problem to which we will return in the next section.

Second, Davies and Tanter and Midlarsky make some rather intriguing references to the Marxian notion of revolution: they argue that their theories have either 'modified' or corrected some of Marx's basic assumptions. Yet upon careful reading of their works, a different result emerges which suggests that they have seriously misread or misunderstood what Marx wrote. Davies, for example, suggests 'that revolutions need both a period of rising expectations and a succeeding period in which they are frustrated qualifies substantially the main Marxian notion that revolutions occur after progressive degradation . . .'.[71] Tanter and Midlarsky suggest that 'the Marxist . . . sees revolution as a product of irresistible historical forces, which culminate in a struggle between the bourgeoisie and proletariat'.[72] The thrust of these two works is that Marx was wrong about revolutions since revolutions do not occur when a class of people is getting progressively poorer and more miserable.

What these theorists have done, however, is assume that the revolution which makes the proletariat ascendant is the prototype of the revolution that makes the bourgeoisie ascendant when, ironically, the type of revolution that they have considered would seem to be precisely what Marx would have called the transition from feudalism to capitalism. As we have seen, Marx suggested that the bourgeoisie was in itself a revolutionary class which began to develop in feudal society and eventually transformed that society into the capitalist epoch. Starting as a class dominated by feudal lords, it eventually destroyed the dominant or ruling class. The bourgeoisie acted to destroy the feudal rulers precisely because those rulers stood in the way of progress. By utilizing the types of examples, or cases, that they do, the theorists in the rising expectations tradition have not debunked Marx at all; instead, they have tended to bolster his argument with regard to the revolutionary tendency of the bourgeoisie but, through what appears to be a misunderstanding of the Marxian notion of revolution, they have failed to grasp this point. This, however, should not suggest that the theory of rising expectations is invalid; it merely argues that the interpretation of the Marxian idea of revolution is mistaken and, therefore, the conclusion that this theory replaces the Marxian theory is untenable.

Where the theory is incomplete is in its failure to determine what is an intolerable gap between expected and actual need satisfaction. While Tanter and Midlarsky do make an effort to explain that the wider the gap, the more violent and widespread the revolution is likely to be, we have not yet come to an understanding why some societies can tolerate a very wide gap and others cannot. Is it due to a tradition of suffering? Is it contingent upon the size and disposition of the armed forces? We are, unfortunately, back to a tautology: the revolution was very violent because the gap between expected and actual need satisfaction was very wide, and we know it was wide because of the violence of the revolution.

But the J-curve specifically, and theory of rising expectations generally, is not uninteresting. While the criticisms stand, with more to follow, the theorists may have found a uniformity among societies that experience risings. One cannot infer from this a general 'feeling' among the people in those countries that they are frustrated or unhappy about impeded progress, but 'the J-curve of actual satisfaction of needs is an analytical tool that historians can usefully bear in mind as they probe the violent social upheavals of the past'.[73]

The Theory of Relative Deprivation

A more recent entry into the field of psychological theories of revolution is the theory of relative deprivation which appears to have gained in acceptance in the wake of the civil disturbances in the United States during the middle and late 1960s. This theory has particular interest for us because it has, ostensibly, been 'proved' through the application of a variety of empirical techniques over a whole range of aggregate indicators of economic performance and social change. Scholars such as Gurr, the Fierabends and Nesvold have constructed elaborate and often ingenious models of social upheaval and stability in order to demonstrate the correctness of this theory. Despite the very impressive work—and, paradoxically, because of the sheer volume of it—numerous questions arise about the validity of the theory and the particular indicators that have been used in order to validate it. At the outset it should be noted that the criticisms that are made here may also be directed toward the J-curve theory that was just examined because the theory of relative deprivation subsumes the J-curve: the latter is merely one example of relative deprivation in a society.

It is exceedingly difficult to cope with the volume of work that is concerned with relative deprivation. We shall only be able to present the theory in brief form and criticize some of its basic assumptions and findings; but it should be realized that the magnitude of work does not relate favourably to the contribution this literature makes to an understanding of why revolutions occur. On balance, we shall see that extensive efforts have produced very little of theoretical interest.

Criticism may be applied to the findings of the scholars at different levels. For example, the professional social scientist would have great difficulty accepting some of the operational indices and statistical methods that some of the main exponents of the theory have utilized. The student of revolution who is generally unacquainted with such methods would be concerned with more general problems. Does the theory fulfil all of the requirements that have been suggested for proper validation of the theory? This would, of course, also be of interest to the social scientist. All would be concerned with the possible triviality of the theory: does the theory really tell us very much?

The standard definition of relative deprivation is provided by Gurr:

> '. . . the necessary precondition for violent civil conflict is relative deprivation, defined as actors' perception of discrepancy between their *value expectations* and their environment's apparent *value capabilities*. Value expectations are the goods and conditions of life to which people believe they are justifiably entitled. The referents of value capabilities are to be found largely in the social and physical environment: they are the conditions that determine people's perceived chances of getting or keeping the values they legitimately expect to attain'.[74]

The definition flows from the frustration-aggression hypothesis which states 'that the occurrence of aggressive behaviour always presupposes the existence of frustration, and contrariwise, that the existence of frustration always leads to some form of aggression'.[75] An important derived hypothesis suggests that the greater the degree of frustration the more aggressive the response is likely to be. This point relates directly to the modification of the J-curve theory by Tanter and Midlarsky as well as to the general theory of relative deprivation. Thus, just as people are likely to react in an aggressive manner when they feel frustrated, 'the occurrence of civil violence presupposes the likelihood of relative deprivation among substantial numbers of individuals in a society; concomitantly, the more severe is relative deprivation, the greater are the likelihood and intensity of civil violence'.[76]

Strictly speaking the theory of relative deprivation is not a theory of revolution; instead, it is a theory that purports to explain civil strife or violence. Gurr has argued that 'revolutions are but one of an extraordinarily numerous variety of inter-related forms of strife . . .'.[77] What Gurr is suggesting is not unlike what Johnson argued earlier: revolution is only one form of violence. For Gurr, as well as for other theorists of relative deprivation, the same factors that may be present when a revolution occurs may also be present in other forms of civil strife.

Gurr has utilized the findings of research by Rummel and Tanter[78] to set up his threefold typology of civil strife. The three categories are turmoil, conspiracy and internal war. Turmoil is the most spontaneous of risings or rebellions which includes such occurrences as strikes, riots or demonstrations. Conspiracy refers to organized activities such as coups, assassinations or 'small-scale guerrilla wars'.[79] Internal war, which might include revo-lution (although a conspiracy may certainly be part of a revolution) refers to 'large-scale, organized, focused civil strife, almost always accompanied by extensive violence, including large-scale terrorism and guerrilla wars, civil wars, private wars and large-scale revolts'.[80] To determine the magnitude of the civil strife Gurr has argued that it is necessary to examine three facets of strife. First, one must examine the extent or 'pervasive-ness' of the strife or how many people are participating in it. Second, how long has the strife lasted? Third, the researcher needs to consider the intensity of the strife in terms of its cost in human casualties.

We need not comment extensively on the obvious difficulties in utilizing such indicators. Body counts that are taken to deter-mine total casualties and measures of how many are actively involved in a strife situation are notoriously inaccurate. But the researchers are aware of these difficulties. What is interesting is that the real question that is being answered does not ask 'why men rebel?' or even 'what are the causes of civil strife?'. Essen-tially, Gurr, the leading theorist of relative deprivation, is really attempting to explain the magnitude of civil strife, i.e. the factors that explain the extent of violence. Thus, his operational effort differs from the original conceptual question rather widely.

The magnitude of civil strife or the extent of violence as

measured by the indicators that Gurr has used is not the same as an attempt to measure, or even predict, the extent of the change that may occur. In fact, a social situation may involve a very great 'amount' of violence and result in very little change in a society. Further, the costs of extensive violence may be very high. Gurr and Graham have suggested that while the Bolshevik seizure of power took Russia out of the war (which they identify as the main 'immediate grievance' of the Russian people), the costs were enormous and included such things as 'civil war, famine, and totalitarian political control'.[81] Of course, it may be suggested that costs are relative just as is deprivation and it is not within the scope of social science just now to weigh the costs to the Russian people of the provisional government's activities which did not involve an ending of the war. It is possible that for the Russian people at the time an end to the war was 'worth' the difficulties that may have been imposed by the new regime. This apparent antipathy to violence may be evidence of the same type of bias in the school of relative deprivation as in the functionalist and mass society schools.

Once the basic definition of the variable to be explained, i.e., the magnitude of civil strife, is understood, some discussion of the operational indicators is profitable because what may be a fundamental flaw in the work becomes apparent. Gurr maintains that relative deprivation is the cause of civil strife. Other factors may enter into the formula, such as legitimacy and social and structural facilitation.

Where a certain amount of disquiet may arise is in the definition of deprivation. In one work, for example, Gurr identifies measures of persisting deprivation and short-term deprivation which account for the magnitude of civil strife. These measures are constructed from a variety of aggregate indicators that are used in much of the research in social science. The indicators of long-term deprivation are (1) economic discrimination and (2) political discrimination, (3) potential separation which attempts to tap the significance of 'historically separatist regional or ethnic groups',[82] (4) the dependence upon foreign capital by the country in question, (5) religious cleavages, and (6) lack of educational opportunity. The short-term indicators are (1) short-term trends in trade values, 1957–60 compared with 1950–7, and (2) the same in 1960–3 compared with 1950–60, (3) inflation in 1960–3 compared with 1958–61, (4) the GNP growth rates of 1960–63 compared with the 1950s, (5) an index of 'adverse' economic conditions 1960–3 which includes factors such as 'crop failures, unemployment, etc.' and 'new restrictions on political participation and representation by the regime'.[83]

These are described only to indicate the range of factors that are included by Gurr in his analysis. Each of the other general conceptual variables such as legitimacy and social and cultural facilitation includes such indices as well. These indices may be criticized for what they include. The legitimacy index, for example, is the sum of 'character' and 'durability' scores. Character refers largely to the origin of the national political institutions and requires judgements concerning the nature of the origins and the reforms that may have changed them. The 'durability' scale examines 'the number of generations the regime had persisted as of 1960 without substantial, abrupt reformation . . .'.[84] We are provided with no definition of 'substantial' or 'abrupt' or 'reformation'. As a result it is rather difficult to comment on the usefulness of such indices and how much they really do explain. Further, Gurr's use of the particular statistical methods with the type of scales that he constructs is at least questionable.[85]

But, as indicated earlier, these questions are more relevant to the social scientist than to the student of revolution who is unfamiliar with some of the basic requirements of research design. What is critical is the question of inferring individual behavioural tendencies, i.e., the willingness to participate in violent activities from aggregate indicators. If relative deprivation is a psychological concept, can an 'adverse trade balance' be utilized as an indicator of such deprivation? As Muller has suggested :

'. . . developing an operational system based on macro-indicators is not the most felicitous way to begin testing a theory conceptualized largely in terms of psychological characteristics of individuals. Even if there were macro-indicators that would permit reasonably valid inferences about the psychological variables presumed to affect political violence, tests based on such macro-indicators would be most useful in the theory confirmation process after the theoretical propositions had been subjected to intensive micro analysis, so that the dynamics of the behaviour of individuals were thoroughly understood.[86]

Muller also has devised his own theory of the potential for

political violence which is based largely on the notion of legitimacy.

But the point that Muller makes is a telling one and one with which Gurr is certainly not comfortable. In fact, Gurr attempts to deal with the problem and writes that 'it is unquestionably necessary to test all hypotheses, including psychological ones, in a variety of ways, for example to determine whether the inferentially-deprived groups are those most likely to engage in strife, and to ask highly frustrated individuals whether they would, or have, taken part in collective violence'.[87] While the identification of 'highly frustrated individuals' may present the social scientist with some intriguing and interesting problems, the thought of wide-ranging surveys covering all countries of the world is probably not a realizable goal even if the problem of cross-national comparability could be overcome, so in the absence of such research, Gurr's findings could be the best we have. Yet 'the best we have' may not be good enough to reach the types of conclusions about relative deprivation that Gurr reaches.

This is not a small problem; but the Fierabends and Nesvold have attempted to confront it. Instead of discussing relative deprivation, they utilize the frustration-aggression hypothesis but raise it to the level of the community and deal with 'systemic frustration'. This refers to

'(1) as frustration interfering with the attainment and maintenance of social goals, aspirations, and values; (2) as frustration simultaneously experienced by members of social aggregates and hence also complex social systems; and (3) as frustration or strain that is produced within the structures and processes of social systems'.[88]

In order to demonstrate the effects of 'systemic frustration' they examine a whole range of socio-economic and political indicators that might explain violence (the 'definition' of systemic frustration) in the society. Their research indicates that countries that are 'modernizing' rapidly are the most prone to violence (although this is not uniform across all variables), and once a particular 'threshold' of modernity is reached the violence is likely to diminish. They suggest that certain variables are better indicators of violence, and they are able to conclude that the probable reason for a high level of violence in the United States reflects the relative development of different subcultures in the country, particularly the black communities.

In addition to the anthropomorphic difficulties that are raised, the notion of 'systemic frustration' operationalized in terms of levels of violence is an interesting one but rather difficult to comprehend. Is it useful to speak of 'systemic frustration' or does this pose the same problem that is found in concepts such as societal goals or the structural-functional notion of the main goal of a system being self-maintenance?

We have raised a number of questions about the theory of relative deprivation that may be reiterated. First, it is not really a theory of revolution, and it may be a questionable assumption to suggest that the same range of factors is responsible for all civil strife. Until we know more, this remains an empirical question. Second, many of the indices of such concepts as short-term and persistent deprivation and legitimacy are highly questionable. Further—and this refers to Gurr's work—the methodological approaches that he utilizes are particularly questionable given the nature of the indices that he has constructed. Fourth, aggregate or macro-level indicators are clearly not adequate when inferring certain individual behavioural patterns.

Finally, an extraordinarily large volume of literature has been produced which says relatively little : when people feel that they are not getting that to which they believe they are rightly entitled they are prone to revolt. The 'theory' cannot establish a proper if → then sequence because the theorists are unable to identify that point at which the populace has 'had enough'. They do suggest that the more 'frustrated' people feel the more violent the response is likely to be, but we are still unable to identify the 'breaking point', and why this 'breaking point' varies from society to society.

Conclusion

In a sense the psychological theories and models of revolution are simply the reverse side of the coin of the sociological theories. They seek to explain why people respond as they do to certain societal conditions. Without some changes in society when such changes are demanded, be it in the environment or the value system, people are more likely to act in a revolutionary or 'violent' manner. Even the studies that focus on the individual revolutionary leader must deal with the notion of that individual acting in the context of his society. If theories of the revolutionary personality are correct, then countless Lenins and Maos maturing in non-revolutionary societies may have become unhappy eccentrics or dissidents, criminals and social deviants, students and academics, or chairmen of the boards of large and possibly dynamic companies. If there is no revolutionary situation there is no revolutionary leader.

The psychological approaches that deal with the masses tend to clash. For Sorokin people revolt when they think that they are miserable. During the revolutionary era they learn that they were not nearly as miserable as they had thought they were, and when they make this discovery they try to re-establish order in an effort to reduce misery—the misery that they have brought upon themselves. For the other theorists the crisis comes when the hopes of the populace are, for some reason, greater than the actual reward that they are receiving. The populace will act then to relieve their situation through violence if the violence is perceived as instrumental in attaining the desired goals.

Implicit in these theories is the same assumption that is found in the functionalist and mass society theories. Revolutions are probably avoidable. If people can be satisfied then the demands for change will subside. If the 'urge' to rebel stems from a feeling that the government is denying valued goods to the individual then a perception that the authorities are acting to relieve certain problems or restraints may relieve that urge provided the needs of the individual are actually satisfied or perceived to be satisfied.

Notes and References

1 Robert Conquest, *The Great Terror: Stalin's Purge of the Thirties*, Harmondsworth, Middlesex, 1971. First published 1968, pp. 97–8.

2 R. J. Lifton, *Revolutionary Immortality: Mao Tse-Tung and the Chinese Cultural Revolution*, Harmondsworth, Middlesex, 1970. First published 1968, p. 22.

3 Lewis J. Edinger, 'Political science and political biography: reflections on the study of leadership, I', *Journal of Politics*, 26, 1964, p. 423.

4 See Lewis J. Edinger and Donald Searing, 'Social background in elite analysis: a methodological inquiry', *American Political Science Review*, 56, 1967, pp. 428–45; and Donald Searing, 'The comparative study of elite socialisation', *Comparative Political Studies*, I, 1969, pp. 471–500.

5 See, for example, William Quandt, 'The comparative study of political elites', *Sage Professional Papers in Comparative Politics*,

ed. by Harry Eckstein and Ted Robert Gurr, *I*, 1970, pp. 179–242.

6 In my own research, I have found marginality to be not particularly useful in explaining the development of the revolutionary elite in Ireland. See A. S. Cohan, *The Irish Political Elite*, Dublin, 1972, esp. pp. 44–9.

7 Lewis J. Edinger, *Kurt Schumacher: A Study in Personality and Political Behaviour*, Stanford, 1965.

8 Erik H. Erikson, *Childhood and Society*, Harmondsworth, Middlesex, 1965. First published 1950, p. 394.

9 *Ibid.*, p. 395.

10 E. Victor Wolfenstein, *The Revolutionary Personality: Lenin, Trotsky, Gandhi*, Princeton, New Jersey, 1967, p. 21.

11 Bertram D. Wolfe, *Three Who Made a Revolution*, Harmondsworth, Middlesex, 1966. First published 1948, pp. 61–5.

12 Isaac Deutscher, *Lenin's Childhood*, London, 1970, p. 26. There are many books that may serve as useful introductions to a study of Lenin. Perhaps the most useful and interesting is Leon Trotsky's *The Young Lenin*, trans. by Max Eastman, first published Newton Abbot, Devon, reprinted 1972. Also very useful is Adam B. Ulam, *Lenin and the Bolsheviks*, London, 1969; first published in 1965.

13 See Erikson, *Childhood and Society*, pp. 239–268.

14 Wolfenstein, *The Revolutionary Personality: Lenin, Trotsky, Gandhi*, p. 41.

15 Erik Erikson, *Young Man Luther: A Study in Psychoanalysis and History*, New York, 1958, p. 123.

16 Wolfenstein, *The Revolutionary Personality: Lenin, Trotsky, Gandhi*, p. 97.

17 James Maxton, *Lenin*, Edinburgh, 1934, p. 17. Emphasis mine.

18 Louis Fischer, *The Life of Lenin*, London, 1965, pp. 11–2.

19 Trotsky, *The Young Lenin*, p. 114.

20 *Ibid.*, p. 118.

21 Maxton, *Lenin*, pp. 18–9.

22 Deutscher, *Lenin's Childhood*, p. 65.

23 Trotsky, *The Young Lenin*, p. 119.

24 Wolfenstein, *The Revolutionary Personality: Lenin, Trotsky, Gandhi*, p. 98.

25 *Ibid.*, pp. 103–24.

26 Wolfe, *Three Who Made a Revolution*, p. 56.

27 Adolf Hitler, *Mein Kampf*, trans. by Ralph Manheim, Boston, 1943, p. 10.

28 Alan Bullock, *Hitler: A Study in Tyranny*, Harmondsworth, Middlesex, 1962. First published 1952, p. 30.

29 Hitler, *Mein Kampf*, p. 18.

30 *Ibid.*

31 Erikson, *Childhood and Society*, p. 320.

32 Bullock, *Hitler: A Study in Tyranny*, p. 392.

33 *Ibid.*

34 See Werner Maser, *Hitler*, trans. by Peter and Betty Ross, London, 1973.

35 Wolfenstein, *The Revolutionary Personality: Lenin, Trotsky, Gandhi*, p. 167.

36 *Ibid.*, p. 168.

37 *Ibid.*, p. 238.

38 Deutscher, *Lenin's Childhood*, p. 67.

39 C. A. Gibb, 'The principles and traits of leadership', from *Leadership*, ed. by C. A. Gibb, Harmondsworth, Middlesex, 1969, p. 210.

40 Peter Kelvin, *The Bases of Social Behaviour: An Approach in Terms of Order and Value*, London, 1970, p. 42.

41 See, for example, Lyford P. Edwards, *The Natural History of Revolution*, New York, 1965, first published in 1927; George Sawyer Pettee, *The Process of Revolution*, New York, 1971, first published 1938; and Crane Brinton, *The Anatomy of Revolution*, New York, 1960. First published 1938.

42 Charles P. Laomis, 'Social change and social systems', from *Sociological Theory, Values and Sociocultural Change: Essays in Honour of Pitirim Sorokin*, ed. by Edward A. Tiryakian, New York, 1963, p. 212.

43 Pitirim Sorokin, *Society, Culture and Personality*, New York, 1969. First published 1947, p. 481.

44 *Ibid.*

45 Arthur K. Davis, 'Lessons from Sorokin', from *Sociological*

Theory, Values and Sociocultural Change . . ., p. 5. See also Lyford Edward, *The Natural History of Revolution*, p. 130.

46 Pitirim Sorokin, *The Sociology of Revolution*, New York, 1967. First published 1925, p. 22.

47 *Ibid.*

48 *Ibid.*

49 *Ibid.*, p. 35.

50 *Ibid.*, p. 80.

51 *Ibid.*, p. 149.

52 *Ibid.*, pp. 179–80.

53 *Ibid.*, p. 367.

54 *Ibid.*, pp. 409–10.

55 Sorokin, *Society, Culture and Personality*, p. 490.

56 Sorokin, *The Sociology of Revolution*, p. 411.

57 Sorokin, *Society, Culture and Personality*, p. 495.

58 James C. Davies, 'Toward a theory of revolution', *American Sociological Review*, 27, 1962, p. 6.

59 Alexis de Tocqueville, *The Ancien Régime and the French Revolution*, trans. by Stuart Gilbert, London, 1966, p. 195.

60 *Ibid.*, p. 190.

61 See Hannah Arendt, *On Revolution*, New York, 1965.

62 De Tocqueville, *The Ancien Régime and the French Revolution*, p. 194.

63 *Ibid.*, p. 196.

64 Brinton, *The Anatomy of Revolution*, p. 33.

65 *Ibid.*, p. 35.

66 Davies, 'Toward a theory of revolution', p. 7.

67 *Ibid.*, p. 6.

68 Raymond Tanter and Manus Midlarsky, 'A theory of revolution', *Journal of Conflict Resolution, 11*, p. 265.

69 *Ibid.*, p. 269.

70 *Ibid.*, p. 271.

71 Davies, 'Toward a theory of revolution', p. 17.

72 Tanter and Midlarsky, 'A theory of revolution', p. 265.

73 Lawrence Stone, *The Causes of the English Revolution: 1529–1642*, London, 1972, p. 16.

74 Ted Robert Gurr, 'Psychological factors in civil violence', *World Politics, 20,* 1967–68, pp. 252–3; see also Gurr, *Why Men Rebel,* Princeton, New Jersey, 1970, p. 24.

75 John Dollard, Leonard Doob, Neal F. Miller, O. H. Mowrer and Robert Sears, *Frustration and Aggression,* New Haven, 1939, p. 1.

76 Gurr, 'Psychological factors in civil violence', p. 254.

77 *Ibid.,* p. 246.

78 Raymond Tanter, 'Dimensions of conflict behaviour within and between nations—1958–60', and R. J. Rummel, 'Dimensions of conflict behaviour within nations, 1946–59', *Journal of Conflict Resolution, 10,* 1966, pp. 41–73.

79 Ted Robert Gurr, 'A causal model of civil strife : a comparative analysis using new indices', *American Political Science Review, 62,* 1968, p. 1107.

80 *Ibid.*

81 Hugh Davies Graham and Ted Robert Gurr, 'Conclusion', from *The History of Violence in America: Historical and Comparative Perspectives,* ed. by Graham and Davis, New York, 1969, p. 812.

82 Gurr, 'A causal model of civil strife', p. 1110.

83 *Ibid.,* p. 1111.

84 *Ibid.,* p. 1115.

85 For a discussion of the level of measurement required for use of regression and correlation analysis see Hubert M. Blalock, *Social Statistics,* New York, 1960, Ch. 2, 17, 18.

86 Edward N. Muller, 'A test of a partial theory of potential for political violence', *American Political Science Review, 66,* 1972, p. 929.

87 Gurr, 'A causal model of civil strife', p. 1123.

88 Ivo K. Fierabend, Rosalind L. Fierabend and Betty A. Nesvold, 'Social change and political violence : cross-national patterns', from Graham and Gurr (eds), *The History of Violence in America: Historical and Comparative Perspectives,* p. 635.

Chapter 9
Conclusion

Unless one is a Marxist, the definitive theory of revolution has yet to be written. We may describe the richness of the literature that deals with the subject, but it is a richness associated with detailed analyses of revolutions such as the French, American, Russian or Chinese rather than the common features that might underlie all of the cases. Unfortunately, the main feature that may be noted about much of the theoretical analysis of revolutions is its thinness and triviality. Effectively, all that the theories tell us is that if people are greatly angered they may have a tendency to rebel. We are left with uncertainty about what it is that angers people, why some groups rebel with apparently little provocation as, perhaps, the colonists did in the American Revolution, or why other groups in society can tolerate great injustice and misery without initiating violent action as in Russian society during the period following the emancipation of the serfs in 1861. With the exception of the Marxian tradition, the theories tend to leave the reader with the fairly disappointed feeling that perhaps the whole exercise of reading and examining the theory was not worth the effort.

The Marxian tradition is probably more satisfactory because of the logic of an approach that begins with an assumption that revolution is the inevitable consequence of certain social forces. Thus, when revolutionary movements develop, the Marxist is not surprised. Yet, as was indicated in Chapters 4 and 5, the nagging questions concerning the mistaken predictions and expectations do remain, and the anticipated rising of the workers in the advanced industrial societies still seems the most unlikely revolution of all despite increasing social and economic problems in those societies.

The functionalist model that we examined is problematical from the very outset because of an inability to decide what a revolution is. Ultimately settling on an implicit definition of revolution as a violent rising which may or may not entail social change, the reason it seems to be able to account for the occurrence of the rising is a failure of values to explain the environment (or vice versa) combined with an elite that is unwilling or unable to cope with the demand for change. Whether we are to assume from this that all other societies are 'functioning' properly, as indicated by the non-occurrence of such risings, remains unstated, yet implicit. But to tell us that the reason a revolution occurs is because there is something (unstated) causing value-environment dyssynchronization and the political elite cannot cope with the new pressures is not particularly adventurous and really not much of a model from the standpoint of establishing causal relationships.

The mass society theorists provide us with more interesting fodder than do the functionalists because they work more closely with an actual case, the rise of the Nazis, and possibly two if we include the aggrandisement of power by Stalin in the Soviet Union. Yet how they reach their conclusions particularly with regard to Germany is something of a mystery. Virtually all of the evidence seems to suggest that the Nazi rise to power was the result of a sharp polarization of class ties rather than the breakdown of the traditional class structure. It is true that the older class leaders may have been swept aside by the events that occurred between 1919 and 1933, but such leaders were replaced by new leaders of the class groupings. That the Nazis and, perhaps, Stalin later 'massified' society once in firm control of the societies they governed is an argument which we need not consider here. What is of importance is that the presence of a mass society does not seem to have preceded the rise of the mass movement. It may, instead, have been the result of rampant pluralism with all of the rules of fair play tossed aside.

The psychological approaches are also problematical. We may dismiss Sorokin's formulation for the moment because, empirically, the perceived repression of the instincts does not seem attractive. Nor does Sorokin's self-proclaimed non-objectivity add a great deal to his incisiveness. The rising expectations, J-curve, and relative deprivation approaches, however, cannot be dismissed so facilely. So much research has gone into the propagation of the theories that great care must be exercised in analysing what they are ostensibly telling us. But a common fault seems to run through all of the analyses, a fault that is most blatantly obvious in Gurr's work. One cannot infer a feeling of deprivation, which is a psychological variable, from indicators which are developed using aggregate figures. To suggest that adverse national trade balances are a legitimate part of an index of short-term deprivation is indeed questionable. Admittedly, it is very difficult to construct an index that may be utilized in the type of cross-national analysis that Gurr attempts. Nevertheless, his indicators do not really tap the feeling of deprivation an individual may have.

If we examine the J-curve approach, it is again questionable whether the lines of expected and actual need satisfaction may be drawn from the types of data that are available. Further, if twenty students were required to apply the J-curve to the Russian Revolution, it is doubtful that any two would come up with the same description even from the standpoint of choosing similar starting dates if the date were not specified beforehand.

A further criticism of all of the theories and models other than the Marxist is that they are not, in the final analysis, concerned with social change. They focus instead on the question of why violent means are utilized by the masses against the political elite. This, in itself, may be an interesting question, but it is not the same question as 'why do revolutions occur?'. Finally, they may not even have answered the question concerning the occurrence of violence very satisfactorily.

The psychological approaches that concentrate on revolutionary leaders are inevitably interesting, if for no other reason than because the aura that tends to surround those leaders holds a certain fascination for students. Yet we are left with very little of theoretical interest once we learn that there is little truth in the attribution of certain characteristics to the revolutionary leader and countless numbers of individuals may have displayed the same characteristics as the revolutionary leaders yet the unknown figures never became revolutionaries. Additionally, we have the understanding that if there is no 'revolutionary situation' the presence of the individual with the revolutionary personality, if such a description is valid, is of no particular consequence.

The Marxian tradition, taken in its loosest sense as a model of revolution, may be the most useful of the notions of revolution that we have discussed. If 'class' is utilized in a wide conceptual sense rather than in the narrower operational sense which specifies a particular class such as proletariat or bourgeoisie, then revolution may be understood as the result of the alienation of a particular class which leads it to an awareness of its own situation of exploitation and, therefore, opposition to the group that is doing the exploiting. Yet still missing is that elusive psychological component which helps us to understand why people feel aggrieved and, even more mystifying, why they do not feel aggrieved even though the observer is able to determine that the people are being subjected to great injustice. It may well be that social forces determine how people behave; but how those forces become operative is still unspecified.

The Marxian approach also goes much further than the other models and theories in suggesting what revolutions entail. As we have seen, the other approaches focus not on social change, but on why a group of people in society may rise up against the established order. Thus, the rising is the dependent variable and certain reasons are sought which might explain the rising rather than social change.

As we saw earlier, a class of scholars has argued that the violent, or illegal, overthrow of the government should be treated as a revolution, which may, according to their view, take the form of simple political change. To these theorists the causes of the risings are the most relevant factors to be considered. Yet whether any other type of change has occurred remains un-explored In fact, research has found that in the case of military coups, which would be considered revolutions by these scholars, the degree of change in socio-economic, economic, and military indicators between civilian and military regimes is virtually indistinguishable.[1] Such findings suggest that radical social change is not necessarily a function of the violent overthrow of the government at all, but may be the result of factors that are not accounted for by the kinds of political strains that are present in a particular society. Or, of course, it may be con-firmation of Sorokin's particular bias (which is shared by virtually all of the non-Marxian theorists) that revolutions accomplish nothing other than the temporary removal of the veneer of civilization from a particular society. Thus, the doubt-ful proposition is posited that change is bound to come regardless of the newness of the political form, so why bother to incon-venience oneself when the end result is inevitably the same?

Does this mean that it is futile to examine revolutions, how-ever defined, as a separate type of social change? Let us refrain from attempting an answer to this question for the time being and examine the implications of such a question. If we work under the assumption that revolution is simply the violent over-throw of the government then we need carry the discussion no further. The question of social change becomes irrelevant because revolution is not conceived as social change. In fact, a revolution may take place in the absence of any social change particularly if the new leaders are drawn from the same social formations as the old.

Where the Marxian tradition differs substantively is in its consideration of revolution not merely in terms of the violent overthrow of the government, but in the establishment of a 'new' society—in other words, what happens after the previous government or ruling group is overthrown. The Marxists, however, are not the only theorists to take this particular view. As we have seen, Hannah Arendt raised the point that the most interesting part of the revolution is not the violent overthrow of the regime, but what happens in the aftermath of that event. For Arendt, the relevant problem is whether the 'foundation of freedom' follows, but that need not be our major concern since confronting such a problem raises more questions than it answers, particularly with regard to what is meant by the term 'freedom'. Nevertheless, revolution is not conceived as an event, but as a process.

Brinton, also, was concerned with what follows the seizure of power by the new elite. He divided the revolution into stages, the most interesting of which were those which occurred after the old regime was destroyed. He was, however, a very cautious historian and social scientist, suggesting that the 'uniformities' that he found in the four great revolutions with which he dealt may have been insufficient to generate the types of 'theorems' that social scientists want and need. But he was aware that he had raised some very important questions that pointed 'to the necessity for a more rigorous treatment of the problems involved, challenging those who find them incomplete and unsatisfactory to do a better job'.[2] He argued that the researcher needed to locate 'facts', and through use of these 'facts' Brinton's very tentative suggestions could be tested and measured against later findings. 'Our first approximation will then lead the way to another's second approximations. No scientist should ask more . . .'.[3]

In returning to Brinton's work and arguing that the intellectual richness of Marx's tradition and Arendt's formulation about what revolution is (even if rejecting her view of the mass society) are far superior to the more recent attempts at 'explaining' revolutions, we are suggesting once again that revolution needs to be looked at as a process which does not end with the violent overthrow of the government, but rather with the firm establishment of the new government, either through a monopoly of coercion, wide-scale support, or, more likely, some combination of the two. This entails a rather different approach to the subject than that which has been taken by most of the theorists whose work we have examined. Above all, it suggests only tentative hypothesizing at the outset which will allow the analysis of 'revolutionary situations' without too many preconceived notions about what such situations may entail. Of course, we may be faced with the rather paradoxical situation (paradoxical because of what we have just said concerning the significance of the violent overthrow of the government as an indicator of revolution) that the way in which we may be able to identify a revolutionary situation is by the probability that the existing regime cannot survive. But the major point is that the violent overthrow of the government is not the dependent variable explained by the events before; instead, the actual overthrow or change in governments can now become an explanatory factor of what follows the change in the elite. Thus, the form of the change in the elite (if it occurs) and the extent of the movement preceding it may help to explain the content of the regime that follows and some of the problems it may confront as well as the particular style it adopts for future performance.

This is not a novel approach; nor is it unexplored since Brinton wrote his major work. It does, however, entail a different way of looking at the aftermath of the seizure of power than many of the more recent works have done.[4] Let us take one example of the type of analysis that may be required. Kautsky has suggested the hypothesis 'that in underdeveloped countries generally there is some link between industrialization, on the one hand, and, on the other hand, the replacement of the leadership of revolutionary modernizers by that of managerial modernizers'.[5] There are aspects of this hypothesis that are of interest, such as the meaning of underdeveloped, but let us leave this on one side. What is of concern to us is the problem of the replacement of the revolutionary leaders by the managers. Implicit in Kautsky's argument is that such an occurrence may be the inevitable consequence of the overthrow of the previous government. In this view, the revolutionaries may actually impede social change rather than aid it once the seizure of power has been effected, because of their inability to cope with the types of problems that might arise in the new order. We have already alluded to this possibility in Chapter 7 where different interpretations of what marginality is were suggested. The major point is that individuals who are skilled at overthrowing governments are not necessarily skilled at building factories and fostering industrial and technological development or coping generally with the types of problems with which they are likely to be confronted.

Stalin, for example, is almost always depicted as a tyrant who presided over a totalitarian regime in which all freedoms were curtailed.[6] The purges of the 1934–8 period may be viewed as the actions of an individual who was determined to hold 'total control' over society by eliminating any possible opponents to his rule. Without excusing the excesses of the Stalinist era, one may also consider Stalin a manager committed to the modernization of the Soviet Union through a process of industrialization. As was suggested earlier, the end result of the Bolshevik seizure of power and ensuing civil war was the weakening of the working class so that the Bolshevik party had to play a custodial role.[7] In order to ensure industrial growth, Stalin was forced to eliminate the old revolutionary participants who had no managerial skills and replace them with individuals who were safe politically and capable of providing the necessary ability to bring about the technological transformation of Soviet society. The old Bolsheviks, in this view, were incapable of bringing the society to a high level of industrial competence.

Chinese society also provides us with an example of the post-seizure situation. Embodied in the Maoist interpretation of the Chinese notion of revolution is a view of permanent revolution that is somewhat different than the view held by Lenin and Trotsky. We saw in Chapter 5 that the motivating idea of the mass line was the involvement of the populace in the decision process. More than anything, the mass line would keep the leadership continually aware of what the 'people' were feeling. Further, through continual rectification campaigns, individuals, particularly leaders, who strayed from the revolutionary path would be brought back into the revolutionary movement through a process of self-criticism.[8]

For Mao, perhaps the most dangerous tendency within the leadership is bureaucratism, the establishment of permanent, rational organization which is not amenable to change. Rather than working to continue the revolutionary process, the new bureaucrats tend to work to maintain the bureaucracy itself. Moreover, the managers are quite likely to stress the importance of doing things in ways which seem contrary to the combined wishes of leaders and masses because the managers may feel themselves to be better equipped to deal with particular problems.[9] To the revolutionary, the social question is more significant than a solution to a problem which is the least costly way of approaching the task.

The Great Proletarian Cultural Revolution, which was the major rectification campaign in the late 1960s, was a 'showdown' between the party bureaucrats, or pragmatists, led by Liu Shao Chi, and the revolutionaries led by Mao Tse-Tung. We cannot debate the results of the cultural revolution here. There are conflicting views, for example, concerning which group took the more realistic view with regard to how economic growth ought to proceed in China.[10] What is not doubted is that one group, the party bureaucrats, perceived that orderly economic growth could be achieved only through firm party control. The other group advocated the belief that 'the collectivist forces of the peasantry, aroused by education and indoctrination, and not by political coercion through the party, would win out over individualist and Kulak trends and make the commune ideal a reality'.[11] Industrial growth might be slower, but revolutionary 'purity' would survive.

The relevant question is concerned with how long the revolutionary zeal will continue. Will it be possible for the Maoists to prevent the bureaucrats who probably see only one possible road to modernization from eventually taking power? If, in fact, there is a 'normal' post-seizure process than it can probably be argued that the revolutionaries will eventually disappear and be replaced by the managers. Of course, in bluntest terms, time takes care of all, and even old revolutionaries must eventually die. Although hundred of thousands of young people, particularly students, participated in the cultural revolution on the side of the Maoists, those who believe that the managers must eventually win would argue that those who did not participate in the formative years of the movement, and the seizure of power, could never understand fully what the revolutionary fervour is really about. Mao has certainly been aware of this problem, and the rectification programmes have followed periods of heavy recruitment into the party ranks. Thus, the rectification programmes have been considered vital in order to continue the revolutionary movement.[12]

Whether such zeal can be maintained in China is an unanswerable question for the present. But the active antagonism toward bureaucratization and elimination of the role of the 'managers' of production may prevent the industrial growth that leaders of other societies seem to value. How long the revolutionaries are able to hold sway will depend ultimately upon the goals that the leaders have. Adherence to the revolutionary 'tradition' in the Chinese case may be adherence to the status quo; managerially-led modernization through industrial growth may be radical social change.

The clash between 'revolutionaries' and 'modernizers' is visible not only in Russian and Chinese societies. It may be seen as a possible consequence of the revolutionary period in countries as disparate as Ireland, Nazi Germany, particularly in the period between 1933–8, Algeria and Cuba. Whatever the outcome of these disputes it should be clear that if the revolution is to be considered synonymous with social change it does not end with the coming to power of the new group; instead, perhaps the most interesting period of the revolution begins with the seizure of power.

Still, one of the two essential questions inevitably remains unanswered. To the question, 'is the violent overthrow of a government the same as radical social change?' we have answered 'no'. There is little evidence to suggest that such an occurrence lead to a greater degree of change than the 'normal' social processes. This is not intended to suggest that violent action on the part of the population or groups within society is never justified. Clearly this is not so, for the very act of rebellion on the part of a group indicates that among members of that group there is a grievance and for that group the grievance is justification enough to rebel. Further, the potential for radical social change may be vastly enhanced by the elimination of the ruling group within the state particularly if that group adheres to policies that inhibit economic growth and changes in the social environment. But, ironically, such change that results from that overthrow may be contingent upon the willingness of those who led the takeover either to step down once power is attained or permit those with the requisite skills to fill certain roles.

The second question is the one that was raised earlier: how useful is the concept of revolution, given all the problems that we have raised throughout this work? Certainly the concepts of revolution that have been discussed by most of the theoreticians are not particularly helpful toward an understanding of why social change occurs or even why people rebel. Perhaps we need to focus less on the political aspects. In our fascination with revolutionary movements and our tendency to half-believe and half-wish that men make their own history we may have forgotten about other factors which might 'revolutionize' societies such as the location of the greatest oil reserves or the world's most extensive deposits of copper or nitrates. In the future these may be the factors that need to be considered if we wish to understand why societies change radically. Political change is but one possible explanation for radical social change.

This is not to suggest that violent political change is uninteresting, for there are many facets of such change that may warrant examination. But whether radical social change follows a violent upheaval is an empirical question, and one which social scientists ought to explore. What they should not assume, however, is that violent political change leads inevitably to radical social change or that revolutionary change may coincide with, or be signalled only by, the rude and sudden removal of the political elite of a society.

Notes and References

1 There is considerable divergence in the work which deals with military regimes. For an analysis of the similarities and differences between civilian and military regimes see R. D. McKinlay and A. S. Cohan, 'A comparative analysis of the political and economic performance of military and civilian regimes : a cross-national study', *Comparative Politics*, forthcoming.

2 Crane Brinton, *The Anatomy of Revolution*, New York, 1957. First published 1938, p. 275.

3 *Ibid.*

4 See Barrington Moore, *Social Origins of Dictatorship and Democracy*, and Ralf Dahrendorf, *Society and Democracy in Germany*, both cited earlier, as examples of the types of work that are concerned with the *process* of revolutionary change without regard to seizures of power.

5 John H. Kautsky, 'Revolutionary and managerial elites in modernizing regimes', *Comparative Politics*, *1*, 1969, p. 441.

6 See, particularly, Robert Conquest, *The Great Terror*, Harmondsworth, Middlesex, 1968.

7 See Chapter 2.

8 For an introduction to the rectification campaigns see Stuart Schram, *Mao Tse-Tung*, Harmondsworth, 1966; J. W. Lewis, *Leadership in Communist China*, Ithaca, New York, 1963. The most impressive work on contemporary China is Franz Schurmann, *Ideology and Organization in Communist China*, Berkeley, 1970, first published 1966.

9 Schurmann, *Ideology and Organization in Communist China*, pp. 70–5.

10 Schurmann has dealt extensively with the Cultural Revolution in the Supplement to his book, pp. 501–92. See also Joan Robinson's sympathetic *The Cultural Revolution in China*, Harmondsworth, Middlesex, 1969, and Tai Sung An's unsympathetic *Mao Tse-Tung and the Chinese Cultural Revolution*, Harmondsworth, Middlesex, 1968.

11 Schurmann, *Ideology and Organization in Communist China*, p. 544.

12 See Schram, *Mao Tse-Tung*, and Lifton, *Revolutionary Immortality*, cited above.

Index